CONTENTS

ABOUT THE AUTHOR

Jackson P. Rainer, PhD, licensed psychologist, is Dean of the Graduate School and Professor of Psychology at Gardner-Webb University in Boiling Springs, North Carolina. Known and respected in the professional community, he specializes in psychotherapy work with individuals, couples, and families dealing with the crisis of loss due to catastrophic, chronic, and terminal illness. A former Chair of the Publication Board for the Division of Psychotherapy of the American Psychological Association, Dr. Rainer currently sits on the editorial boards of seven psychotherapy journals and is a consultant with the CMI Education Institute.

Frieda Farfour Brown, PhD, is Professor of Psychology and Counseling at Gardner-Webb University, Boiling Springs, NC, and Adjunct Professor of Psychology and Education, Davidson College, Davidson, NC. She has taught crisis counseling at the graduate and undergraduate levels since 1983 and has over 30 years of experience as a practitioner, program developer and evaluator, and trainer and supervisor. A leading contributor to the field, her well-received model for crisis counseling has recently appeared in *Innovations in Clinical Practice.* A licensed clinical psychologist, Dr. Brown joined mental health professionals in efforts to work with victims of Hurricane Katrina in 2005 and currently maintains an active practice.

Preface

Tragedy is now visibly evident in our community. Crisis intervention as a clinical technique is moving in the direction of being seen as a social movement in response to a personal accident, trauma, and hardship. As a technique, it relies on models comprised of a variety of strategies integrated from psychology, medicine, sociology, and theology. As a social movement, it is employed as a response to the general cultural trend of greater personal isolation in an indifferent society. Crisis intervention operates under the fundamental notion that an individual's resistance to stress is finite and idiosyncratic, so that under certain circumstances, every person will find his or her coping mechanisms inadequate to sustain psychological equilibrium. Crisis treatment involves systemic efforts to supplement the personal resources of the individual who is failing under stress, rather than assuming that the individual is in the presence of a disease process.

Practicing crisis intervention requires the clinician to make fundamentally difficult choices regarding the offering of help. The clinician is obligated to shelve some of the traditional psychotherapy techniques in which he or she has been trained in favor of new models and paradigms. In crisis work, there is an assumption that an occurrence of some external precipitant or event has proved distressing and disabling to the individual. The outcome of contemporary crisis practice is defined in terms of restoration of the individual's pretraumatic level of overt functioning.

This book is written as a text, reference, and resource book for clinicians working in the area of crisis intervention. It is assumed in the discussion that crisis is accompanied by temporary disequilibrium that contains potential for human growth. The successful resolution of the crisis may lead to positive and constructive outcomes, such as self-enhancing coping ability, a decrease in negative, self-defeating,

Crisis Counseling and Therapy
© 2007 by The Haworth Press, Inc. All rights reserved.
doi:10.1300/5953_a

dysfunctional behavior, and a return to the precrisis level of functioning. It is the authors' bias that the essence of the human dilemma found in the presence of crisis will combine elements of danger and opportunity. Applied from an experiential viewpoint, the systemic model discussed in this work subscribes to the truth that no single theory or strategy will prove useful in all crisis situations.

The text presents a specific model for crisis intervention, developed by the authors and based on the definition of crisis as "a perception of an event or situation as an intolerable difficulty that exceeds the person's resources and coping mechanisms" (Gilliland & James, 2005, p. 3). By definition, a crisis is time limited. This distinctive model will address time constraints for helping an individual and will address the system's need to integrate the crisis in order to return to maximum functioning. By necessity, the time-limited dimension of the crisis state will limit the frame for intervention to a maximum of six to eight weeks. Rather than conforming to the traditional once-a-week therapeutic hour, interventions are to be determined and applied by the degree of disequilibrium the system is experiencing. The model is innovative since it allows the practitioner to be flexible in session length, theoretical approach, and determination of subjective therapeutic goals. The systemic crisis intervention model has three phases with goal-specific substages drawn from multiple theoretical perspectives. The model is easily incorporated into the clinician's practice, and provides a paradigm for effective, strategic intervention.

Chapter 1

An Introduction to the Systemic Model of Crisis Counseling

INTRODUCTION

December 7, 1941—The Japanese attack Pearl Harbor.
November 22, 1963—President John Kennedy is assassinated.
September 11, 2001—Terrorists attack the World Trade Center and the Pentagon.
December 26, 2004—Earthquake and tsunami hit Indonesia, wreaking havoc on thousands.
August 29, 2005—Hurricane Katrina drowns a U.S. city, New Orleans, Louisiana.

Five dates, powerfully and collectively imbedded in memory. Even for those individuals who were not born at the time of the Pearl Harbor attack or John Kennedy's assassination, a sense of tragedy can be communally felt. Each event was horrific and left indelible scars.

Consider the terrorist attacks of September 11, 2001; our world was terrified as live television images of the events surrounding the World Trade Center, the Pentagon, and the Pennsylvania cornfield were played and replayed. The nation was stunned as terrible acts of violence and destruction created widespread crisis. The aftermath of the event still lingers and is lodged in the social consciousness of victims and observers. Professionals remain entrenched in an ongoing debate concerning the implications of the attacks and their lasting personal, political, psychological, and sociological impact.

Crisis Counseling and Therapy
© 2007 by The Haworth Press, Inc. All rights reserved.
doi:10.1300/5953_01

There was never any disagreement regarding the need to support the healing process for everyone involved. Despite symptoms of distress, as a group, no one was labeled with psychological disorders. All touched by the crisis of the terrorist attacks were viewed with compassion, concern, respect, and admiration for their collective ability to exist in the midst of such abject suffering. In the subsequent months and years, there has been a great deal of talk about the nature and need for closure, and how those touched have or have not recovered and created new lives with new normal rhythms of the day.

The immediacy of the crisis of the terrorist attacks is now over. Rescue efforts have been addressed and the cleanup is complete. However, it is now clear that many of those involved in the tragedy continue to have difficulties reconciling the pain related to the multiple losses that were individually and collectively experienced. One heroic rescuer committed suicide. His family reported that he was unremittingly troubled by the crisis and had been unable to resolve the residual trauma. The rescuer is not alone. The pain of his distress has been troublesome for many to accommodate. It is a truism in American culture that it is easier to elevate heroes than to embrace suffering.

Tragedy in so many forms is now visibly present locally, nationally, and internationally in our communities. Crisis intervention, a clinical technique, is currently moving in the direction of being seen as a social movement in response to personal and communal tragedy. As a technique, it relies on models comprised of a variety of strategies integrated from psychology, medicine, sociology, and theology. As a social movement, it is employed as a response to the general cultural trend of greater personal isolation in an indifferent society.

Crisis intervention operates under the fundamental notion that an individual's resistance to stress is finite and idiosyncratic, so that under certain stressful or traumatic circumstances every person will find his or her coping mechanisms inadequate to sustain psychological equilibrium. Crisis treatment involves systemic efforts to supplement the personal resources of the individual who is failing under stress, rather than making the assumption that the individual is in the presence of a pathological disease process.

Practicing crisis intervention requires the clinician to make fundamentally difficult choices regarding the offer to help. Clinicians are obligated to shelve some of the traditional psychotherapy techniques in favor of new models and paradigms. In crisis work, there is an assumption that an occurrence of some external precipitant or event has proven to be distressing and disabling to the individual. The outcome of contemporary crisis practice is defined in terms of restoration of the individual's pretraumatic level of overt functioning, return to precrisis equilibrium, and incorporation of the immutable changes caused by the crisis event. This understanding dates back to the research of Lindemann (1956), who gave clinicians an understanding that victims, in the presence of trauma and loss and with no history of psychological diagnoses, would still exhibit symptoms that appear to be pathological. He recognized that behavioral responses to crisis associated with grief and loss are normal, temporary, and amenable to alleviation through short-term counseling intervention techniques. While Lindemann focused on resolution of grief after loss, Caplan (1964) expanded these constructs into the larger field of traumatic events. He viewed crisis as a state resulting from those impediments to life goals that cannot be overcome through customary behaviors and that arise from both developmental and situational events. Both Lindemann and Caplan dealt with crisis intervention following trauma using an equilibrium/disequilibrium paradigm. The stages in the Lindemann paradigm include (1) disturbed equilibrium, (2) brief therapy or grief work, (3) the client's working through the problem or grief, and (4) restoration of equilibrium (Janosik, 1984). The focus of treatment is narrowly defined and the time frame for completion is short term. The goal of treatment is to help the individual restore his or her characteristic and typical level of coping.

DEFINING CRISIS

In contemporary practice, crisis is best defined by examining the nature of the crisis state. Simplistically, the definition could be left wholly phenomenological and subjective, that is, "I'm in a crisis when I say that I am." For the practitioner, understanding crisis is a more in-depth and interesting journey adding objective elements and requiring a stance as participant-observer with the client in his or her psychological, sociological, and spiritual functioning. The practitioner is obligated to extend the work from a diagnostic frame in order to determine the depth and nature of the crisis and its impact on the individual and the surrounding system. Classic diagnostic paradigms are insufficient and at times counterproductive to the immediate reconciliation and integration of crisis. Young practitioners of crisis intervention often find this to be difficult and experience the application of any model or paradigm to be unwieldy. One such counselor, who worked in a crisis center following an environmental disaster, reported it this way: "I found that a client was just not interested in spending time to pursue the avenues of treatment that were recommended. Another person said that my levels of intervention weren't sophisticated enough to meet his needs. He said that he was surprised how straightforward my work with him was. I didn't feel valued in my professional efforts. That hurt my feelings."

On closer examination and with a good diagnostic eye, it becomes clearer that in the first case, the client was not in crisis, but was suffering from an extreme stress response. In the latter case, the client was, in fact, experiencing a traumatic response and needed a more profound level of intervention than was offered. Since "one size does not fit all," how then can appropriate interventions be identified? This initial question begs a second: What is crisis and what is not?

In the psychological and stress literature, crises have typically been discussed in terms of two major dimensions: the time of life at which they occur and the intensity or cataclysmic dimension of the event (Schneidman, 1973). What often was left out of early clinical discussion was the personality of the victim. Historically, crisis intervention theories were oriented to environmental manipulation as a favored strategy for achieving the reestablishment of equilibrium and balance. Caplan was one of the first researchers who extended the working definition of the goal of crisis intervention to elimination of the cumulative cognitive, emotional, and behavioral distortions that precipitated the psychological trauma in the first place.

James and Gilliland (2005) define crisis as "the perception of an event or situation as beyond the coping mechanisms of the individual" (p. 3). Three components can be discerned from this definition: a precipitating event occurs, the perception of the event leads to subjective distress, and the usual coping mechanisms fail, leading the person experiencing the event to function psychologically, emotionally, or behaviorally at a lower level than before the precipitating event occurred (Kanel, 1999). Using this definition, the practitioner assesses the process and content of the crisis state while empathically joining the person who has experienced the crisis event. The therapist listens closely to verbal and nonverbal cues suggesting high levels of anxiety, fear, or depression; feelings of loss of control; others' losses of relationship, security, or status; and a generalized sense of being overwhelmed. There is a corresponding loss of effective self-care and management of the situation.

This being said, differentiating stress from crisis is more than a matter of degree. Mature individuals who are resilient, having life experience, and personal, financial, and social resources are less likely to be thrown into crisis. Vulnerability is heightened when an individual is in frail health, has family-of-origin dysfunction, or is socially isolated. Multiple losses also increase the risk of critical impact from an event. Perhaps the most relevant and often overlooked benchmark is the developmental state of the individual. Depending on the age and stage of the person, there is the potential that a developmental crisis will enhance the likelihood of an adverse impact from an external precipitant. In order to integrate crisis, which is a developmentally sophisticated task, it is incumbent on the person to intellectually and emotionally abstract meaning from the experience. The younger the individual in crisis, the less likely this will occur.

Ultimately, an individual in crisis must be willing to accept help, which oftentimes is difficult. As one college professor said, "My son died in an automobile wreck. I was so confused by my disequilibrium after the accident. I was completely out of sync. I thought that each day I would get better, and that if I 'toughed it out,' that one day I'd wake up and it'd be all over. It certainly didn't happen like that. I did my best not to let others know—not to let it show that I was so upset. Keeping my feelings locked inside nearly destroyed me. It was the worst thing that I could've done to try and stay quiet. What I really needed to do was talk it all out, but I didn't know how." The professor is not alone. Many people choose not to accept help and cannot fathom that they might share their thoughts, feelings, and beliefs with others who might perceive them as vulnerable, psychologically weak, or impaired. Yet much of crisis work is oriented to normalize experience. The clinician offers reassurance in response to a stressful event that it is normal to feel abnormal.

Several clinical indicators help the counselor listen for signs of crisis. When individuals are overwhelmed and feel threatened by the presence of danger, they will intuitively seek to survive. This can be understood as a mechanism for incorporating contemporary experience with past learning. Theories of learning teach that repetition is the most functional way of "taking in" an experience. Therefore, if individuals learn from crisis, they must tell, retell, and tell again the story of the event and its impact. One client described her experience "like an old-fashioned sifter. You know what I mean. The flour has to be sifted over and over until all its ingredients are smoothly mixed together. So many people told me to forget about it, and that I needed to stop thinking and talking about what happened, but I couldn't help it. That's all I wanted to talk about." In the presence of trauma, the retelling of the tale allows the individual gradually to accept the facts and truth about the situation and that the crisis is life changing, for better or worse.

In a crisis situation, an individual will often demonstrate a type of thinking more characteristic of young children. Called magical thinking, such a state allows the individual a flight of fancy out of the immediacy of the trauma. "Why did I ever let my child go to that concert? She wouldn't have been exposed to drugs," a mother cried when her child overdosed on Ecstasy at a rock event. In an ideal world, we would be able to test our decisions and have prescient knowledge regarding the satisfaction of choice and consequence. The child's father echoed his wife's pain, saying, "You know, hindsight is always better. Truth is, it only happens in the movies. We can only live our lives forward, not backward. You would think that I could do a better job of protecting my family. Now my child is dead and my wife is destroyed."

An individual in crisis consistently scans personal decisions, actions, and reactions, searching for the direction that might have made a difference in avoiding the crisis situation. The rape victim wishes she had not walked alone. A mother regrets allowing her drowned child to swim in a nearby creek. The cancer victim believes that a diet richer in broccoli and vitamin C might have protected her. Such behavior is an attempt to bring control to an out-of-control situation, by wishing "I could go back and do it differently," as a woman in a hunting accident said.

People in crisis feel alone. Like the latency stage adolescent who yells to anyone who will listen that "no one understands me," there is a cloying sense that crisis leaves the individual feeling misunderstood in personal thought and affect. One woman said angrily, "No one can possibly understand what's going on. I don't want one more person to tell me 'I know how you feel.' They don't. They won't. That kind of jabber just infuriates me." In such an isolated state, it is regrettably natural for the individual to turn dystonic feelings inward, increasing the risk of depression and self-harm. Such internalization of unwelcome feeling states can heighten emotionality, which decreases control and leads to an erosion of self-worth and self-esteem. The crisis clinician provides a therapeutic service in helping the person in distress to discover that idiosyncratic behavior is not "crazy." As one counselor told his client, "I would worry about you right now if you didn't feel crazy. Craziness, in my book, is a normal response to an abnormal situation. Given all you've been through, crazy is a normal feeling right now."

The repetition of storytelling, regression, and feelings of aloneness are noted characteristics of the cognitive and affective functioning of people in crisis and are benchmarks for diagnosis. Often, individuals regress to levels of functioning below what is typical of their daily functioning. This disruption of normative age functioning erodes the individual's feelings of self-efficacy and competency. The loss of a feeling of mastery then undermines belief in personal and fundamental ability to solve problems, particularly those concerns precipitated by the crisis.

CRITICAL MOMENTS OF DEVELOPMENT

Erikson's (1959) model of development serves as an effective paradigm for understanding how crisis resurrects previously integrated distress and dilemma. In crisis, individuals lose a sense of trust of self, others, and the world. They suffer from feelings of vulnerability and inadequacy that cause a loss of independence and self-sufficiency. Without sufficient resources, the person typically is unsuccessful in attempts to reconcile the situation and will retreat from using personal initiative and preferred coping strategies. Such a lack of adequacy fosters feelings of inferiority, which impacts the individual's ability to provide self-care. As a young fellow who was suspended from college said, "I just lost it. I couldn't take care of myself anymore. I quit bathing, dressing, just about everything. I was such a little baby. I was a mess."

The role of the crisis therapist is to help the client restore developmentally age-appropriate levels of functioning and to help the individual discern impact of the event in all areas of life's functions. Such a process takes patience as the individual constructs, deconstructs, and reconstructs the event in "the mind's eye." From such a mental model, an identification of the presence of vulnerabilities in cognitive, emotional, and psychosocial functioning unfolds. The therapist then helps bring focus and a meaningful understanding to the event to place it in proximity and concert with the individual's value system.

The wife of a deceased astronaut described her process this way: "I was overwhelmed with feelings of sadness, anger, and resentment. The only way I survived was to remind myself that his work was what he wanted to do. He died doing his life's mission. So many people have reached out to me with cards, letters, and phone calls. I'm in mourning, I think. Do I consider this a crisis? Yes and no. I am heartbroken that he died, but what he has given the world will continue to contribute. My grief is shared by the world."

Crisis counseling is a short-term approach with departures from the brief therapy treatment model. Most notable are distinctions in client characteristics, therapeutic techniques, client-counselor relationships, and the process of termination. Historically, practitioners of brief psychotherapy have not recognized the significance of crisis counseling as a distinct approach and intervention paradigm. Marmor (1980), for example, in reviewing the approaches to brief psychotherapy, does not include crisis counseling in his schema until his later work. For a comparison of crisis intervention with brief psychotherapy, see Table 1.1.

Traditional approaches to counseling and psychotherapy are based on understanding human suffering from an intrapsychic or interpersonal frame of reference. The field of crisis counseling has developed from the impact of external sources of distress and disequilibrium. The focus of the work is on the external as it is experienced on an internal level by the client. Culture, gender, ethnic, and class conditions impact the trajectory of the crisis and its resolution.

TABLE 1.1. Comparison of Crisis Intervention with Brief Psychotherapy

Selection	Crisis Intervention	Brief Psychotherapy
Onset	No diagnosis	Traditional diagnoses
Focus	Immediate	Current or long standing
Goal	External stresses	Underlying internalized issues
Technique	Restore equilibrium; enhance coping	Treat symptoms; develop more adaptive coping mechanisms
Structure of Therapy	Problem solving; supportive	Confrontational; intensive intervention techniques
Transference	Brief assessment with focus on goals and the individual in context	Standard approach with extensive assessment and one-on-one intervention on a weekly basis
Termination	Not a part of crisis work; regression expected in crisis	Use of transference interpretations common
Selection	Goal oriented following approximately six to eight weeks of counseling	Conflict resolution usually after twelve to thirty-six sessions; termination issues addressed

Source: Adapted from Marmor (1980).

Consider a benign example. A late-middle-aged man retired. The retiree later experienced a transitional crisis when the stock market dropped, jeopardizing his financial security. Because of health problems, he had to stop playing golf. He also found that he was much lonelier than he expected. A woman peer retired at the same time. She developed a strong support system outside of the workplace and found that retirement offered her more time with friends, giving her great sources of nurturance, where the male retiree found himself at an existential crisis of loneliness.

THE SYSTEMIC MODEL OF CRISIS COUNSELING

The model discussed in this book views crisis from an applied systemic perspective, keeping the individual's restoration of functioning paramount while working with available social and environmental supports. The goal of the counseling process is to bolster a healing return to baseline and to facilitate integration of trauma into personal understanding. The professional heritage of systems thinking provides a perspective for understanding both the function and consequences of a crisis event. Systemic thinking increases examination of the function of relationships in growth and health. This school of thought leads to a focus on people not as isolated individuals but in the context of their lives. It is a view in which human systems are seen as resources for helping in the process of change. Understanding the structure and flow of relationships allows for perspective in the presence of crisis and facilitates constructive and reparative intervention strategies. The systemic thinker makes a paradigm shift that considers all aspects of human behavior within the multiplicity of contexts in which they occur. Systems thinking views behavior as most understandable when conceptualized as a function both of the multilevel, reciprocal relationships and sociocultural context in which the problematic behavior is embedded. Systems thinking challenges the clinician to enlarge diagnostic, explanatory, and intervention focus to the level of relationship and into the larger matrix of social relationships and organizational processes. To be a systems thinker, the clinician must evaluate contextual, cultural, and developmental components of the crisis at hand.

The approach is transcendent of any particular theory, technique, or population. The systemic features of circularity, feedback, and internal regulation are informative in the process of understanding, planning, and integrating change. Attention to systems dynamics enables the clinician to modify data gathering and intervention in order to achieve a more collaborative goal with clients.

Approaching crisis intervention as a systems theorist is a viable option for the clinician. Many counselors will report, as one fellow said, "My theory? It's hard to say. I guess I fly by the seat of my pants. In the middle of a crisis, I do what I think is right. Could I fully explain or repeat the process? Maybe yes, maybe no. Each time I feel like I handle the crisis differently." This is risky territory for the clinician. The demand for expediency and the press of outside forces during a crisis argues against substantive understanding of theory. These demands frequently push to minimize theory in the service of practicality, leading to more of a "knee-jerk" response to the situation at hand. However, practicality not grounded in good theory is not practical on a long-term basis. Systems thinking reaches and embraces a broad range of human experience. It is rooted in natural order and can reveal considerable information that enhances the individual's understanding of self and place in the world.

It is assumed that all people experience psychological stress that can turn into crisis at different times in their lives. Only when the event is subjectively experienced as a threat to need fulfillment, safety, or meaningful experience does the individual enter into a state of crisis (Caplan, 1964). It is further assumed in this discussion that a crisis is accompanied by temporary disequilibrium rather than potential for human growth. The successful resolution of the crisis may lead to positive and constructive outcomes, such as self-enhancing coping ability, a decrease in negative, self-defeating, dysfunctional behavior, and a return to precrisis levels of functioning.

The essence of the human dilemma found in the presence of crisis will combine elements of danger and opportunity. Applied from an experiential viewpoint, the systemic model discussed subscribes to the truth that no single theory or strategy will prove useful in all crisis situations. To work in the presence of crisis means entering a world of ambiguity. A clinician said it best: "Early in my career, I started doing crisis work looking for a quick fix for my clients. Now I've learned that although the dictionary's primary definition of 'fix' means 'to repair,' a second definition is more applicable to my stance in crisis work. I use the photographic definition of 'fix,' which means 'to clarify or stabilize an image.' This gives me much more room to be helpful. I never want to fly by the seat of my pants, but I know that anytime I look for a 'right way' to deal with a crisis, I get into a bigger clinical mess than I entered."

There are no clear-cut answers or simple cause-and-effect directives in the overarching theory of crisis work. Specific crises demand specific interventions that span the entire continuum of therapeutic strategies. Good practice of crisis intervention calls for creativity and the capacity to adapt to rapidly changing conditions in the therapeutic moment. This requires a sense of therapeutic art, often overarching therapeutic science. This being said, it remains important that the clinician be well-versed in a therapeutic schema so that appropriate interventions and techniques might be applied in a systematic fashion. Such scaffolding enables the clinician and propels the client's movement into therapeutic contact with the helping person and environmental supports.

After being held hostage in a bank robbery, a woman was offered crisis intervention services. Following the initial debriefing, she said, "In the midst of my confusion, I was offered a crisis counselor. She was like a safe haven for me. I had a place and a person I could go to figure out why I felt so bad and what I could do to get over the feelings. I'll never forget how helpful she was to me."

CHARACTERISTICS OF THE CRISIS COUNSELOR

The crisis clinician, regardless of discipline, needs to have an ability to analyze, diagnose, and synthesize. By definition, a crisis brings imbalance into a system and potentially engulfs the individual in emotionality and irrationality. Clinicians are called on to make themselves big enough to assess and hold multiple forms of distress and disability, and to order facts, truths, and opinions related to the crisis in manageable and effective ways. To do so, the clinician must maintain a stance of equanimity, known as an ability to stay calm and comfortable in fractious situations. From the Latin words *aequus* and *animus,* literally translated as "equal mind," the ability to muster equanimity, to maintain composure in the presence of adversity, is a cultivated skill.

The crisis clinician also needs to have an ability to think globally and act locally. It is important to have personal assessment skills and be familiar with the process of referral. The knowledge of how to "move systems," that is, to access and utilize resources, provides modeling of efficacy for the victim of crisis. One individual said it best: "I didn't know where to go or what to do. When you don't have a place to live, you get emotionally wiped out, which is a huge problem. My therapist walked me through contacting the agencies that could help until I could do it for myself. I never would have known how to find the help I needed." Such a skill is enhanced by quick mental reflexes, a creative approach to problem solving, and flexibility. One clinician described the skills this way: "In the middle of a crisis, I know how far I can bend before I get bent out of shape. I can size up resources and learn to speak in the client's language. I learn who holds the authority for decision making and bide my time so they don't feel pushed until I get what I need to help them."

An effective crisis counselor is a caring individual. To many, this statement will seem simplistic and superficial. Caring in this case is meant in its most profound sense. The fundamental meaning of the word *care* is "to grieve, to experience sorrow, to cry out" (Rainer & McMurry, 2002, p. 1423). To care for another is an invitation to enter into that person's pain and suffering. In crisis, suffering is inevitable. How an individual responds to suffering speaks of personal value, character, and the ability to grow mentally, emotionally, and spiritually. It is the responsibility of the crisis clinician to help relieve suffering and offer hope. Even when the crisis is sufficiently devastating so that recovery is long, the counselor can encourage a meaningful attitude and give the gift of choice as open and available to the individual.

A counselor made a visit with a client whose parent was placed in a nursing home. The counselor said, as he met with the family in the center's recreation room, "I understand that it is my job to go where the client is, rather than waiting for them to come to me. As a practitioner during crisis work, I have the flexibility to work along a continuum of intervention styles, from being a very direct authority to becoming a collaborator with the client as he or she seeks to regain sense of control in the subjective world. I assess the degree of disequilibrium in the system and make my judgment regarding the amount of intrusion I will make on the client's behalf."

Crisis is contagious. As an event and process, it disrupts the normative functioning of individuals and their social support systems. To enter the sacred space of crisis and to preserve the integrity of the therapeutic relationship and process, the clinician is well-advised to prepare both personally and professionally for the role.

The purpose of this book is to lay the foundation for understanding the crisis theoretically, then build a structure for intervention, and close with a reflection on protecting the person of the therapist. No work can be more meaningful or more dangerous. The therapist can be left with a sense of purposeful involvement or frustrated needs. As one young therapist said, "I feel like I am in a whirlwind when I work with clients in crisis situations. I sometimes don't know who is more confused, my client or me. In many ways, I see my work as occurring in the eye of a hurricane. I can't address one problem without many others taking its place."

A more seasoned counselor described her work: "Every time I enter into the world of an individual's crisis, I am intimately aware of my own mortality. To interface with people at such a powerful juncture, joining and journeying with them through the complexities of the crisis, leaves me feeling humbled and grateful. Having experienced these feelings many times, I covet the opportunity to do this work."

Chapter 2

Contemporary Standards and Models of Practice

INTRODUCTION

Models of crisis counseling can be confusing even for experienced practitioners. Ranging from a simple referral to a self-help group to the intensity of critical incident stress debriefing (CISD), such models can be as short as a single session or extended into six to eight weeks. The confusion about models can be reconciled by examining the current terminology describing crisis-related circumstances and developing a scaffolding for classifying treatment approaches. A three-by-three model is presented as structure for understanding the dimensionality of crisis intervention. Table 2.1 organizes the three dimensions with intensity, type, and treatment. Treatment examples are included.

The literature is rich with examples for responding to almost any type of crisis. The key to making effective use of these resources is a clear understanding of how closely client needs mirror those of the described patient population. An example will illuminate this point. If an individual has a terminal illness, guidelines for intervention will depend on several variables. Included in the formulation of a treatment plan could be a referral to hospice, possible plans for palliative care, or simply helpful reading for the individual and family. A structure that highlights the factors and variables contributing to the choice of treatment will be instructive. The models of treatment shown in Table 2.1 organize these approaches to treatment according to three

Crisis Counseling and Therapy
© 2007 by The Haworth Press, Inc. All rights reserved.
doi:10.1300/5953_02

TABLE 2.1. Models of Treatment

	Type		
	Developmental	**Situational**	**Systemic**
Stress	School entry [relaxation training, stress management]	Cancer Unemployment [self-help groups]	Burnout Compassion fatigue [psychoeducation; wellness programming]
Crisis	Retirement Midlife crisis [crisis counseling]	Separation Divorce [crisis counseling]	Family disintegration [crisis counseling]
Trauma	Child sexual abuse Child neglect [psychotherapy]	Car accident Shooting [CISD]	Stockholm syndrome WTC terrorist attacks [crisis counseling, psychotherapy]

dimensions: the impact or intensity of the event, the type of crisis, and the range of influence, that is, whether individualistic or systemic. The clinician considers these factors as critical to the evaluation of the utility of a particular approach. The value is found in the determination of "fit" between client situation and chosen approach.

The following sections of this chapter will closely examine these dimensions. Treatment modalities will be discussed in an effort to give clinicians information and guidance regarding choice of intervention. The stress, crisis, and trauma continuum will be examined, then the types of crisis, and finally the models of intervention first from an individualistic perspective, then with a systemic perspective.

THREE DIMENSIONS

The first dimension in the continuum of impact or intensity of the event ranges along three points, from stress to crisis to trauma. Specific questions must be asked: Is this a situation that is simply stressful? Does it cause disequilibrium, which qualifies it as a crisis? Or does this threaten the existence of the individual, which places it in the realm of trauma? Stress, crisis, and trauma have much in common. The symptoms of one are shared with the others, making differentiation difficult. Components of treatment planning overlap for the three. However, it is clear that the clinician must identify the degree of impairment in the individual affected by the event so that appropriate interventions may be brought to bear.

The second dimension to be considered refers to the type of crisis and is measured through markers identified according to developmental, situational, or existential events. If developmental, the individual will experience the event as a passage from one life stage to another. These events are normative and expected. They do create a certain vulnerability to other external crises because of the stressful nature of the developmental challenge, from a lack of coping mechanisms, or due to the dysfunctional response of family members. A situational crisis is one that arises from events external to the individual. These environmental events arise from a variety of phenomena, including forces of nature, accidents, or intentional harm. Intentionality is predictive of crisis. An existential crisis is based on a struggle with the meaningfulness of life. These crises can interface and influence each other.

The third dimension focuses on the identified client either as an individual or as an individual in context. If the person is viewed in an individualistic frame, treatment is confined to the direct impact of the crisis on the victim. As a systemic perspective is adopted, the counselor focuses on the individual and on systemic factors contributing to the life of the individual.

Since crisis is determined by how the individual perceives a life event, the sense of loss of control and predictable coping mechanisms, the evaluative process is quite subjective. A given situation may be a crisis for one and only stressful for another. For example, consider a couple divorcing. Depending on the maturity, history, personality of each spouse, and context of the event, the termination of the marriage may be stressful or may escalate as a crisis. "I felt a sense of relief when we finally separated. We had spent so many years arguing, in truth, we separated long ago," the recently divorced man admitted. "Our only problem now is dividing up property, and deciding who gets what." This is in comparison to a woman, married thirty years, whose spouse came to her and said he was divorcing and remarrying. "My whole world came crashing down. I couldn't function for days. All I did was cry." The stresses of the first case would likely be alleviated with a support group and psychoeducation. The latter will require crisis counseling.

Distinguishing between crisis and trauma is also relevant. Two men were injured as a bridge collapsed. One struggled with changes in his marital relationship, loss of income from work, and physical disabilities. His faith and support system sustained him. He was in crisis but did not experience trauma as the second fellow did: "I couldn't eat or sleep. I had nightmares about the accident and at times during the day, I felt as if I were being crushed again by that bridge. I became irritable and depressed, and overreacted to everything." Treatment for the two will have many similarities as well as important differences. The man in crisis can be helped with traditional crisis counseling, while the fellow with a post-traumatic stress disorder will need more pronounced intervention.

Stress

The term *stress* is now in the fabric of our everyday lives. It takes on a range of definitions.

The young wife who is cooking for her in-laws tells her husband that she is "stressed out." A middle-aged man who has a heart attack and whose health and well-being is compromised is told by his physician that "it was stress-induced." A teenager tells his mother, "Don't stress me. I need to chill." The teenager's mother in turn vents to her friend, "I'm going to show him what stress really is. He doesn't know stress until he sees how much I can stress him upside his head!"

The parent of stress theory, Hans Selye, defined stress as "the non-specific response of the body to any demand made of it" (1975, p. 5). What that "demand" might be will vary idiosyncratically from mild discomfort to severe debilitation. Two of the most important factors of the definition relate to the "response of the body," including physical, emotional, and psychological response, and if the "demand" occurs internally or externally.

On a biological level, the stress reaction causes a rush of the hormone adrenaline to be released into the blood stream, arousing and alerting the body for its well-known "fight-or-flight" response. Under stress, an individual will notice an increase in heart rate and will be aware of a heightened sense of activity in the autonomic nervous system. Increased blood flow to the brain, muscle turgidity, and increased respiration and perspiration signal the demand for a more focused perceptual attention. This adaptation response increases blood sugar. The body begins to produce more platelets, so that blood may clot with increasing speed—a remarkable adaptation of the body to prevent hemorrhage in case of physical injury.

Stress also impacts the cognitive, psychological, and behavioral functioning of the individual. Stress triggers physical symptoms of headache, chest pain, fatigue, insomnia, muscle aches, nausea, and gastrointestinal distress. Cognitively, stress exacerbates confusion, disorientation, loss of a sense of humor, diminished mental acuity, ruminations, and a reduced capacity for concentration and memory. Psychological symptoms of stress include affective disturbances precipitated by anxiety, leading to depression and anger. There can be complicated interpersonal disruptions of withdrawal, isolation, and diminished sexual desire. Behavioral indicators may be evident through eating disorders, use of alcohol/drugs, aggressive behavior against others, or uncharacteristic patterns of daily living. Stress management literature directs the individual toward lifestyle changes that enhance health and balance. Stress management also encourages new forms of rational thinking. As Albert Ellis (1980) teaches, learning problem-solving skills, challenging negative thinking, eliminating perfectionist thought, and developing a sense of humor enhance a sense of realistic resilience to the adverse impact of stress. Meditation, prayer, and internal reflection increase a sense of self-control.

Like dining at a smorgasbord, victims of stress can pick and choose from a variety of self-help and self-directed techniques that improve their ability to cope and bounce from the negative impact of stress. The old adage "If at first you don't succeed, try, try, try again" is not helpful in meeting the adverse effects of stress. A more appropriate proverb might go something like this: "If at first you don't succeed, do something different." Simply by acting on alternatives, an individual is likely to feel a regaining of control from distress.

Crisis

Aguilera and Messick's (1986) model (Table 2.2) of the relationship between stress and crisis defines stress as an individual's need to respond to the disruption of equilibrium resulting from the occurrence of a problem or difficulty. The problem is solved and equilib-

TABLE 2.2. Aguilera and Messick's Model

EQUILIBRIUM
⇓
PROBLEM
⇓
STRESS

INADEQUATE BALANCING FACTORS	ADEQUATE BALANCING FACTORS
⇓	⇓
CRISIS	RESOLUTION
⇓	⇓
RESOLUTION	EQUILIBRIUM—With:
⇓	Factual and realistic perception
NEW EQUILIBRIUM—In the context of:	Adequate Support
Inadequate perception	Good coping mechanisms,
Inadequate social network	adequate for problem
Inadequate coping mechanisms	Other assets

rium regained through the use of balancing factors (more commonly known as stress management tools), including a factual and realistic perception of the problem, enough helpful and supportive people, and effective coping mechanisms to deal with the problem. If there are missing or inadequate balancing factors, the situation moves from stress to crisis. "Inadequate" is not normative in definition. Rather, it is subjective. What is inadequate for one may not be for another. An example will illustrate.

Two college students experienced the same problem: both had been to a fraternity party one night before an early morning lecture class. Both came to class hung over and were reported to the disciplinary committee of the university after being suspended from the class. Later in the day, the first student went to his professor, apologized, told him of the circumstance of his poor judgment, voluntarily went to the counseling center for an alcohol and drug assessment, and agreed to remedial activities to complete the course in a timely manner. The second student, as he described it, "went nuts." His indignant and self-righteous proclamations that "this just wasn't a big deal" landed on deaf ears. The situation escalated, and the young man eventually failed the course, losing scholarship money for the year. The first student responded to the stress of the circumstance; the second student found himself in crisis.

Diagnostically, using Aguilera and Messick's model to differentiate between stress and crisis by the presence or absence of balancing factors, the practitioner can evaluate the problem or circumstance and the client's perception that it is beyond his or her coping abilities. Interventions can then be prescribed in response to the intensity of the crisis. Education and support, such as a referral to a self-help group, may be all that is required for an individual in transitional stress. Individuals in increasingly intractable situations may benefit from crisis counseling.

Trauma

The third term frequently associated with crisis counseling is trauma. Most textbooks and training models refer to trauma as one example of a crisis situation necessitating treatment. There is, however, a significant difference between crisis and trauma. A traumatic event threatens the physical or psychological life of an individual and, on an emotional level, causes intense and powerful feelings to emerge, potentially overwhelming and disorienting the individual with affect.

> Traumatic events are extraordinary, not because they occur rarely, but rather because they overwhelm the ordinary human adaptations to life. Unlike commonplace misfortunes, traumatic events generally involve threats to life or bodily integrity, or a close personal encounter with violence or death. They confront human beings with the extremities of helplessness and terror, and evoke the response of catastrophe. The common denominator of trauma is a feeling of intense fear, helplessness, loss of control, and threat of annihilation. (Herman, 1992, p. 3)

Webster's New Collegiate Dictionary defines trauma as an emotional shock that creates substantial, lasting damage to the psychological development of the individual. Current research suggests that the physiological impact of trauma alters the cognitive functioning of the individual in ways that will respond only to certain types of treatment. Crisis counseling may be helpful, but not sufficient, for the treatment of trauma.

One of the benchmark variables influencing the success of intervention approaches is the presence of psychological support in the aftermath of the traumatic event. It is impossible to adequately and fully treat the needs of a traumatized individual within a brief framework without accounting for the physical impact of care and support. In contrast to the six- to eight-hour brief therapy guidelines for crisis counseling, treatment for trauma may extend into much longer periods. The goal of crisis counseling is to restore equilibrium, that is, to return the individual to the precrisis state of functioning. An individual is changed indelibly by trauma. Rather than looking to assist the individual with restoration of equilibrium, the more appropriate goal for treating trauma is to reintegrate a sense of a new "normal." Metaphorically, crisis counseling is first aid and trauma psychotherapy is major surgery. Stress is a bruise, crisis a cut, and trauma a wound.

Consider this case. A young woman in her early thirties presented in a therapist's office and tearfully said, "I'm in a mess. This is the biggest crisis of my life. I'm married, have two children, a good husband, and a good job. I've been depressed most of my life, but it hasn't been bad enough to stop me from taking care of my obligations. I've known that I had a pretty rough upbringing and that there have been blocks of time where I just don't have any memory. I'm a jumpy sort of person and have always been suspicious of others. I'm moody much of the time, but just wrote it off to PMS. However, about a month ago, my husband and I were watching a made-for-TV movie and a child was sexually molested in the story. I started crying and began to have nightmares almost every night. Since then, I've begun to remember some horrible things about my childhood and now believe that I was sexually abused for several years when I was a young girl. This may answer a lot of the questions that I have about family secrets and my trouble 'staying in my own skin.' I'm scared to death to find out what I'm afraid that I already know and need your help. I'm so embarrassed to be here." In the telling of the story, this young woman begins to enter into excavation and exploration of a history of abuse and maltreatment from early caregivers.

Early life trauma is one of the most well researched and explored areas in social science and psychological literature. Such trauma, including treatment for sexual abuse and child neglect, warrants discussion, since treatment has different trajectories that can be achieved as a result of a brief intervention.

SELF-PSYCHOLOGY THEORY

Self-psychology theory is the preferred model for discussing and treating early life crisis and trauma. Affect deregulation, as noted earlier, is seen as a primary issue for survivors with trauma-related attachment problems. Contemporary experiences, such as the young woman's exposure to the provocative stimulus of the movie, produce overwhelming and out-of-control emotional states, which in turn create feelings of shame and guilt.

Theories of early childhood trauma support the notion that abuse at one stage of development, if unresolved, carries with it the potential for creating new problems at other stages of development (Friedrich, 1991). As the theory goes, disrupted attachment makes the child more vulnerable to abuse.

Self-psychology, as a disciplined theory, is able to indicate how the human infant cues an empathic self-object, that is, parents and primary caregivers, to perform caregiving functions which are then transmuted into self-functions, ultimately forming the psychic structure of a cohesive self. The psychological functions of infants are organized to respond to their need to be affirmed, admired, and stimulated, and to merge with the power and generosity of an idealized figure. The infant who moves in a normative way through childhood develops an unfolding transference onto the parent, not as a target of incestuous aims, but as a self-object who performs missing intrapsychic functions infants are unable to perform for themselves. These functions, through transmuting internalization, gradually become the child's own, ultimately allowing the growth of a cohesive, vigorous, and harmonious self that is capable of monitoring stress and regulating self-esteem on the journey to an enjoyable adulthood.

The process of self-object identification and differentiation begins at birth, when the infants' temperament cues others to their needs. The adult caregiver responds to the child, and, ideally, each merges with the other's calmness and competence. If this process happens effectively, the child grows and develops with creativity and good humor. If there is an absence of the capacity for self-soothing, a pervasive anxiety develops. The process of self-object identification and differentiation continues throughout the child's and adolescent's life. Each new phase of development provides the opportunity for further deepening and strengthening the self-structure and for improving its resiliency. As the individual grows into mature years, there are transitions that severely test the cohesiveness of the self, resulting in periods of lessened vigor, loss of purpose, and continuity. Self-objects play a role both in sustaining an individual during a period of such reverse and in tempering the excitement of success. The capacity of the individual to seek and find appropriate self-objects is the hallmark of health.

Wexler (1991) discusses four personality patterns resulting from faulty self-object environments. The first is the *understimulated self.* This pattern is characterized by the prolonged absence of stimulating responsiveness from central figures in the individual's life. Boredom and internal deadness become a chronic underlying state for the adult, and a sense of joy and satisfaction is rare or nonexistent. The individual is compelled toward excessive self-stimulating activities, such as drug use or compulsive sexuality. The result of such understimulation leads alternately to a severe defense against emotional life, characterized by an impoverished internal life and a disavowed sense of internal feeling states. A client described this state: "Life just doesn't excite me. If I don't have something to stir me up, I just feel like there is nothing inside." This client was self-described as a "cynic." He was a polysubstance abuser who initiated treatment for exposing himself while he urinated in a public park.

The second pattern is characterized as the *fragmented self.* In this incidence, there is a profound absence of experiences in response to the diverse emotional states of the child, known as a disturbance in the affective bond. The parent or primary caregiver is thought to have been overwhelmed, providing inadequate emotional responses to the child, so that the ability to stay organized and cope with emotional states is underdeveloped. Such early deprivation creates susceptibility to narcissistic injuries to the extent that the individual is unable to reintegrate effectively following a contemporary crisis. A narcissistically impaired client described his experience in this way: "I don't ever expect to get my needs met by one person. I'm just too big for that. I don't see anything wrong with having several relationships going at any one time. If the woman can't handle that, then I've always got a backup. Keeping several going keeps me from getting too involved with any one of them. I don't trust women, so I certainly don't want to get too attached." He presented for help when a woman rejected him, causing a crisis of monumental emotional proportion in this fellow's life.

The third pattern Wexler describes is the *overestimated self,* caused by the primary parent's or caregiver's excessive or overwhelming responses in the direction of exorbitant praise, adoration, or relentless mirroring. The personality pattern resulting is cast in a grandiosity that leads to chronic dissatisfaction with normal pleasure. A client presented for help resulting from a marital crisis. The client's wife demanded that he "grow up" in the context of their marriage. In his midforties, he was in a managerial position with a good deal of referent authority and responsibility. "What does she want?" He said, "I help her out and I really do care for her. I've got a big job though and think that she should take the lead in this. People love me in my work. Is it too much that I ask her to love me like I am?" His infantalized behavior in his primary relationship led to the crisis of attachment.

Finally, the fourth personality pattern is called the *overburdened self,* which has its genesis in the child's deprivation of the normal experience of being able to merge with a protective caregiver. Such a state predisposes the individual to difficulties with self-soothing. Vulnerability is a constant experience, leading to hypersensitivity, somatic disturbances, fear of risk taking, and withdrawal from normal interpersonal life. Julie* was such a client. She presented at regular intervals to her primary care physician with multiple complaints that had no physiologic genesis. She could not be soothed and at one point told her physician, "I know that you are keeping something from me." She was unwilling to accept a referral to a regional university teaching hospital, reporting that "going to a new doctor" was "too scary," and that she had no friends who were "close enough to accompany me in such a private matter." She reluctantly presented for therapy when her physician insisted that she be evaluated.

All such experiences are thought to be exploitive, which creates a sense of powerlessness and helplessness. The individual in turn develops an attribution style for negative events, all of which are distortions to the actual circumstances surrounding a contemporary event. Some will internalize and respond to crisis with the theme "It's all my

---

*The names of all clients mentioned in this book have been changed to maintain anonymity.

fault." Others will have more of a sense of stability about a crisis, saying, "It will always be this way." A third group will have more of a global attribution style and believe "It is this way for everything."

Long-term trauma survivors repeatedly perceive visual, tactile, kinesthetic, or olfactory memories of the traumatic event. They will engage in repetitive reenactments of aspects of the trauma in play and relationships. The long-term survivor is likely to develop trauma-specific fears (such as sex fear or anger fear) and will have pervasively changed attitudes about people, life, and the future (such as a sense of danger or untrustworthiness). Early trauma survivors will report a primary and pervasive violation of intimacy and a generalized sense of betrayal. By definition, early trauma will translate into an interpersonal experience that changes the fundamental view of the world. The goal of treatment is to form linkages among multiple realities of different self-states to facilitate relatively fluid ease between the states, to focus on relational and cognitive restructuring, and to create and maintain a cohesive self. Treatment goals are achieved when the individual has "the capacity to tolerate paradox" (Gartner, 1999, p. 83).

Early trauma is typically treated as a longer-term psychotherapy issue. In her seminal text, Miller (1994, p. 2) defined the crisis through a "trauma reenactment syndrome," which she equated with "hidden pain, visible hurting." In this paradigm, the individual who experiences early trauma begins to see the physical body as an enemy, which provides an illusion of control and a distorted sense of relief. Personal and familial secrets maintain the liveliness of the trauma because of its social and behavioral unacceptability. The secrecy is incorporated into a survivalistic defense where the symptom becomes "friend" and the child is loyal and protective of the incidence of abuse. Regretfully, this translates into a poor internal sense of protection, and a fragmented sense of the self. Ultimately, such fragmentation impairs relationships because of an inability to engage in reciprocal intimacy and a loss of permeable boundaries.

Symptoms and Treatment

Treatment for early life crisis and trauma is typically oriented to the creation of a sense of safety and empowerment. Safety is built in intrapsychic, interpersonal, and environmental ways. The individual is taught how to trust others outside of seduction or aggression. Boundaries are developed and responsibility is clarified. Empowerment then helps the individual to regain a sense of personal power and an ability to acknowledge strengths and validate survival skills. This allows the individual to learn and integrate new skills, particularly in the ability to acknowledge emotional states, which serves to anchor psychological and psychosocial growth. The individual progressively reclaims "lost" or "stuck" parts of the self and finds a new sense of cohesion and "wholeness." Much of the work is accomplished through examination of ego states and unconscious conflict. The theory suggests that the victims must learn a sense of internal empathy and find the ability to reparent themselves while anchoring the adult state in present resourcefulness. Work is considered long term and intrapersonal. Until the individual feels more of an internal sense of efficacy, empathy, and safety, there is no move to take resolution into a systemic response. Precipitous movement into exploration of the trauma without stabilization of ego defenses and preparation for the approaching traumatic memories may lead to negative therapeutic outcomes.

Unresolved early life trauma is also thought in self-psychology terms to lead to compulsivity. Compulsive behavior is believed to come from an identifiable source and operates in a predictable pattern (as opposed to impulsivity). In the self-psychology theory, compulsions serve as clues to the deeper life story of the individual's wounds. The compulsion is used in service to the ego to cover an interior emptiness. It is seen as a control mechanism providing an escape route from some memory or feeling that is ultimately inescapable and unavoidable. Furthermore, the compulsion represents an attempt to compensate for an internal sense of low self-esteem and powerlessness. The immediate agenda of a compulsion is to maintain a sense of basic survival in the face of what feels like annihilation. The frequency of the behavior displayed is dependent on the depth of one's pain and/or current difficulties in life. Ultimately, engaging in compulsive activity creates the illusion of control and the pursuing of illusions creates an internalized sense of betrayal.

Carnes and Rening (1994) describe dimensions of early childhood trauma as manifesting in eight different ways:

1. Trauma reactions—physiological and/or psychological alarm reactions from unresolved trauma experiences
2. Trauma repetition—repeating behaviors and/or seeking situations or persons that re-create the trauma experience
3. Trauma pleasure—seeking/finding pleasure in the presence of extreme danger, violence, risk, or shame
4. Trauma blocking—efforts to numb, block out, or overwhelm residual feelings due to trauma
5. Trauma abstinence—compulsive deprivation that occurs especially around moments of success, high stress, shame, or anxiety
6. Trauma shame—profound sense of unworthiness and self-hatred rooted in trauma experience
7. Trauma splitting—blocking traumatic realities by "splitting off" experience and not integrating into personality or daily life
8. Trauma bonding—dysfunctional attachments that occur in the presence of danger, shame, or exploitation

The challenge to treatment for compulsivity is to offer new, positive images of the self, coupled with positively reinforcing statements. Often, there is confusion occurring when the individual feels that the thought or image actually leads to better feeling and that it helps the individual behave in the way that the individual wants. Oftentimes, a compulsive behavior is coupled with a thought or image that leads the individual to feel that his or her productive movement through the early trauma and engaging in the compulsive behavior may actually improve contemporary relationships.

DEVELOPMENTAL AND NORMATIVE CRISES

As noted, it is a helpful distinction when looking at models for treatment to discern types of crises. Developmental crises are normative events requiring successful completion of a psychological task in order to grow and mature. Movement through school, the advent of puberty, menopause, and death are considered developmental crises, since they are typical and expected of all human beings. What moves them into nonnormative events is the pervasive sense of loss of control, anxiety, depression, and the sense of helplessness that throws the individual into a different type of crisis.

Erikson's (1963) model of psychosocial development is instructive in understanding situational as well as developmental stress, crisis, and trauma. Erikson organizes development around eight critical relational milestones (see Table 2.3). Failure to achieve any of these eight milestones results in deficits in subsequent psychosocial characteristics that will enable the individual to adapt and adjust to emerging demands, and to experience resiliency in the face of change. He believed that these eight milestones are representative of a normative passage that was defined as crisis. These developmental crises are times of vulnerability for the individual and the family system. Understanding the stages enables the clinician to explain how particular events may precipitate distress and how each particular stage has a different precipitant. Table 2.3 organizes these stages around types of situational crises that may intersect with developmental crises, also known as milestones, creating challenges of adjustment. Normative response to developmental issues provides important diagnostic and treatment information for counselors. A brief review and examples will be helpful.

At birth, the infant is dependent on care from adults in order to meet basic physical and emotional needs. Failure to meet these needs impacts the infant's sense of security and trust in the outside world.

TABLE 2.3. Developmental Challenges to Adjustment

	Impact		
	Stress	**Crisis**	**Trauma**
Trust vs. Mistrust	Newborn; adoption colic	Adoption	Child abuse SIDS
Autonomy vs. Shame and Doubt	Toilet training	Moving	Parental abduction
Initiative vs. Guilt	Night terrors	Broken bones	Abandonment
Industry vs. Inferiority	Learning	Learning disabilities; school refusal	School violence
Intimacy vs. Isolation	"Coming out"	Rejection by family	Hate crimes
Generativity vs. Stagnation	Retirement	Unemployment	House fire
Integrity vs. Despair	Assisted-living placement	Alzheimer's disease	Death of spouse

The infant may resolve this crisis by becoming vigilant and self-protective, discounting relationships as a source of safety and security. At the same time, the demands of a newborn change the relationship between the parents. An unplanned or difficult pregnancy, the birth of a stillborn or handicapped child, or the disruption of work and loss of income due to the pregnancy may throw a developmental milestone into crisis.

As children biologically become capable of self-care around the age of two, they begin to move away from their parents, beginning the process of self-differentiation. The parents' "job" is to be present to "catch" the child as they experience the dangers of separation. Such a task allows the child to experience risk. Progressively, as they are successful, the children look forward and know that a loving parent is present to break the fall of failure and to lift them up and begin again. The increased autonomy also presents dangers. As a parent cried, "I only fell asleep for a few minutes and he disappeared. When we found him at the bottom of the pool, I was devastated. How could I have been so stupid?"

Around the age of three, the development of language, movement, and imagination creates a sense of wonder within the child. Curiosity provides the impetus to intrude into the adult world. The child begins to take an active part in shaping the world, even as the child is shaped. Parents find their child's emerging personality taking its own character, separate from the adult. This initiative is either welcomed or shamed by the parent. If shamed, the child (and later the adult) is unwilling to take risks. Perfectionism becomes an illusive goal, one that sets the child up to experience inadequacy as a lifestyle in later ages and stages. Those situations that require action may instead paralyze the individual. Coping with new challenges becomes overwhelming.

At about age five, the child's attention moves from home into the world of school. Here the crisis of industry, also known as mastery, takes on new dimensions. Children compare their strengths and weaknesses with those of peers in academic, social, and emotional arenas. This begins a lifelong process of acceptance of limitations and an increased capacity to embrace those coping mechanisms that will become the basis for adjustment throughout life. If the child experiences failure, the parents are also affected. As one parent said, "The diagnosis of John's learning disability shattered our hope that he would follow his father's footsteps into medicine. All of us had to revisit our cherished dreams."

At adolescence, the questions of "Who am I? How do I fit in the world? What do I believe? What of my parents' teachings will I accept/reject?" create a crisis for both the family and the teenager. This crisis of identity has ramifications for social, vocational, and spiritual choices. Failure to make choices, to make choices too soon, or to abdicate the choice to others can significantly change the course of the adolescent's life. The power of the peer group shapes these choices and oftentimes leaves parents at a loss as to how to regain an enjoyable relationship with their teenager. The advent of puberty and the choices about sexual expression are particularly sensitive areas in the family. Lack of communication skills for honestly addressing intimate areas leaves both parents and teenagers lacking a sense of security. For example, an adolescent's "coming out" as gay or lesbian has left many families hurt and broken.

In young adulthood, the individual moves away from parenting. The tasks of adolescence have been met and should provide a foundation for independence and choice. Decisions around work, marriage, and residence either move the young person toward developmentally appropriate options, or not. Failure at this stage leaves the parent feeling unsuccessful in "job" completion and the young person is left diminished. One parent told a heartbreaking story: "My son had a closed head injury following a motorcycle accident," the father said. "He's now partially paralyzed and intellectually compromised. His girlfriend has rejected him and he lost his job. We feel like we have a child to raise all over again."

The middle-aged adult, challenged by unmet goals and beginning physical decline, will find this stage to have meaning as teacher, mentor, coach, or guide to the rising generation. If this does not happen, the individual becomes dissatisfied and disillusioned by life's lack of meaning. The "midlife crisis" often speaks of the impulsive and destructive attempt to find meaning outside of commitments to family or work. There are many examples of a spouse leaving a long-term marriage, taking up a second career, or buying youth through plastic surgery or expensive gadgets that make this crisis all too apparent. Children are not spared from the impact as their beliefs about life and love are challenged in light of the parents' distress. As one young adult said, "I couldn't believe that my father left my mother just when they could begin to enjoy life. I've lost trust in him and feel responsible for my mother. How in the world am I supposed to manage this?"

Finally, the last stage of life demands meeting the needs of failing health, loss of spouse and friends, impending death, and disruption of family support. The elderly need the advantage of resolution of the preceding developmental crises to successfully negotiate this phase. Done well, reflection and acceptance will create existential resolution. Problems with this phase result in depression and despair.

SYSTEMIC CRISES

Crisis occurs in context. Family systems theory teaches that a stone thrown into water changes both the stone and water; neither will remain the same. When stress, crisis, or trauma occurs to an individual, a family, the community, or, as in the circumstance of the 9/11 disaster, a nation or world, the practitioners are obligated to expand their scope of the systemic response to the event. The greater the scope, the more systemic the impact, including placing the crisis counselor at increased vulnerability resulting from entrance into the crisis situation.

Using the models of treatment paradigm (Table 2.1), the crisis counselor can evaluate treatment approaches required by the nature and depth of the event and its impact on the individual and his or her social system. An example may clarify. Developmental sources of stress can be identified and treated using a tool such as the Life Change Index Scale (Holmes & Rahe, 1967). Treatment for a normative crisis might focus on limiting the number or types of changes in the life of the person. Physical or emotional ill health could be understood by the degree and depth of life change units experienced by the individual. As one fellow said after picking up his white chip at Alcoholics Anonymous, "I now understand why I'm not supposed to make any major life decisions this year. Staying sober is going to be hard enough for me. I can't imagine adding the stress of a new job or a new relationship right now. I really hear the message: One day at a time."

Examples of situational sources of stress include health-related conditions, such as cancer, or a work-related source of stress, such as unemployment.

Systemic sources of stress would occur in a family involved in elder care for an aging parent, or caregiving for an injured family member. The necessity for physical care, the impact on finances, and/or the loss of role-related responsibilities may lead to exhaustion and compassion fatigue.

Crises can also occur from developmental, situational, or systemic sources. For example, a seemingly stable and successful professional man was denied an expected promotion. He experienced a midlife crisis, which led to a decision to separate from his wife. He later said, "I broke up my family. It's not like things weren't bad enough. I had my head buried in the sand and thought that if I didn't get the promotion that I was doomed on my career track. Now look what I've got—a lot of lonely time to think about what kind of mess I've gotten myself into." Developmentally, he is vulnerable to crisis. His wife, who had no part in his decision-making process, but suffers from the impact, finds herself in a situational crisis, and the family members, in their helplessness to change their father's decisions, experience a systemic crisis.

Trauma can also occur on a developmental, situational, or systemic level. On a developmental level, the most relevant example of such a crisis is the sexual abuse of a child. Self- and ego psychology is the recommended and recognized treatment for such trauma. Situational trauma, occurring from an automobile accident, an accidental shooting, or a brutal rape, will lead to the treatment response described by trauma theory. As an initial therapeutic response, critical incident stress debriefing is prescribed. Systemic trauma can occur when a family or entire community is disrupted by a life-threatening situation, such as a natural disaster or the tragedy of the World Trade Center and Pentagon. Coordinated community services must be mobilized to meet these needs.

It may be the successful management of stress that prevents its movement into crisis; appropriate interventions for stress may prevent or ameliorate trauma. Research efforts, comparing and contrasting types of treatment designed to neutralize the severity of stress from different sources of impact, may allow the practitioner better understanding of the effectiveness of differing models of treatment. Looking at crisis in a continuum benefits the practitioner throughout the course of treatment. Initially, such a stance allows the counselor entrance into the system, then adds options as time and circumstance change the nature of the crisis as it unfolds. Ultimately, viewing the crisis as a process helps guide choice and option as the client returns to normative states of functioning.

Tuesdays with Morrie (Albom, 1997) is a lovely example of a systemic view of crisis. The anticipation of death is common to all who will take the time to recognize human mortality. The impact of impending death on Morrie leads him to recollect and to teach final, important lessons of life. Many would find such a circumstance so frightening that they might lose functional abilities. Morrie, however, took the time to direct his remaining life energies in directions that provided meaning for the greater good.

MODELS FOR INTERVENTION

Treatment planning for any psychological problem is based on the practitioner's theoretical understanding of the problem's precipitant and development. Interventions are based on empirically supported data that assess functional impairment, coping styles, goal consensus, and collaborative variables generally categorized as relational attributes. Treatment outcome is based on clinical and observational data reflecting changes made, as prescribed by theory and intervention. Depending on the theory's stance, limits are placed on the scope of the problem and identification of what constitutes symptom resolution.

The many different trauma theories illustrate this perspective. As noted, a precipitant is defined, its impact on the individual identified, and treatment interventions chosen based on the needs of the client in concert and collaboration with the practitioner. One definition of trauma says that an event "causes disrupted pathways and memory patterns" (Shapiro, 1996, p. 209). Such trauma can be treated using a hypnotic approach called eye movement desensitization reprocessing (EMDR). This and other biologically based approaches alter physiologic impact through perceived shifts in encoding memory. The rapid eye movements, coupled with suggestions from the therapist, are designed to alter the experience of the memory of trauma, giving the individual a sense of mastery in place of the sense of loss of control.

EMDR is founded on Pavlov's theory that an excitatory-inhibitory balance in the brain underlies normal functioning. Trauma disrupts

this balance, causing an overexcitation of the nervous sys
perceptions and sensations of the trauma are encoded in the
system and are capable of disturbing the individual long a
trauma has ended. EMDR allows the processing of this perc
and sensory information so that information of value can be retained
and that which is destructive eliminated. Using rapid eye movements,
coupled with suggestions that the individual change the focus of
attention to different aspects of the traumatic event, the synaptic path-
way of the traumatic memory is thought to be disrupted. In addition,
the individual explores thoughts, feelings, and behaviors influenced
by the trauma.

Francine Shapiro (1996), founder of the technique, admits to a lack
of scientific data to fully support the theory but points to extensive research supporting its success in the treatment of trauma. She points
out that there are more controlled studies of EMDR than of any other
method used in the treatment of post-traumatic stress disorder (PTSD)
(Shapiro, 1996). Her literature review found only six other controlled
clinical outcome studies of psychological interventions in the entire
field of PTSD (Solomon, Gerrity, & Muff, 1992).

Another definition of trauma can be conceived of as "massive psychic disruption, which involves an attack on ego-coherence and the experience of the 'death imprint'" (Lifton, 1993, p. 11). Such a definition
corresponds to intervention from a psychodynamic perspective and is
directed at avoidance of repression and a reduction of psychic anxiety. A similar approach is Lindsey's brief-term psychodynamic intervention approach to trauma (Lindsey, 2005). His interventions examine
the trauma within a historical context. With emphasis on the therapeutic relationship, change is measured through the integration of
the altered sense of self. Another approach is the behaviorally based
theory of Edna Foa (1998). The brief behavioral intervention proce-
dure incorporates exposure-based treatment with anxiety reduction
methods, helping victims "overcome" the trauma. This model has its
critics, however. Gilfus (1999) argues that Foa's approach is too victim oriented. Other approaches emphasize cognitive-behavioral technique. The model of Van der Kolk, McFarlane, and Van der Hart
(1996) includes components for stabilization, deconditioning of traumatic memories and responses, restructuring of traumatic personal
schemas, and reestablishing secure social connections in order to en-

hance interpersonal efficacy and the accumulation of sensitive emotional experiences.

Finally, a similar model, the WITS Trauma Intervention Model (Eagle, 1998) integrates two approaches. Combining psychodynamic and cognitive-behavioral perspectives, trauma is understood both as impacting the psychic structures of individuals and influencing their ability to solve problems. In this model, trauma is conceived as a complex experience, including the impact of the external stressor experienced by all involved, and its interface with the individual's psychic response to the threat of death. The components of the model include telling the story, normalizing symptoms, addressing blame and survivor guilt, encouraging mastery, and facilitating the creation of meaning. Myer (2001) admits that the approach has not been subjected to rigorous research but believes that the client feedback and clinical evaluations demonstrate success. The face validity of this model comes from experience with the unique nature of trauma, coupled with the literature that presupposes the universality of the symptoms of trauma.

The CISD model is a treatment approach widely used to reduce the psychological impact of trauma. This single-session approach, designed for groups, has the twofold purpose of mitigating crisis survivors' post-traumatic stress responses and identifying individuals who may need additional psychological support (Everly, 1995). This intervention method is designed to facilitate effective cognitive processing through immediate human contact. It allows for catharsis, provides a forum to reconstruct and verbalize the trauma, facilitates support of the group for each individual participant, and offers practical information for understanding trauma response. CISD treats physical and/or psychological symptoms associated with exposure to trauma. Two components, debriefing and defusing, define the intervention. Debriefing allows individuals to talk about the traumatic event and to explore the meaning of the experience in their lives. Defusing allows for the expression of deeply felt affective states and the processing of thoughts and beliefs about the event. This intervention is designed to be used twenty-four to seventy-two hours after the impact of the event. Davis (1998) outlines the approach:

- The debriefer assesses the impact on survivors and support personnel.
- Issues of safety and security are managed.
- Ventilation and validation allow the individual to discuss exposure, thoughts, and feelings related to the event.
- The debriefer guides the individual through predicting, preparing, and planning for future events that may cause physical and/or psychological problems.
- The debriefer does a systematic review of the impact on the physical, emotional, and psychological functioning of the individual.
- Information on community resources is provided with a plan for future action.
- Debriefing assists in the systematic review of the events before, during, and after the trauma.

Early outcome studies have generated controversy regarding the outcome of the approach for ameliorating post-trauma morbidity (Everly & Mitchell, 2000). Empirical evidence comes from a variety of studies. Campbell and Hills (2001) examined the effects of CISD among robbery victims. One group received immediate debriefing, within ten hours of the incident, while the second group's debriefing was delayed. Those immediately debriefed reported fewer and less severe symptoms at days two and four, as well as two weeks after the incident. A study by Mayor, Elhers, and Hobbs (2000) found no significant difference in avoidance and intrusion symptoms between individual road traffic victims who received debriefing and those who did not. In fact, the debriefed group reported more severe psychiatric symptoms, such as higher levels of pain, hostility, anxiety, depression, and obsessive-compulsive symptoms. These individuals typically recovered to a lesser degree physically and rated the quality of their daily living at a lower level in a three-year follow-up study. Single-session psychological trauma debriefings with trauma reviewed by Rose, Bisson, and Wessely (2001) conclude that this treatment did not reduce psychological distress or prevent symptoms associated with PTSD. They interpret results as evidence that CISD is not an effective intervention technique for trauma.

Again, the complexity of the traumatic event, individual characteristics of victims, and training and competency of the professional
providing treatment are moderating variables that significantly alter
the results of studies of CISD (Altmaier, 2002). The perspective of
the research, models of treatment, and the subjective value of treatment impact its effectiveness. Therefore, rather than discounting the
value of this approach, it would be helpful to evaluate the type of traumatic incident and determine what therapeutic techniques provided
by a trained clinician might best serve each individual crisis victim.
Consider the following example of how the same intervention led to
significantly different responses from multiple victims of one traumatic incident.

A vice president of human resources died of a heart attack early
one morning during a staff meeting in his urban office. Nine staff
members were present. That afternoon, members of the employee assistance program (EAP) conducted a CISD. The session went well,
with varied individual responses. One member of the group said, "It
really let me know that our company is interested in our group's wel-
fare." Another said, "I thought it was pretty intrusive that the company tried to tell me what I should be feeling. It was none of their
business." A third came to the EAP counselor within the week, reporting an increase in nightmares, a loss of appetite, and generalized
anxiety. "My father died of a sudden heart attack. I thought I had gotten over it, but when it happened to the boss, I had a flashback to my
own dad. I've not been able to get the images out of my mind and I
feel like I'm going crazy." Clearly, individual characteristics of the
victims will vary the effectiveness of CISD intervention.

Brewin (2001) provides the most compelling theory regarding the
contradictory nature of the research on debriefing following trauma.
He theorizes that immediate intervention following trauma may interrupt the natural healing process of the body. When a traumatic event
occurs, the immediate emotional responses include fear, helplessness,
and horror. Once the immediate threat has passed and the individual
has had time to intellectually process the meaning of the event, secondary emotions, such as guilt and shame, may emerge. Some traumatic events, such as a car accident, may occur so quickly that only
emotional, not cognitive, responses may be present. Other traumatic
events that occur over a longer period of time, such as combat, allow

a wider range of emotionality, coupled with cognitive responses. When stressful events are maintained over a longer period of time, the body secretes endogenous opiates, in effect creating psychological numbing. Cognitive responses accompany this intense emotional response. It is not unusual for the individual in this state to experience a sense of helplessness, which may be so overwhelming it leads to a type of mental defeat (Ehlers, Macrecker, & Boggs, 2000). The individual simply gives up and waits for whatever fate has to offer. Once the threat passes and individuals begin to recover, they may be left with residual hypervigilance to guard against similar threats that might occur in the future. This is the body's natural and primitive defense against high levels of stress. The neurological functioning of the individual is automatically aroused, specifically in the prefrontal cortex and the hippocampus areas of the brain. Attention becomes narrowed, thinking is more rigid, and confusion and disorientation occur. Feelings of depersonalization and derealization cause a disruption to normal states of consciousness. The victim of such a process typically feels detached from consensual reality. Such was the description of a woman who experienced a bank robbery: "I was minding my own business, on a perfectly fine, ordinary day. Then the robbery occurred and it was like everything happened in slow motion. I was aware of everything but could remember none of it. I was amazed when the police questioned me how little I remembered. I was lost, out of sorts, and irritable the rest of the day. It brought new meaning to the old saying, 'I didn't know whether I was coming or going.' I literally didn't know up from down for a couple of days."

These neurological and psychological changes explain why individuals have difficulty recalling details of a traumatic event. Brewin (Brewin, Dalgleish, & Joseph, 1996; Brewin, 2001) has proposed a "dual representation" theory, describing the memory of events as stored in two separate memory banks, labeled as verbally accessible memory and situationally accessible memory. Verbally accessible memory contains information about the event that is encoded using the present language capacities of the individual. These capacities are integrated with previous memories about the past, representations of the self, and beliefs about the world. Situationally accessible memory is encoded through sensory pathways, including visual, auditory, olfactory, and touch receptors, and acts in accord with the emotional and physiological changes of the individual's experience. Memories from the situationally encoded pathways are retrieved when the individual is exposed to stimuli similar to the traumatic event. In this way, responses are generated from the original response. "I was assaulted outside of a gay bar," one man described. "Several weeks after the mugging, a friend came to visit my family for dinner. He had on new cologne that sent me into a terrible emotional flashback. Once I caught my breath, I recognized the same scent my attacker had worn. It just brought the whole experience back."

As the individual relives the traumatic event, a variety of affective and emotional states may be evoked from memory. Magical thinking may be employed as a defensive strategy, leading to the belief that alternative behaviors could have prevented the catastrophe. It is also possible that, as the individual moves toward an irrational belief about the ability to foretell the future or to forestall the disaster, shame, guilt, and depression will emerge. As one woman said, "It was my fault. I should've seen it coming. I am simply a bad person for ignoring all the signs that I should've spotted." Alternately, when responsibility is shifted exclusively to others, common responses evoked include anger, rage, and resentment. Following an arrest for road rage with physical altercation, a man screamed at the police officer, "It was not my fault. It was all theirs. People can be such jerks. They had it coming. I should get some medal or something for this, not arrested."

Following trauma, flashbacks—or vivid memories—are known to occur with increasing frequency. Brewin (2001) theorizes that such flashbacks arise from situationally encoded memories having no reference point to past or present. As the individual is able to bring language to bear in the telling and retelling of the story, insight and understanding begin to take hold. A sense of safety ensues as the individual realizes and clarifies the flashbacks as representations of past experience, not present danger. A woman said, "I wish I didn't go back to the night that I was stabbed. At least now, years later, I can use the memory as a warning sign, and I don't get immobilized by my fear. When I flash back, I wonder what in my present situation is reminding me of danger, and I look for environmental cues until I'm reassured that I'm safe."

The dual model for understanding the encoding of memory reflects the complexity of the traumatic crisis experience. Original traumatic memories are encoded and can be accessed at a later time. New representations of the event are created in the verbally accessible memory system and consolidated through behavior rehearsal.

The normal course of adjustment occurs in the days following a traumatic crisis experience. Immediate symptoms hopefully will disappear and become less powerful. Interventions that interfere with this normal healing process may, in fact, create rather than heal symptoms. The appropriate role for the clinician is to ensure a sense of personal and environmental safety so that the victim can develop "in" sight without the burden of environmental hypervigilance. The practitioner is further obligated to recognize the impact of the crisis in the life of others surrounding the individual. "Spreading the wealth" and creating a safe zone allows for the normal processing of traumatic experiences without disruption. Failure to have this type of safe time and space leads to repression of memory, which will cause continuing problems with the trauma. Finally, information is a powerful source of security. Facts of the experience, as well as perceptions and intuitions, allow the individual a road map to recovery in a natural, authentic sense. While more pointed external interventions, such as critical incident stress debriefing, may be helpful, it is strongly suggested that the natural healing process be monitored to determine at a later time if additional treatment is indicated.

The "screen and treat" (Brewin, 2001) is an instrument designed to determine if additional support might be needed. It consists of six questions:

1. How many of the intellectual functions are capable of minimally adequate operation?
2. What interpersonal assets are available?
3. What emotional resources are available to contain the disorganization?
4. What are the dimensions of the hope structure? Can it be activated for the purpose of control?
5. How much motivation does the individual have to help himself or herself?
6. To what degree has the individual himself or herself reacted or aggravated the crisis situation?

The crisis counselor uses this screening device to determine needs for treatment.

MODELS OF ASSESSMENT

First, the decision of which model of crisis intervention and therapy is most appropriate begins with methods of assessment. Assessment may consist of a structured, standardized approach to understanding the situation at hand or may unfold in a more traditional approach, using the clinical interview as a means of answering relevant assessment questions. Since a *Diagnostic and Statistical Manual of Mental Disorders* (DSM; APA 2000) diagnosis is not needed for crisis counseling, the assessment is conducted to determine lethality, that is, suicidality or homicidality, and to examine vulnerable victims, establishing treatment needs and goals. The challenge of the assessment phase of crisis work is held in the balance of the clinician's need for information and the client's need to feel heard and understood. Most researchers agree that any assessment model should first be parsimonious and user friendly (Myer, 2001). If the assessment is difficult or extended for too long a period of time, both the client and the clinician may become distracted from the tasks of quickly developing a therapeutic alliance.

Second, an assessment model for crisis intervention should be flexible enough to meet the needs of clinicians working within a variety of crisis situations and contexts. It is rare that a practitioner will see only one type of client. Having different models for different clients or types of situations puts the clinician at risk for becoming overwhelmed with treatment scaffoldings and demands externally imposed by differing theoretical persuasions. A codified model allows clinicians room to flex their therapeutic muscle in ways that are congruent with training and experience.

A third consideration in comparing models of assessment in crisis intervention relates to the need to include multiple dimensions of the crisis situation. Ignoring important dimensions may compromise the long-term success of the approach or can defeat the immediate intervention efforts. A client told a profound story: "I was at my doctor's office for a physical. During the workup he found a critical problem and demanded that I go to the hospital immediately. He couldn't understand why I was so reluctant to follow his directions and check myself in right then and there. I had other obligations that I had to attend to. I had left an elderly mother babysitting with my four-year-old child. My mother could not drive and had a fair amount of physical impairment. My wife was out of town for several days. Until I got the demands of elder care and child care met, if I had a living breath in my body, I couldn't leave my mother and son stranded. The physician kept saying, 'This is a time that you have to look out after yourself.' I kept saying, 'I know, I know, but there are other things that are just about as important as my getting to the hospital immediately.'"

Finally, to make a good assessment of the crisis situation, the counselor must be culturally sensitive. Culture speaks to shared meanings and ways of a group of people. Cultural competence is known as the capacity to work effectively with people of a variety of ethnic, cultural, political, and religious backgrounds. Such competence requires the counselor to be acutely aware of how individual cultural influences affect one's view of others. Client perceptions of what constitutes a crisis and beliefs about what can or should be done about it are shaded by culture. Cultural sensitivity is the integration of knowledge about individuals into specific practices and attitudes that increase quality of services, thus producing better outcomes. This is a view that recognizes race/ethnicity and intersects with other factors, such as gender, socioeconomic class, history, and current oppression. These aspects impact the individual's values, perceptions, and expectations for seeking help and for health and wellness beliefs. Such culturally rooted health beliefs influence help-seeking behavior. They also impact the individual's tolerance for stress and coping capacity for the perception of crisis. The counselor must use cultural sensitivity to assess the individual's presentation at treatment, access to treatment, and response to treatment. It is incumbent on the competent crisis therapist to understand culturally different others and the dynamics of working with individuals of similar cultural backgrounds.

Assessment Tools

Myer's (2001) Triage Assessment Model and his Triage Assessment Form: Crisis Intervention (TAF) reflect an appreciation of the aforementioned characteristics of assessment. The TAF assesses crisis in three domains: behavioral, cognitive, and affective. In the behavioral stage, responses are considered to be one of three types: approach, avoidance, or immobile. Cognitive responses are identified as those thoughts of loss, threat, or transgression. In the affective realm, feelings of anger/hostility, anxiety/fear, and sadness/melancholy are assessed. Research on the reliability and validity of the TAF by Walters (1997) compared the average rating of groups of individuals with crisis intervention experts, using vignettes of role-plays between crisis counselors and clients. Inexperienced students in undergraduate programs, recruits from the police academy, and experienced graduate students had a 97 percent agreement with experts using the TAF assessment model.

This model is believed to be superior to other current models of assessment. For comparison's sake, the Hoff (1995) model assesses safety and the ability to function. Information on difficulty in managing feelings, suicidal or homicidal behaviors, substance abuse, legal involvement, and the inability to effectively use available assistance assessed from affective, cognitive, and behavioral realms gives a comprehensive picture of functioning. His model, though, is long and cumbersome to use. The Slaikeu model (1990) is a multidimensional model based on the BASIC-ID model of Lazarus (1981). This model is adapted to include the BASIC components along with a B factor, reflecting the behavioral responses to the crisis, particularly regarding activities of daily living and lethality tendencies. All those involved in the support system of the client are invited to provide assessment information. This assessment model is as cumbersome as the Hoff model. The assessment task involves completing a twelve-page comprehensive form. It is not efficient or adaptable for emergencies or brief work.

The Hendricks and McKean model (1995) includes two types of assessment. Initially, one is completed by first responders, such as medics and police officers. Those individuals are asked to determine continuing threats to individual and environmental security. The second portion of the assessment is completed by the crisis clinician. This person, once the crisis scene is safe, uses a "who, what, when, where, and why" approach, identifying necessary information needed to effectively intervene. This model gives little direction to the responders; therefore, its utility is marginal.

The genogram is a tool of choice in family systems work. It allows the clinician to assess the functioning of the individual within the context of family and history. Used in a crisis situation, the genogram allows a collegial approach between the therapist and client as they collaboratively search for meaning of the crisis while tracking historical information that will identify strengths and vulnerabilities in the system. Use of the genogram allows the clinician to identify and incorporate idiosyncratic cultural information. The creation of the genogram allows the client a "working test" for regaining a sense of control. It is a competency-based tool, allowing the client to re-create a sense of previous success and a restoration of precrisis identity. If gathered in the process of listening to the client's recounting of the crisis, creating a genogram takes no time away from the interaction between counselor and client.

These assessment tools help quantify the degree of disorganization and symptom formation by the victim of crisis. Familiarity and comfort with the use of these tools will enhance the counselor's ability to set goals and determine treatment.

MODELS OF TREATMENT

The techniques of crisis intervention must also be defined and delineated so that different approaches can be evaluated. The approach most like traditional crisis counseling is brief psychotherapy, but there are distinct differences. Table 1.1 clearly distinguishes the differences. Most notable are the comparisons of client characteristics, therapeutic techniques, the client-counselor relationship, and termination. Practitioners of brief psychotherapy were not apprised of the significant role of crisis counseling as a mode of treatment until after 1960. In fact, Marmor's earlier review (1980) did not include crisis counseling as a type of brief psychotherapy. His later reviews give considerable attention to this approach.

Crisis intervention is not stress management, nor is it simply short-term psychotherapy. To clearly identify what is and is not crisis counseling, it is necessary to look at the evolution and history of a variety of models and to compare theoretical models most similar to the approach under study. Traditional scaffolds of counseling and therapy are based on understanding human suffering from an intrapsychic or interpersonal frame of reference. The schema of crisis intervention, in context, has developed from the impact of external sources of distress and disequilibrium.

A Justification for a New Model of Treatment

It is a commonly held psychological truth that an individual's resistance to stress is finite and idiosyncratic. As has been said, under certain circumstances, every person will find present coping mechanisms inadequate to sustain psychological equilibrium. This state will cause emotional disorganization, internal confusion, and distress. A benchmark for the presence of crisis is the individual's experience of loss, defined as a state of being deprived of something one has had or valued (Rainer, 1998). Crisis treatment will involve systemic efforts to supplement the personal resources of the individual who has "lost" and is failing under stress, rather than assuming that the individual is in the presence of a disease process.

Oftentimes, an individual's losses during crisis are ill defined. The elusive nature of such loss only compounds the sense of erosion of resources within the system. These are known as ambiguous losses. They create a powerful block to coping and are predictive of symptoms such as depression, anxiety, loss of mastery, hopelessness, and conflict, all of which can undermine the individual's sense of self in relationship (Boss, 1999).

In her research, Boss (1999, 2001) discusses family stress and cites five reasons why the ambiguity surrounding a crisis can make people feel helpless and more prone to symptomatology:

1. Ambiguity surrounding the crisis keeps the system confused. Such confusion impedes the ability to make effective decisions. When individuals are cognitively immobilized, they may choose irrational responses that provide relief without healing or integration.
2. Ambiguity surrounding the outcome of crisis prevents a reorganization of family roles, rules, and rituals. All the members of the system retreat to an "as they were" stance without accounting for the impact of the crisis. An example will illuminate this. A nine-year-old child disappeared one morning on her way to school. There were never any clues to the mystery of her ab-

sence. Months later, the family was interviewed by the local newspaper and the mother of the missing girl said, "We move through the day like we need to, but she is always on our minds. Just because we talk less about it today than we did a month ago doesn't mean that it isn't what weighs heaviest on my mind and heart."

3. Without customary markers of loss, due to the extraordinary nature of crisis, the system's distress remains unverified. With no validation, any changes of adaptations are considered premature, so the system stays frozen in place. In the same interview, the father described the family's inability to celebrate holidays and to honor family traditions. He said, "We just don't know what to do. Time passes, but we don't seem to."

4. Ambiguity surrounding the crisis causes even the strongest of individuals and families to question their view of the world as fair and just. The search for meaning requires discussion as well as personal contemplation. An older fellow described his private experience of his son, a Vietnam veteran and prisoner of war for several years: "I was always a patriot, and supported my country. I was proud of my son for his military service. When he was lost, though, I railed at the government, the politicians, and everybody else, trying to find some sense of fairness and justice. It was just as hard when he came home, because he was so changed by the experience. His grandfather would go around saying, 'It doesn't fit.' That's where I finally came to rest with it—it just doesn't fit."

5. Ambiguous loss of long duration becomes physically and psychologically exhausting. Symptoms of fatigue become increasingly relevant for consideration. The mother of the missing child complained of being "bone tired but unable to rest."

Moving from ambiguity to clarity is a significant determinant of healing. Techniques for accomplishing this goal are crucial for therapeutic success.

Restoration of Functioning

Crisis treatment involves systemic efforts to supplement the personal resources of the individual who is failing under stress, rather than assuming that the individual is in the presence of a disease process. Life experiences of individuals differ from person to person and will impact the effectiveness of any intervention. Response to crisis will vary, not only according to intrapsychic variables, but also because of gender, ethnic, and cultural factors that will influence psychological and social trajectories of healing and integration. Quick fixes are not applicable.

As time and technology change the emerging face of psychotherapy, new models for service delivery are also obligated to bend and mold to current demands. The systemic model of crisis presented is comprised of a combination of traditional models, integrated to meet the unique needs of the person/family/system in crisis in today's world. It is influenced by the recognition that life in the twenty-first century is different and continues to change from even our recent past. Twenty-four-hour media coverage of new crises threatens individual senses of safety and security. A pseudobond develops between people in different areas of the country and world, resulting from the immediacy and repetition of the reporting. The mobility of contemporary society robs individuals of the comfort of lifelong family and friends who are available to help negotiate life transitions. The increasing lack of mental health resources creates a gap in service delivery.

The foundation of the systemic treatment model, based in theory and technique, is one focused on healing the wounds precipitated by crisis. Its novelty is found in integration and process, reflecting the progression of the needs of the individual in crisis. In a real sense "the old is new again." Family systems thinking, cognitive-behavioral therapy, existential-experiential treatment, and narrative psychotherapy have long been the standard of care for many psychological needs. Each represents a dimension of the systemic model, and without each dimension, the model would lose its power.

A systems, rather than individual, approach to crisis counseling expands the perspective beyond the direct victim as patient and into an understanding that others are directly and indirectly impacted by the event. Imagine, for example, the distress experienced by the spouse of the rape victim, the family members of the terminally ill, and passengers in a car accident that claims the life of the driver. All involved in the crisis may need help, as they become a part of the personal support system available to the direct victim. Even those who are distanced from the direct impact of the crisis can suffer from vicarious traumatization. Watching the television coverage of the 9/11 terrorist attacks in New York, Washington, and Pennsylvania caused most people around the United States painful, deep-seated distress. Many reported that the repetitive exposure to the events caused psychological dysfunction. Such an event reaffirmed the fundamental truth in crisis work that crisis never occurs in a vacuum nor is limited in impact only to the direct victim. One young man in a southern state presented for therapy two months following the 9/11 incident. He reported that he was ". . . depressed. I can't understand how my school just goes on like nothing is happening. Can't they see that the world has changed? Can't they see that we have all changed?" The teenager's despair was disruptive to his daily experience and required profound intervention, not unlike what was offered to family members of individuals working in the Pentagon on that fateful September day.

Understanding the developmental level of crisis victims allows the clinician to collaboratively set age-appropriate interventions and establish stage-appropriate goals. The rapes of a ten-year-old, a teenager, a forty-year-old, and a senior citizen are not the same developmental experiences. Differences in the developmental foundation of the individual in crisis lead to vastly different psychological, emotional, and spiritual resources that can be brought to bear in the process. The senior citizen who was raped reported to her therapist "that it wasn't the sexual act that was so terrible. I'm an elderly woman," she said, "and the sexual violence wasn't the worst part of it for me. What I have been robbed of is something different. I never thought much of my age; now I do. The rapist has made me old. That's the tragedy." Developmentally, this is a very different experience from the younger woman who adopted a vigilante stance in response to her rape when she said, "I will find him and bring him down."

The systemic treatment model allows for collateral help from many resourceful people. The bringing together of multidisciplinary professionals and paraprofessionals requires a flexibility based on levels of training, theoretical approach, and therapeutic technique. A nurse sees crisis through different eyes than a minister. An EMT will approach crisis at a different pace than a psychologist. A contemporary model must accommodate for these differences.

The world today lives by the maxim "Time is of the essence." Time-limited, briefer models of therapy are in vogue. Paradigms of treatment should make room for the rhythms of daily living. The model presented allows for a clear resolution, and for the therapeutic relationship to "play itself out" should the client need longer-term work. It is not unusual that individuals will discover new and creative parts of themselves as a result of crisis and will want more help to integrate the new life lessons into their psyche.

There is much room for creativity in this systemic treatment approach to crisis intervention. The clinician may assign homework, create rituals, and direct enactments that facilitate movement for the client. One clinician called this his "bag of tricks." He was sanctioned by a peer, who said clearly, "There are no tricks of the trade for me. I need many tried-and-true tools that will help me be productive if I am going to be insightful and intuitive and to lead my client to the same source of healing."

Integrating Four Approaches

The integration of the four theoretical approaches combines powerful dimensions of the healing process. From systems theory, the family developmental approach highlights the intergenerational negotiation of shared life cycle transitions. Problems presented by the crisis are interwoven into the ongoing work of surviving and thriving in everyday life (Shapiro, 2002). The importance of changes in one part of the family system influencing all other parts leads the therapist to look actively for the implications of change in the entire family system during crisis. An understanding of the family's status quo, that is, their preferred state of being, allows the counselor to explore and understand the history of the family's functioning. Such exploration creates an environment that paces change and recognizes the predictability of the possibility of sabotage of change efforts. Such a possibility is not experienced as oppositional, but as a way the family arms itself for survival. The need to remain self-differentiated as the power of the system pulls the therapist into a distorted frame of reference challenges the counselor to be part of the system but not blinded by it. The joining of the past as it intersects with the present creates the crisis context. Family systems work even supplies the language for change—disequilibrium to equilibrium is the stated goal of treatment. The approach identifies the system as client and shapes clinical perspective, guides assessment, and defines goals.

Cognitive-behavioral psychology gives the clinician the tools of change. Reframing the crisis as an opportunity to address old beliefs and induct new ones leads the crisis counselor to engage the thoughtful mind of the crisis victim on behalf of change. The individual's cognitions, meanings, and perspectives regarding the precipitating event clarify and direct an understanding of the affective response to the crisis. Structured approaches to challenging irrational beliefs and converting self-defeating inner dialogues into problem-solving formats help the client overcome negative feelings of overwhelming intensity. The restructuring and reframing of the maladaptive cognition (Peake, Brodiun, & Archer, 1988) restores the individual's confidence to resume control of daily life.

The existential-experiential focus to crisis ultimately guides the crisis client toward construction of meaning and significance from the painful experience. The approach examines how individuals perceive events, what meanings are attributed to those events, and how the crisis relates to an overall sense of liveliness and mortality. Discovering a congruent, authentic expression of what is figural in the individual's contemporary life draws the crisis victim away from a destructive incorporation of the experience and toward the construction of a philosophical, spiritual, life-enhancing meaning. The experience of anxiety, a key tenet of the theory, is viewed as a motivator that encourages redirection and risk, rather than as being alien and disruptive. Choosing between danger and opportunity as it is presented in the crisis situation restores and teaches the client the power of living life in a forward motion. Consider the case of a young medic whose legs were severed as he was pinned between one vehicle and a runaway truck. As he processed the experience, he emerged with the support of a community that cared in tangible and loving ways. He said, "I got prayers, e-mails, money, food. . . . I really have seen that I am valued. I will stand ready to serve my community again, even if it is on artificial legs."

The narrative approach to crisis provides the tools the therapist employs to travel to those interior places of the client's subjective experience. The subjective, according to Bugental (1987, p. 7), is "that inner, private realm in which we lie most genuinely." Rather than objectifying or marginalizing people through the label of diagnosis, narrative theory humanizes and normalizes experience. The therapist facilitates the sharing of the stories necessary for healing. Narrative approaches facilitate successful life stories as the client moves from victim to problem solver. New stories are developed and new solutions created as major life themes are unraveled and rewoven.

These four theories are utilized in the three phases of the systemic model and are designed for the therapist to track the progression of the management of crisis. The model is not meant to confine the counselor or the client. As trust develops, the story will change and deepen, or as new stories are told, truths about earlier stories are revealed. Overpowering anxiety may be initially alleviated through medication, later by meditation or relaxation training. The resolution of one problem may uncover or create another that must be confronted. Initial goals may be met with concurrent desires to go beyond recovery to new levels of adjustment and personal growth. Therefore, the model brings some structure to an otherwise chaotic process, guiding, not girding, the work of the clinician. The environmental, social, and psychological demands of the precipitant define its value.

The outcome of crisis treatment, facilitated by the systemic model, is defined in terms of restoration of the individual's pretraumatic level of overt functioning. The model guides the client further toward self-enhancing coping abilities, a decrease in negative, self-defeating, dysfunctional behavior, and enhanced insight into personal life. Essentially, as one client said, "I learned the lessons I needed to get out of the crisis. I wish there had been easier ways to learn, but you take what you get."

Caplan (1964) spoke of seven characteristics of effective coping behavior, that is, the "lessons" that are called insight:

1. The individual actively explores reality issues and searches for information.
2. The individual freely expresses both positive and negative feelings and tolerates frustration.
3. The individual can actively invoke help from others.
4. The individual can break problems into manageable bits and work through them, one step at a time.

5. The individual is increasingly aware of fatigue and can pace coping efforts while maintaining control in as many areas of functioning as possible.
6. The individual feels a sense of mastery of feelings where possible and is increasingly flexible and willing to change.
7. The individual finds more of a sense of trust in self and in others and has an increasingly basic sense of optimism for living in the world.

Crisis counseling "teaches" these coping behaviors in ways that shape the outcome of crisis toward opportunity and away from danger.

Chapter 3

Profile of an Individual in Crisis

INTRODUCTION

Individuals live in character, in and out of crisis. Enduring personality traits and patterns of behavior do not change. Human nature, in response to stress, moves us to what is most familiar and predictable as a way of restoring personal safety and balance. One woman said it this way: "I was my mother's primary caregiver during her elder years. That, in and of itself, was stressful and demanding. She began to have a series of small strokes but wasn't ready for a nursing home, so I brought her back to my home. Her personality changed in subtle, but distinct ways. I got more and more worried but believed I could handle it. I always did in the past. Unfortunately, all the tried-and-true approaches didn't work. I couldn't believe that those ways that I knew to help weren't working anymore. By the time I finally got it through my thick skull I had to do something different, I was in terrible shape trying to care for my mother."

To understand the woman in context and to provide help, it is incumbent for the clinician to know how to enter into her private experience. In order to do so, the clinician must have a way to understand the larger perspective of the client. Crisis intervention does not diagnose in a traditional sense; however, an organized manner of seeing and understanding the client's worldview is useful and worthy of discussion.

Diagnosis comes from two Greek words meaning "to split knowledge." In its contemporary connotation, diagnosis is a descriptive statement that speaks of what can be noticed about a client's state of

Crisis Counseling and Therapy
© 2007 by The Haworth Press, Inc. All rights reserved.
doi:10.1300/5953_03

being. It carries further weight, since a diagnosis goes beyond the present and implies a pattern of behavior and a prediction of future behavior. It may or may not include notions of causality. To diagnose is to enlarge the picture, to move from what is observable now to what is habitual. It includes a schema not only of what needs to be observed but also the patterns in which these observations are organized.

As noted, formal diagnosis has its critics who state that a system of labeling is not relevant to crisis intervention. On the other hand, many practitioners hold the belief that in all mental health work there must be a process of arriving at an absolutely correct diagnosis and that the practitioner cannot proceed until such a process is complete. Others will say that this is unnecessary in every incidence. Experiential theorists, for example, believe that how an individual organizes what is observed is the fundamental process of meaning making, and that meaning making is unique to each individual, including each client and diagnostician, and to each situation. Therefore, there can be no absolutes in the diagnostic process. Despite these strongly held beliefs, theorists and practitioners report compelling reasons for diagnosing in a more formal and narrow manner.

First, a diagnosis gives a road map and describes possibilities of how a person can evolve and grow. The therapist benefits from the structure, since it provides a compass to help organize information, provide clues, and a direction to navigate through a vast sea of data and information.

Second, the process of diagnosing allows the therapist to control anxiety. By distancing from the data, the therapist maintains a state of equanimity while working with salient information. The process is thought to be grounding and keeps the practitioner from jumping precipitously into the unknown. It creates intentionality rather than supporting impulsivity.

Third, formal diagnosis links the clinician into varied bodies of research and theory. It is an efficient way for the therapist to make predictions without waiting for data to emerge from the therapeutic encounter (Melnick & Nevis, 1998).

Diagnosing during crisis is derived essentially from the current state of the client. It provides the keys to intervention, interpersonal process, and change. By paying attention to the phenomenon presented by the client in the context of the event, some aspect of behavior emerges and becomes of particular interest. Something stands out and a pattern unfolds. This is the entrance point for the clinician, who then begins to explore, based on the diagnostic impression. This type of diagnosis has value, since it relies on observable behavior and calls on the therapist to define a piece of work that can be completed successfully during an initial encounter. One practitioner described her experience this way: "I met the client for an initial session and she told me, over and over again, that she was 'lost.' Diagnostically, this metaphor was my point of entry. We explored fully what being 'lost' meant to her and began to look for a path that would help her find her way. Is that overly simplistic? Maybe, but I consider this the essence of therapy when we can focus on the 'pattern-making' process that the individual brings into the situation. Were I to have begun in a more prescriptive place, I would have been functioning more as a teacher than my client was requesting."

In crisis work, it is not vital to the process to label individuals in terms of long-term, ongoing, and fixed characteristics. Certainly, blocks to the therapeutic process, such as avoidance, are explored but are seen as systemic attempts to regain balance and equilibrium. By staying with symptomatic behaviors in contemporary time and locating them as having value to the survival and recovery of the individual, the clinician adopts a therapeutically optimistic stance. This stand is more likely to support change in people who might otherwise be restricted by more traditional and permanent diagnostic categories. A clinician said, "It may be helpful for me to frame my thoughts in terms of an individual's personality disorder; however, in crisis, I need to focus on what is 'out there' and most immediate. Regardless of a person's character structure, in crisis the focus is on restoring equilibrium with some degree of efficiency and elegance. Traditional diagnosis doesn't allow me the perspective to facilitate this."

Diagnostics in crisis work focus on immediate change. It therefore becomes helpful for the clinician to diagnose with verbs rather than nouns. A client "ruminates" rather than "has ruminations." A client is "suspicious and ill at ease accepting help from others outside of her intimates" rather than "the client has a paranoid personality." Once the noun is used, the person is lost in the label and more than the behavior is characterized, which becomes a two-edged sword. Not only is the behavior characterized, but also the person, and the diagnosis is a prediction of the moment but also a subtle prediction of the future, essentially locking in the trajectory of change. Identifying observable patterns, as opposed to character flaws, gives optimism and hope to the process of change.

It is incumbent on the clinician to assess the premorbid functioning of the individual in crisis. However, just as individuals function before a crisis, they will demonstrate "more of the same" during and after the crisis. Each person is seen as continually moving through an overlapping series of experiences that are organized into beginnings, middles, and endings. In the presence of crisis, such defining points are blurred. Understanding the individual out of the crisis state gives the clinician a sense of perspective on the client's motion and movement through the present circumstance. The individual who has the capacity to understand the world realistically and act on it to meet personal and social needs will function more effectively in the presence of stress. The same is true for the individual who is a member of a strong social support system. The more natural help that is available, the more resilient the individual is in distress. A lone person will struggle more in crisis and will tend to depend on outside support systems rather than the ones that can be personally mustered.

The metaphor of music can be employed to help understand this concept. In activities of daily living, an individual lives by a given rhythm and listens to a familiar tune. A crisis creates disharmony, a cacophony, and disrupts predictable patterns of daily life. Given the magnitude of the stressor, the individual will fail in restoration of his or her own personal song style. There will be noticeable disruptions in previous patterns of behavior and an increasing number of ineffective behaviors working in service to the restoration of familiar rhythms. The caregiver who began her story earlier continued, saying, "I thought we'd just get mother settled and things would go back to the way they were. I guess that was true for her, but I had to be busier than ever. I had to go see about her more often during the day and night, all while trying to take care of my own family and work. She was forgetful about recipes, so I'd try and provide her simple things she could cook. It didn't dawn on me until later, if she was forgetful about recipes, she was also in trouble when it came to remembering how to use the stove. One day she nearly burned the house down. It didn't bother her, but I was a wreck. It was that day that I realized that I was in more of a crisis than she was."

T. S. Eliot spoke of the disruptive nature of crisis. He said, "None of these previous things have ever been created to last forever. The joy of life is in the creation of the new and not in the preservation of the old. And the universe goes on living because it renews itself endlessly" (1936, p. 85). If this is true, then health is associated with feelings of well-being, vitality, and a vigorous pursuit of life goals. Disruption leads to feelings associated with helplessness, discomfort, and a narrowness of attention and constriction of goals (Rainer, 2002). Therefore, the individual who has the capacity to "bounce" will feel healthier in the presence of distress. Bounce, which is the operational definition of efficacy, is enhanced by an accurate understanding of the crisis, and its psychosocial, systemic, and environmental consequences (Shapiro, 2002). It is critical for the clinician, regardless of a preferred definition of diagnosis, to remember that it is simply a tool for change. Its purpose is not to burden the client or therapist with constricting and irremediable labels, but to focus on the process of awareness, growth, and health.

The woman caregiving for her mother speaks about an identifiable response set to the crisis she experiences. Response sets are identifiable, predictable patterns of communication and behavior that are indicative of an individual's adaptive coping style. To the degree that the crisis clinician can help the client put a finger on the response sets brought to the crisis, awareness, understanding, and change may be facilitated. Response sets can be illustrated through thematic analysis in four realms of psychological functioning: affect, cognition, behavior, and spirituality.

AFFECT

Early psychological theories emphasized the importance of the abreaction and catharsis of emotion. Symptoms were thought to represent repressed memories and associated emotions (Freud & Breuer, 1895/1955). Remembering certain experiences and expressing associated emotions was thought to be curative in and of itself. Later, affects, especially affects such as anxiety, guilt, anger, and shame, were considered to be signals functioning to monitor danger in the internal or external world. In contemporary life, affects/emotions not only are considered signals but are viewed as a way to communicate with others; affects are considered to be intersubjectively regulated between two people (Spezzano, 1993). Increasing awareness of underlying emotions that are accompanied by insight and self-understanding is viewed as an important avenue for the individual to clarify personal experience and come to terms with problematic life situations.

A person is a symbolizing, meaning-creating being who acts as a dynamic system, constantly synthesizing information from many levels of processing and from both internal and external sources into a conscious experience. Three major levels of processing—innate sensory motor, emotional schematic memory, and conceptual level processing—are identified as critical to this function (Greenberg, Rice, & Elliott, 1993). Individuals are seen as organizing experience into emotion-based schemas that play a central role in functioning and in the creation of meaning. Integration of experience, particularly in crisis work, is viewed as a synthesis of emotions in a coherent fashion. Therefore, the experience of affect in crisis work is more than "I am aware of my feelings" or "I understand what is going on with me." Rather, it is the lucid and harmonious sense of "my self," which is a form that successfully organizes aspects of experience together in a lively way that meets the demands of the crisis situation.

One woman described her experience in this way: "Before, I never saw myself as an angry person, but after my home burned, I was enraged. The feelings in my heart and soul seemed so foreign. I couldn't function because of my anger. It took a fair amount of work to understand the source of the intensity of my emotions before I was able to begin to move, to problem solve, to take care of the things at hand. I'm much better able to handle my anger now. I've found out a lot of things about myself I didn't know."

Reclaiming the emotional experience results in the integration of its various aspects in the client's awareness. When affect is evoked, emotions do not act singly but produce a feeling experience that is dynamic, interactive, and a progressively synthesized process where the external is symbolically made internal. This emotional scaffolding creates meaning that further influences and is influenced by new experiences. It is also open to reflective processing and is used in reasoning about and explaining the person's circumstances.

Gestalt theory proposes an experience cycle (Zinker, 1977) that illuminates the dynamics of emotionality and affect. The primary assumption of Gestalt psychology is a theory of perception, which theorizes that humans create a figure (organization) out of the ground (experience). This is done through scanning, evaluating, and assessing the internal and external environment. Gestaltists believe that humans are predisposed to organize the continuous, disorganized, sloppy, and overlapping realms of experience in order to make meaning. Meaning making begins with energy.

Emotional energy is a physiological response to stimulation. Sensory awareness involves all experiences taken in by the senses. The individual must be able to sort out awareness from all the internal and external stimuli impinging on the senses. In crisis, the individual is overstimulated and unable to provide such a clean sense of awareness, which limits the accuracy of sensory experience. Such overstimulation further limits strong contact with the self and others, leaving the individual overexposed to the internal and external environment. The emotionality of crisis prohibits a sense of closure, defined by reviewing, summarizing, reflecting, and savoring experience and meaning making. As one young man said, "I felt wired. I couldn't make decisions, complete my work, or really connect with other people. It was like everything was too bright. I was completely unable to sort out what was more important from what was less important."

In this view of emotion, the person is seen as an active agent, constantly organizing and configuring experience and reality into meaningful wholes (Mahoney, 1995). Discovery of elements of experience, including affect, and creation of new meaning operate in tandem, neither process being privileged over the other (Greenberg et al., 1993). In addition, both emerging internal experience and external validation, bridged through affect, are seen as active ingredients in the process of change. Feelings, then, are the product of this symbolization of experience and reveal the cognitively felt meanings of one's experience. Emotions are the physical sensations or reactions that are a response to various environmental stimuli and reveal the prereflective importance or significance that things have for the individual (Watson & Greenberg, 1996). Feelings and emotions, taken in concert, make up the realm of affect.

Gendlin (1974), in his early writings, suggested that change or movement in therapy consists of the client's internal shift in experiencing as a result of accurately representing an internal "felt sense." He conceptualized experience as a process, and the occurrence of change fully dependent on whether the ongoing living and experiencing process moves further as the individual's inner sense is continually articulated. "The motor that powers change is a direct sensing into what is concretely felt and allowing that to form and move" (Gendlin, 1974, p. 240). He developed a technique called focusing to assist clients to recognize and clarify their feelings. He observed that clients need to turn their attention toward inner experience. He said that within each individual there is a flow of experiencing to which that person can have full access to discover the particular meaning of those inner experiences. Gendlin further said these inner experiences are full bodied, rich in detail, immediate, intense, fluid, and capable of differentiation. As the individual focuses on the figural, the clinician's primary tool becomes one of reflection. He argued that it is through the use of reflection that the therapist can check the understanding of the client's experience and stay in tune with what is being said. Such internal processing in the presence of another oftentimes gives rise to a moment of strong feeling and allows for flow or motion as the individual translates inner potential into a new life script or scene.

Gendlin states that experience is a dialectical construction. Change is an inherent aspect of all systems, and meaning is created by human activity and in dialogue. If it is constrained by a bodily felt emotional sense, then affect is a synthesis of experience and symbol. Emotional experience is seen as both creating and being created by its conscious symbolization and expression. This view allows clients to see themselves as creators of the self. Flowing from this foundation, emotional experience, seen as a basically healthy resource, is viewed as capable either of providing health-adaptive information based on the biologically adaptive emotion system or, in certain instances (such as a crisis state), of becoming maladaptive through learning and experience.

The most basic process, then, for the individual in a crisis state is one of reflecting on and evaluating what is healthy and what is maladaptive in terms of feeling functions. Once the individual is aware of the adaptive and healthy, which can be used as an affective guide, understanding and transformation of what is maladaptive and unhealthy can occur. Transformation is achieved by exposing the maladaptive experience to newly accessed and symbolized adaptive, interpersonal experience (to other parts of the self) and to new corrective interpersonal experience. Transformation comes by integrating maladaptive experience (such as worthlessness or shame) with adaptive internal resources (such as anger at violation and pride in self) to form a new, more balanced whole (such as self-worth and assertiveness). This, combined with corrective emotional experiences that will challenge and disconfirm erroneous beliefs about the self ("If I am weak, I will disintegrate"), allows for healing.

In crisis work, the therapeutic task brings emotions and their associated action tendencies into awareness. Affect allows the individual to pay greater attention to the questions that are posed as meaning making occurs. Affect is viewed as a marker that indicates troubling aspects of experience. One client described her global emotional response to crisis in this way: "After the initial blow of the crisis, I was just as puzzled as I was troubled with the numbers of problems that I had against me. I could go so many directions, each with a different outcome. I was overwhelmed with doubt about how I should proceed. I stayed stuck too long and began to have bad feelings about myself because I couldn't choose a path. I got increasingly upset because of my uncertainty and began to wonder what in the world I actually believed to be right. What an awful mess."

Once these parameters were heard, the therapist was able to intervene and help the client to make differential decisions, using the conflicting emotional energies to pick a course of resolution the individual could live within and progressively trust. Evoking clients' emotional reactions helps to identify the impact of events, symbolize reactions, and discover needs and goals and the action tendencies inherent in their emotional reactions. This allows clients to become aware of links between the external environment, their inner experience, and initiation of behavior. These links can then be examined in light of current goals, values, and environmental contingencies. Once the data from emotional and rational systems have been integrated, clients are in the position to choose among alternative ways of acting to enhance their adaptation and growth and facilitate resolution of the crisis state, moving into new life tasks and goals (Watson & Greenberg, 1996).

Expression of emotion is healthy for people in crisis. Clients should be allowed a free berth to their feelings, provided they are not harmful to themselves or others. The clinician is obligated to find a place of empathy in order to join the client and establish a therapeutic alliance. As one clinician said, "If I can't share the pain, I have no business working with the client."

Ordinary stress can have a profound impact on the psyche of the individual. As has been previously discussed, acute stress is a response to imminent danger. Physiologically, it turbocharges the body with powerful hormones. Chronic stress is caused by constant emotional pressure the victim cannot control, which ultimately produces hormones that can weaken the immune system and damage bones. When the brain detects a threat, a number of structures, including the hypothalamus, amygdala, and pituitary gland, go on alert. They exchange information with each other and then send signaling hormones and nerve impulses to the rest of the body to prepare for fight-or-flight. Adrenal glands then react to the alert by releasing epinephrine, which makes the heart pump faster and the lungs work harder to flood the body with oxygen. The adrenal glands also release extra cortisol and other glucocorticoids, which help the body convert sugars into energy. Nerve cells release norepinephrine, which tenses the muscles and sharpens the senses to prepare for action. When the threat passes, epinephrine and norepinephrine levels drop. At a cellular level, this is the experience of feeling, or affect.

Circumstances don't always define emotional states. People can learn to manage their grief, even in the face of tragedy and crisis, and not allow it to overwhelm them.

COGNITION

In contrast to the discussion of emotion and affect, the realm of cognition emphasizes the powerful role that negative, irrational thought plays in affecting mood and movement through crisis. When exploring the realm of cognitive thought, there is a de-emphasis on emotionality in order to focus upon the distortions and dysfunctional beliefs that drive maladaptive patterns of affect and behavior. Cognitivists are particularly interested in those thoughts called "hot cognitions" that are emotionally charged and connected to erroneous attitudes and thoughts.

In ordinary language, cognition refers to the thoughts or ideas that we have about the world around us. In the broadest sense, cognitions are internalized, individual symbols that help an individual to make sense of the world. Understanding an individual's cognitive functioning helps the clinician address how a person gathers information about events and how it is processed, in order to act on the environment. Cognitions provide internalized rules that guide an individual's capacity to behave, believe, and feel in the larger world. These are the rules used in decision making. Some theorists have discussed maturity as a cognitive concept: that the mature individual is one who is capable of making use of information in a meaningful way. Others discuss cognition from a social learning perspective and incorporate constructs such as expectancy, imitation, verbal and pictorial imagery, and memory.

Traditional learning theorists discussed cognition as a response to need. In this view, individuals in a quiescent state start to experience bodily needs for food, water, and sex. These needs tend to motivate them to seek objects that reduce their tensions so that they can once again exist in a homeostatic balance. Incentive was then seen as motivation to work toward the attainment of certain goals for reinforcement. Contemporary theorists have taken the stand that humans are constantly in process and continually seek to accurately predict events in the world around them. Rather than being passive, controlled by cyclic internal urges or external demands, they are seen as active, curious, and creative beings who continually seek to increase their understanding of the world. Motivation is, therefore, based on cognition, rather than on biological drives rooted in cellular needs. In contemporary thinking, cognitive processes control behavioral actions. This thought is a rejection of the empirical law of effect, which states that behavior is more likely to recur if it is followed by a positive reinforcer and less likely to recur if it is followed by a punishing stimulus, because this law suggests that only external influences control behavior. What seems more important is the individual's anticipation of events and subsequent validation of predictions. Cognitive treatment focuses on identifying, monitoring, and modifying negative thinking and utilizing persuasive interventions to help individuals to see their own self-defeating patterns of behaving. The goal of the work is to change negative self-evaluation and faulty cognitive components of negative affects.

Underlying the basic notion of cognition is the assumption that humans are capable of changing or replacing the present interpretation of events. Specifically, humans are known to be able to change their minds. According to this belief, behavior is rarely completely predetermined. The freedom exists to reinterpret experience. Further, humans do not merely react to experiences but act on them by interpreting and reinterpreting them in an idiosyncratic way. Cognitions, then, are used in attempts to predict and control events. The individual continually evaluates experience and uses those interpretations to understand and be in charge of the surrounding world. The individual is habit driven and wants the world to be more predictable and, if a crisis develops, will work to change concepts or thoughts in order to be able to function effectively. This highly personalized view of reality, used to make judgments, is private and rarely open to the scrutiny of others. Cognitions take on a fairly commonsense view of the self and the world, which makes for great possibilities in distortion and error. Most people will shift views of reality to fit data.

To build a system of personal cognitions that gives structure, purpose, and organization to the world, an individual will place a general interpretation on similar events. The construction of the meaning of events is an abstract process. Using these abstractions, the individual is able to deal with new information from the environment. These interpretations become an idiosyncratic reality and determine how the individual will act in a predictable way. They are also highly personalized. One person may have the same experience as another but will interpret it differently. A seasoned psychotherapist talked about this and described his way of gaining a therapeutic alliance with adolescents: "My office was right across the street from an art museum," he said. "Early in therapy, I would take my teenage client to the museum and we would look at sculpture from different sides. We would talk about what we would see and try and see it from each other's points of view. It is always an interesting exercise to begin to see what an individualistic notion of the world each of us has. It is so true that we each have our own set of eyes and a mind to use in interpretation."

Cognitivists teach that the beliefs and constructs that are formed and used to deal with new experiences are based on previous experiences. In their abstract form, they involve contrasts and similarities with previous experience. They are open to the application of personal labels to describe the same experience. One woman described her pain to a physician as "uncomfortable." A second patient with similar problems described her pain as "hurting like hell." This capacity of each individual to interpret experience is thought to be innate and a continuing definition and elaboration of the major beliefs the individual has about the world. It is not mechanistic, which would state that individuals simply react to the environment. Instead, an individual actively, uniquely, and systematically construes the world and uses these constructions to anticipate events. Previous experiences are used to create hypotheses about possible new outcomes. Cognitions are more than responses to the environment in order to maximize pleasure and avoid pain; they are the mechanisms used to actively strive for individual accuracy of view.

The process of forming cognitions is interesting. In the first of a three-stage cycle, individuals begin to introspect. They carefully consider all the possible ways of interpreting a given situation and use all previous learning to help to deal with the situation at hand. In the second stage, individuals reduce the number of available possibilities and seriously consider only those possibilities that will help solve the problem at hand. Finally, they decide on a course of action by choosing a single interpretation that seems most useful.

This process is relevant in crisis work. Cognitions are formed under "typical" conditions. A crisis is extraordinary and throws the individual out of the "tried and true." In crisis, an individual is likely to invalidate what has worked previously and will need to form new cognitions to meet the demands of the situation at hand. This directs the crisis practitioner to become aware of previously held beliefs and constructs in order to help the individual formulate new, more satisfying choices that will effectively help to meet the demands of the environment. The practitioner works to help the client open to the possibilities of continual change as a result of the crisis. For major change to occur, the individual must think through new possibilities, so that the new thoughts are internally consistent, externally validated, and communicated in such a way that the individual in crisis maintains an active role in the process. Anxiety is used as a guiding energy to help the individual to mobilize, since it challenges what is outside the range of convenience within the individual's worldview.

BEHAVIOR

The world of the mind seems very different from the one inhabited by our bodies. Thoughts and emotions that seem to color reality are the results of complex electrochemical interactions within and between nerve cells. The sense of well-being and distress that is felt affectively is intricately tied to the same neural pathways that manifest through behavior. In addition, the influence of the physical, social, and cultural environments on individuals guides and directs specific behavioral manifestations. According to most behavioral theorists, individuals are not static but are in the process of unfolding and becoming. While situational influences have an effect, it is the individual's own perception of those influences that determines behavior. Therefore, even behavior that seems to be controlled by external forces, that is, crisis, is really controlled by internal forces. The old adage becomes "What you see *may* be what you get." Behavior is the manifestation of the cognition and the energy of affect. In crisis, since there is such an unexpected situation that moves the individual into a state of distress, it is in the clinician's best interest to look at internal characteristics as determinants of behavior.

Given this, there are several limits placed on an individual's ability to maneuver through crisis. Physical and intellectual capacity will markedly influence behavior. Developmental factors will also impact the person's capacity to meet the demands of a crisis. A fire at a nursing home created multiple dangers for residents who were unable to care for themselves and move away from danger. One resident with a sense of humor who survived the fire said, "I was hoping that my walker would walk me faster than my feet would go." Intellectual capacity is a further mitigating factor in crisis. As people mature, changes occur through interactions with the environment and the accompanying learning process. It is thought that with this growing maturity, the individual becomes increasingly active, creative, self-reliant, and rational, all of which largely results from learning experiences. The individual becomes increasingly capable of making conscious and deliberate choices among alternative behaviors.

Some theorists talk about the notion of behavioral traits that shape the self as the person continues to move and grow throughout the life span. Traits are "a generalized and focalized neuropsychic system, peculiar to the individual, with the capacity to render many stimuli functionally equivalent and to initiate and guide consistent forms of adaptive and expressive behavior" (Allport, 1937, p. 295). This sophisticated definition can be easily translated: Traits, which are unseen, are located in certain parts of the nervous system. Their existence can be inferred by observing the consistencies in a person's behavior. As one clinician succinctly said, "People live and die in character." An individual who typically sees himself or herself as shy will respond to crisis in a similar fashion. A young college man said, "It is just so true of me not to ask for help because I get so easily embarrassed. Here I was, in a huge crisis, and I felt too ashamed and awkward to ask for assistance." Such a sense of self can be treated as an actual entity that can direct behavior. It is common to hear, for instance, "She has such a strong sense of herself. It is no wonder that she was able to take the bull by the horns and make it through such a rough time."

The sense of self gives behavior motive. Fundamental motives are impulses and drives, which provide an individual with a striving toward immediate gratification of needs and the reduction of tension. When an individual is hungry, he will eat. When she is thirsty, she will drink. These are simple and automatic acts aimed at reducing tensions. As the person grows and develops, there is an increasing sense of the deliberate nature of behavior. Behavior is ego involved and is characterized by the progressive unification of movement toward life goals. Such maturity is seen as related to the development of conscience. In the child, the evolving conscience is related to the "must," which is rule governed and driven. Children begin to internalize their parents' values and standards and feel guilty if they violate these rules. As people mature, there is a marked change in the perception of the world and of other people. The "ought" conscience develops. At this stage, obedience to the external standards of authority gives way to internal, or self-generated, rules. Conduct and behavior are guided by the person's own values and self-image. The shift from a "must" to an "ought" conscience is not automatic. Many chronological adults are still children in conduct. They continue to react in terms of parental prohibitions and suffer from unresolved guilt feelings and rehash old conflicts with authority figures. They have not learned to rely on their own judgment and to orient themselves toward the attainment of challenging goals. This is an adult task, in which the individual is capable of integrating all prior aspects of experience into a unified whole. The task is for the individual to emerge as functional, autonomous, and independent.

Crisis causes an individual to shift experience and, in many cases, to regress into less mature strivings. This guides the individual into behavioral distress that may or may not address the functional needs of the person. In terms of behavioral philosophy, people are innately curious and seek to understand themselves, others, and their environments. This creative quest for growth, meaning, and selfhood is a part of human nature. However, in the presence of crisis, an individual is prone to become increasingly self-protective and to close in with a "bunker" mentality. This robs the individual of creativity and limits behavioral manifestations for self-satisfaction. One client expressed his frustration: "I keep hearing people ask me, 'What do you need?' I feel like a child pitching a temper tantrum. If I knew what I needed, I wouldn't be in the mess I find myself. All I know how to do is to behave like a scared five-year-old. It's not very becoming of a forty-year-old man, let me tell you." This fellow has a significant amount of insight, since he knows that his behavior is incongruent with what he needs in order to feel satisfied. The crisis at hand has led him to regress into earlier stages of behavior that may have been functional at one time but are unhelpful in meeting the demands of the current circumstance.

Behavior, then, can be considered as the abilities and skills that a person brings to bear when dealing with the complexities of a given situation. In general situations, the individual learns what is needed to acquire and maximize long-term and realistic satisfactions. In crisis, the individual moves into emotionally unstable territory, which in turn influences the behavioral manifestation of need. Typically, individuals in crisis are too anxious and exhibit more fear than is helpful to make a goal-directed behavioral response, other than to fight or flee the situation. In crisis, social rules are suspended, which compromises the individual's "set" for a given response. The individual is unable to effectively adapt, which causes behavior that is harmful to the self or others. In crisis, individuals become *dis-abled* to make good behavioral decisions for themselves.

Behaviorists will teach that repeated trials of such *dis-abled* behavior will cause the individual in crisis to become progressively dysfunctional. In order to eliminate unhelpful behavior, individuals must learn counterconditioning. This is how they learn a new response to a stimulus that elicits maladaptive behavior. In theory and practice, the new response is antagonistic to the old one. Modeling is a tool to modify behavior in prosocial ways. In crisis, the individual is in the presence of an adverse circumstance. The crisis counselor behaves with equanimity and calmness and provides a good model for the individual to follow. The demonstration of this behavior by the clinician allows the client to imitate it.

Modeling serves as the major vehicle for transmitting new styles of behavior. It instructs people in these new styles through social, pictorial, or verbal display. Models serve to legitimize innovation, particularly in the presence of crisis. The acquisition of innovation, defined as the incorporation of new behaviors into an individual's repertoire, is necessary but not sufficient for their adoption in practice. For new behaviors to be incorporated, they must be practiced with stimulus inducements in order for the behaviors to be tried in a variety of situations. Adaptive behavior is known to be highly susceptible to reinforcement influences. When individuals receive tangible advantages for their behavioral display, adaptive behavior will be more evident. However, because benefits cannot be experienced until the new practices are tried, the promotion of innovative behavior draws heavily on anticipated and vicarious reinforcement. As one client told his therapist, "You remember the old joke about the child standing at the New York City crosswalk, asking the police officer, 'How do you get to Carnegie Hall?' The answer is the same for me as it was for that kid: 'Practice, practice, practice.' I have to have a visual image that I'm going to be better because of the practice."

Adopting new behavior is partially governed by self-generated consequences to one's own conduct. A client reported to her counselor, "I'm scared of shooting myself in the foot." The counselor aids the client in crisis to determine which behaviors are praiseworthy and which will violate his or her personal, social, and moral convictions. Behavior changes must be defined and refined in acceptable terms and according to social convention and prohibition.

The primary determinants of learning and adopting new behavior are the influences closely tied to it, including environmental stimulus inducements, the anticipated satisfactions, the observed benefits and risks, the self-evaluative derivatives, and any social or economic constraints. Adopting new behavior in crisis is best analyzed in terms of controlling conditions rather than in terms of personality type. A client told his story: "After my child died so unexpectedly, I had no idea what to expect out of myself, my marriage, or the world. For the longest time, nothing interested me and I learned how seductive depression can be. It wasn't until months later that I was able to kick myself in the butt to get going again. Then, every step I took seemed to make things worse than they were before. I am grateful I had a good therapist who was able to be an extra set of eyes and ears for me, and who could help me make good decisions. Eventually, I was able to chart a more healthy path for myself, and then things began to get better. Make sure you heard me right: things began to get better. I'm still pretty miserable and am struggling with my child's death, but I'm hanging on and don't feel like the other shoe is going to drop."

SPIRITUALITY

Spirituality and religion can have a powerful and important influence on human health and behavior. However, this realm of functioning is the one most often ignored in understanding the individual's process of coming to terms with crisis. About 95 percent of Americans recently professed a belief in God or a higher power, a figure that has never dropped below 90 percent during the past fifty years; nine out of ten people also said that they pray, most of them (67-75 percent) on a daily basis (Gallup & Lindsay, 1999). Over two-thirds (69 percent) recently reported that they were members of a church or synagogue, and 40 percent reported that they attended regularly (Gallup & Lindsay, 1999). The numbers support the importance of addressing this dimension of crisis. In particular, the subjective importance of spirituality increases among those who are dealing with the crisis of serious illness (Miller & Thoresen, 2003).

The spiritual nature of the client provides an understanding of the belief system and of larger coping mechanisms the individual may employ in the presence of helplessness. The spirit is thought to be the connection to the greater universe. Spirituality gives the individual some degree of internal coherence that accurately represents reality. It helps the person to reach for a higher degree of abstraction, so it is capable of influencing an extensive range of perception, evaluation, and action. The spirit also allows the individual to contact and hold personal frailty and to understand the human condition, to diagnose personal and social problems, and to offer remedy (Jones, 1994; Schneider, 1998). The nature of an individual's spirit provides a superordinate, "overriding reference value," which has the greatest and most pervasive control over self-regulated behavior (Carver & Scheier, 1990, p. 13).

The term *spirituality* has had a long and diverse evolution. William James (1961) regarded religion as "the feelings, acts, experiences of individual men [*sic*] in their solitude . . . in relation to whatever they may consider the divine" (p. 42). In essence, he equated religion with spirituality and ignored institutional religion. The *Oxford English Dictionary* offers a substantial ten pages of reference material on the concept of spirituality. Two related themes seem to dominate: First is the notion of being concerned with life's most animating and vital principle or quality, often described as giving life or energy to the material human elements of the person. William James and others throughout the twentieth century related the spiritual to a person's character, personality, or disposition, often with an emphasis on the person's social and emotional style and manner of living (e.g., chronic anger or inner peace). Clearly human experience is central in understanding spirituality. Second, spirituality includes a broad focus on the immaterial features of life, regarded as not commonly perceptible by the physical senses (e.g., sight and hearing) that are used to understand the material world. Major religions have similarly used spiritual terminology to refer to that which is experienced and considered to be transcendent, sacred, holy, or divine.

Assessment in the spiritual realm is complex. The 1996 Summit on Spirituality, sponsored by the American Counseling Association's

Task Force for Spiritual, Ethical, and Religious Values, defines spirituality as this:

> Spirit may be defined as the animating life force, represented by such images as breath, wind, vigor, and courage. Spirituality is the drawing out and infusion of spirit in one's life. It is experienced as an active and passive process. This spiritual tendency moves the individual toward knowledge, love, meaning, peace, hope, transcendence, connectedness, compassion, wellness, and wholeness. Spirituality includes one's capacity for creativity, growth, and the development of a value system. Spirituality encompasses a variety of phenomena including experience, beliefs, and practices. (Position Paper, n.d., para. 3)

Searching for understanding and imposing meaning on the circumstances of crisis compels the therapist to explore this dimension. In crisis and trauma, perhaps as in no other psychological state, the presence or absence of a sense of spirituality can be both a part of the etiology of the crisis as well as a profound source of healing. To enter effectively into this realm, therapists must first address their own integration of spirituality, organized religious practices, and the comfort derived from these systems in order to bring integrity and authenticity into a discussion. The importance of the cultural meaning and influence on the experience of spirituality is central to this understanding, both for the therapist and for the client. In the midst of disaster it is not unusual to see the African-American community lift themselves in prayer and song searching for comfort and connection. The role of the Catholic Church in the lives of Latino families makes it an important part of the understanding of what has created, and what will heal, crisis. The sense of betrayal felt by those victimized by the abuse of a priest is made more intense and powerful as the central role of the church as a source of authority and guilt for wrongdoing is a significant foundation for this culture. The crisis worker will find sensitivity to diverse cultural understandings of spirituality and religious practice and recognition of personal belief systems to be important in the joining with the client in the midst of crisis.

The Greek origin of the word *psychotherapist* comes from two words: *psyche,* meaning "soul" or "breath of life," and *therapeia,* meaning "attendant" or "servant." The role of the counselor as attendant to the client's soul is rare. In crisis, such a role is central to resolution of distress. In order to bring such clarity, as the individual seeks to impose meaning on suffering and loss, questions are formulated from a spiritual perspective. Richard and Bergin (1997) outline the goals of a spiritual assessment as

1. understanding the spiritual perspective of the client;
2. obtaining knowledge regarding the health of the spiritual perspective and how it will influence the individual's issues and concerns brought into counseling;
3. determining possible resources for support;
4. determining possible interventions relying on spirituality that can be used in the counseling process; and
5. clarifying the level of need to address spiritual or religious issues in counseling.

Miller's (2003) reference on spirituality in counseling provides helpful guidelines for identifying spiritual resources in the life of the individual. Refuge, ritual, safe places, and a strong sense of community are identified as important aspects of a spiritual life. First, therapists assess the spiritual refuge and sanctuaries in the individuals' lives that give hope and meaning. They are asked where they might "catch their breath" in the stress of living, what makes them spiritually transcendent, and what blocks prevent them from relying on those places to the degrees that are needed. The second area of exploration relates to ritual. Questions related to rituals that revive hope and a desire to live are paramount. The individuals are invited to explore those activities that elicit excitement for life and realization, and to place these in a spiritual context. The therapists are encouraged to assess self-destructive or self-harming rituals, such as the numbing of emotion through substance abuse. Once identified, these can be reframed as efforts to escape suffering, and new behaviors can be constructed with more meaning and health. The power and importance of ritual will be addressed more fully in the model for treatment in subsequent chapters.

Different religious traditions have varied rituals that are a part of the healing process. Barriers to participation in these activities and traditions require exploration and examination. As one mother painfully shared, "I couldn't show my face in church after my son's suicide. I felt nothing but shame and humiliation. My therapist insisted that I join with others who have experienced similar loss. Fortunately, in a survivor of suicide group, I was able to find the courage I needed to eventually return to long established sources of peace and healing."

Once environmental safety and tradition are explored from a spiritual perspective, the individual's trusted support system, identified as those places where self-disclosure is welcomed and confidences protected, is assessed. In the context of these relationships, the individual is allowed the freedom to reflect on hurts and to seek comfort. Issues related to the experience of forgiveness are of primary focus.

Finally, the overall sense of community is assessed from a spiritual perspective. Myer's (2000) research reveals that people of a mature religious faith handle crisis more effectively because they can answer questions of meaning and significance, are more likely to feel hopeful in the face of loss, and are more prone to rely on the support of a social system. Knowledge of the individual's spiritual community and its denominational practices will aid the therapist's formulation of intervention. The spiritual community can also serve as nonjudgmental witness to individuals in crisis and their struggles toward healing.

Spirituality is viewed as a source of morality, an agent of potent psychological transformation and integration, a master motive, and an expression of that which is best and more creative in humanity (Allport, 1950; Fromm, 1966; Jung, 1938; Maslow, 1971; Rogers, 1980). Collectively, the study of spirituality in the process of crisis work suggests that religion is an enormously important aspect of culture that must be included in culturally sensitive work by the practitioner (Shafranske & Malony, 1996). Contemporary practice softens the boundary between religion and psychology. Even though religion and psychology take on different surface forms, at a deeper level they are structurally very similar (Shafranske & Malony, 1996), specifically in the correspondence between a humanistic or transpersonal psychotherapeutic orientation and the spiritual or mystical. The humanistic tradition is to seek and trust one's own immediate, inner experiencing. To do so connects the individual with a universal, but subjectively experienced, self-actualizing tendency. This derives from or parallels the mystical directive to find God, which causes individuals to find their essential identity, rightful places in the world, and true direction through meditation, contemplation, and prayer (Menahem, 1996; Vaughan, Wittine, & Walsh, 1996). Such a "looking within" to find God or a universal essence through such disciplines as prayer and meditation is considered a self-actualizing, healing tendency (Rogers, 1980). This view is consistent with the belief that affirms the definition of spirituality as "the courage to look within and trust" (Shafranske & Gorsuch, 1984, p. 231), which is a favorably identified positive outcome of crisis resolution. Such a belief reaffirms the trustworthiness of human nature, as God is perceived as a force residing within humanity.

To know God is, according to many traditions, the central function of religion. Systems of religious belief, practice, and relationships are designed to help bring people closer to the transcendent, however that transcendence may be defined. It is important for the therapist to recognize that, to the religious or spiritual mind, the connection with a universal being is of ultimate value. Attachment theory suggests that people who experience a secure connection with their higher power should also experience greater comfort in stressful situations and greater strength and confidence in everyday life. Consistent with these predictions, the research literature reports that those individuals who report a closer connection to God experience less depression and higher self-esteem (Maton, 1989), less loneliness (Kirkpatrick, Kellas, & Shillito, 1993), greater relational maturity (Hall & Edwards, 2002), and greater psychosocial competence (Pargament Smith, Koenig, & Perez, 1998).

As has been noted, many aspects of life, when viewed in a spiritual light, can be perceived as sacred in significance and character. In crisis, this sense of the sacred may represent an important source of strength, meaning, and coping. The spirit of an individual's belief system can provide a road map and a sense of ultimate life destination, often by association with a larger religious framework. Spiritual strivings are empowering. People are likely to persevere in the pursuit of transcendent goals. Spiritual strivings can provide stability, support, and direction in critical times, as the individual holds on to a sense of ultimate purpose and meaning in the midst of disturbing life events. Such strivings offer a unifying philosophy of life that gives more of a sense of coherence to personality in the face of cultural, social, or environmental forces that push for fragmentation.

Religion and spirituality orientations offer the individual a sense of ultimate destinations in living and viable pathways for reaching these destinations. In an effort to sustain themselves and their spirituality during crisis, those with stronger religious frameworks are likely to have greater access to a wide array of religious coping methods, such as rites of passage and meditation. In pursuit of spiritual growth and a relationship with the transcendent, the individual will be more likely to practice virtues rather than to nourish pain or distress. This is indicative of a greater purpose of life, better life satisfaction, and higher levels of well-being.

MULTICULTURAL ASPECTS
OF CRISIS COUNSELING

To some extent, all therapeutic relationships require sensitivity to cross-cultural characteristics. Also called multicultural, the term refers to preparation and practices "that integrate multicultural and culture-specific awareness, knowledge, and skills into counseling interactions (Arredondo, 1996, p. 43). Researchers suggest that multicultural refers to five major cultural groups in the United States: African American, Asian American, Caucasian, Hispanic, and Native American. Each has important characteristics that define person, place, and purpose in the world. Understanding what it means to be a man or woman, the role of authority, the value system, and role of the family and community, is crucial information for guiding the joining and treating of the crisis victim.

Gender also seems to be related to help-seeking attitudes. Johnson (1988) found women to be more tolerant to the stigma related to receiving personal counseling; therefore, they seek help more often than men. Many researchers have found that gender and its interaction with ethnicity are related to an individual's willingness to seek help. All research suggests that there will be a difference in attitudes toward the crisis clinician and the process of receiving help among various ethnic groups and between men and women. To be effective, the clinician must be sensitive to these differences.

While it is beyond the scope of this text to do justice to the differences of all major cultural, ethnic, and gender-specific research, a more realistic approach emphasizes consideration of cultural differences and impact in the process for responding to any crisis. The counselor is obligated to entertain cultural hypotheses and carefully test these possibilities from multiple sources before accepting cultural explanations. The consequence of this movement toward cultural sensitivity increases the clinician's likelihood of accurately understanding the role of culture on the client's functioning.

For the clinician to move to a multicultural view in interactions with the crisis client, questions are asked that identify distinguishing characteristics related to culture. This is easily accomplished in early interviews or as a genogram is developed. The counselor places himself or herself in the role of student with the client, remembering that perception and behavior are central to crisis. Culture impacts behavior and perception as it ascribes meaning to behavior and situations. Questions are raised to teach the counselor to understand how the client's cultural background shapes the life and experiences of the individual. Respectfully seeking guidance on the influence of cultural experience strengthens the therapeutic relationship through a vulnerable exchange of information. This is particularly important in working with individuals from oppressed minority groups who justifiably tend not to trust or feel comfortable in formal organizations.

Pedersen and Locke (1996) suggest that a culture-centered perspective is not "subtractive" or competing with other theories but is "additive," as it integrates with other psychotherapeutic approaches to enhance the therapeutic work. This perspective allows the crisis counselor to become increasingly aware of the complicated and dynamic cultural forces that impact the experience and resolution of crisis into the fabric of the individual's life. Sensitivity to stereotypes and recognition of personal bias places the counselor in a respectful position in relation to the client.

An illustration will be helpful to integrate this thought. Consider an African-American individual who faces the crisis of death. Barrett (1995), an influential African-American expert on death and dying in the black community, suggests an inferential model of practice including three variables: cultural identification (defined as the extent to which a person identifies with traditional African values and embraces cultural African roots), spirituality, and social class.

He suggests that counselors should assess important variables which are indicative to the extent that the individual and family subscribe to and embrace social tradition. The social standing of the family is seen as a confounding variable as the affluent tend to become less traditional while the poor are more likely to follow conventional and traditional practices (Perry, 1993).

Spirituality is a defining dimension of the African-American approach to dying. Profound beliefs in the afterlife are characterized by the dead who do not live in a distant heaven but remain among the living. This view is comforting to survivors who believe that their ancestors remain present in times of joy and sadness. Funerals, therefore, are not seen as goodbyes, but as a "home-going service" in celebration of the transition from the world of the physical into the world of the spirit (Barrett, 1998).

The rules and regulations in medical and health care settings often are at odds with the needs of the African-American community. In this tradition, families gather and hold a felt need to literally surround the dying individual. Hospital policy may not embrace this family ritual. There is a strong sense of obligation to gather at the time of death. Elder and family members meet for prayer vigils, oftentimes encircling the dying individual to comfort and support the transition into the spiritual world. To describe this process as dying is much less representative of the process. In the African-American tradition, the point of death is known as a "passing."

By remembering systems theory, the crisis counselor can identify any rules established by ethnic identification and diminish the possibilities of resistance. In a multicultural perspective, the counselor is obligated to work within the rules of the system unless it is blatantly pathological. There must be a good reason to want to change the rules of the system, and the change must fit within the framework of the cultural heritage and social and economic perspective of the client. The crisis counselor must identify family roles and allowable behaviors of the cultural group; these may be different from mainstream roles and behaviors. Imposing mainstream theories of pathology on other cultures may create a different type of crisis and is often counterproductive.

Chapter 4

The Systemic Crisis Intervention Model

PHASE I: REMEMBER

1. Share the story
2. Validate the emotional impact
3. Evaluate the context of the crisis
4. Protect vulnerable family members
5. Negotiate a solvable problem
6. Network with relevant resources

PHASE II: REORGANIZE

1. Formulate a plan for change
2. Identify developmental issues
3. Engage therapeutic tools
4. Assign homework
5. Support systemic rules, roles, and rituals

PHASE III: RESTORE

1. Track progress toward goals
2. Acknowledge indicators of the time to terminate
3. Address future sources of stress
4. Refer for continuing treatment
5. Exit the system

Crisis Counseling and Therapy
© 2007 by The Haworth Press, Inc. All rights reserved.
doi:10.1300/5953_04

INTRODUCTION

The systemic crisis intervention model is based on an integration of four theories: narrative, cognitive-behavioral, family systems, and experiential/existential. By definition, a crisis is time limited. According to crisis theory, if the crisis extends longer than a brief time period, the system will rest by incorporating symptomatology. Practiced over time, the symptoms become chronic and progressively entrenched in the activities and rhythms of daily living. By necessity, this dimension of the crisis state limits the time frame for intervention to a maximum of six to eight weeks. Rather than conforming to the traditional once-a-week therapeutic hour, sessions are determined by the degree of disequilibrium experienced in the system. Within this framework, most crisis counseling occurs in ten to twelve sessions over the six- to-eight-week time period. During this time, the therapist makes efforts to allow for flexibility in time and session length.

The model is presented in a fairly linear fashion and is applied in a stepwise manner. A brief description of the four theoretical perspectives and of how trauma is logged into memory will facilitate a deeper understanding of the model and its application. Pragmatic application of the model will follow.

NARRATIVE THERAPY

With its roots in the metaphor of stories, narrative therapy promotes fluid rather than rigid movement within the individual. Narrative therapy is based on the belief that humans interact in a storied, moral universe. The use of language and telling of relational (self and other) stories are embedded in social and cultural contexts that change as the contextual frame unfolds. In this theory, reality is defined as an intersubjective phenomenon constructed in conversation among people. The goal of narrative therapy focuses on the unique story of personal experience. Stories are acknowledged as subjective constructions and not as universal or immutable truths. All of what is defined within the individual is context driven. Each and every behavioral action is known as a "performance of meaning" (Bruner, 1986) that simultaneously re-authors past experience and frames subsequent experience. Said in other words, the observer cannot be separated from the observed, so there is no such thing as objectivity. Stories are seen as socially constructed through engagements, also known as discourse, with the culture. They are composed in the dual landscape of action and consciousness. The concept of the self is also a social construction rather than being seen as a stable, observable entity. Furthermore, the unique historical movement of the system fosters certain stories and neglects or marginalizes others. Narrative therapy focuses on the tendency for dominant discourses in the system to quietly obscure other stories that are at odds with those dominant descriptions of reality. This leads to a systemic imbalance of power. Individuals can become oppressed by certain dominant discourses, and their capacity to generate more preferred stories remains choked or limited. Context plays a major role in how humans develop their stories, which by implication states there is no universal standard for normal development. Emotionality is also seen as determined by context, rather than known as internal, stable states.

The key therapeutic practice of narrative therapy involves a radical shift that externalizes the person's problem as a property of social discourse, not of the individual. Such a focus leads to the client's ability to take problems out of a self-identity narrative and to re-author new ways of being. This focus gives therapy a twofold task: first, to deconstruct the dominant discourses and, second, to construct more preferred stories. The therapy is accomplished by both deconstructing the story of how the externalized problem affects the person and then constructing the story of how the person affects the problem. Erving Polster (1995) emphasized the storyline in therapy, saying "The story, well told and palpably experienced, is an essential therapeutic tool for countering the emptiness of experience . . . therapy, therefore, is the process of getting out the vote for oneself or another by restoring the events of the person's life story" (pp. 110-111). These new accounts of the influence *of* the problem and the influence *over* the problem occur in the "landscapes" of action and consciousness. Imes, Clance, Gailis, and Atkeson (2002) restated this principle, saying, "By listening to complex and interwoven stories, the therapist can help to bring a light to a multiplicity of selves who are all contributing to the person's life" (p. 1370). Narrative therapists tend to favor intervening through questions in order to bring forward redescriptions of behaviors, thoughts, intentions, identities, and relationships in increasingly vivid ways.

These practices have a number of beneficial effects. One consequence is to depathologize the client. By deconstructing the contexts and conditions in which problems occur, the person is able to fully separate from the problem. The telling of those occasions when he or she has influence over the problem deepens an alternative, more preferred, narrative construction. The richer the alternative descriptions, the more effectively they constitute identity and experience. Therapeutic focus is placed on how the individual views the situation/crisis as a problem, known as the "problem determined system" (Anderson, Goolishian, and Windermand, 1986). People are members of the problem determined system and are invited to have conversations about how the problem exists. It is particularly important in the theory and practice that all participants agree that the consensual view of the problem has impeded any successful means of resolution. Essentially, there should be agreement by all members of the system that a problem exists. One family member said, "When my grandmother died, we had the family fight that had been brewing for years. Once the dust settled, we had to survey the damage done, which was considerable. Then we were all able to sit down and take stock of things and agree that the fight was bigger than we were. Things started falling back into a more acceptable place."

In narrative therapy, once the problem is organized through the telling of the story, it is *de-constructed,* which *dis-solves* the system, as it exists. The client is invited to describe the system, which is organized by the belief that is held in the problem. The *dis-solving* occurs through conversation. The role of the therapist is to open the doors for clients to explore new meanings in life as a result of the problem context. This process implies that clients, over time, must be engaged in slightly different conversations than the ones that they usually have around the problem or crisis at hand.

Michel Foucault (1980) said that constructed ideas have the power to shape people's lives. When members of a system maintain a dominant story about a problem, they fail to see those times that they have not had the problem. Certainly this is true in crisis. Many clients will report not being able to see the forest for the trees. One woman said, "Everything I knew was only in relation to the trauma of losing my home in that hurricane. I couldn't see, remember, or even think about a time that life was normal." These times become "problem saturated descriptions of life" (White & Epston, 1990). Periods of success in the clients' history with similar problems become subjugated stories that are banished to the edge of awareness. "The structuring of a narrative requires recourse to a selective process in which we prune, from our experience, those events that do not fit with the dominant evolving stories that we and others have about us. Thus, over time and of necessity, much of stock of lived experience goes unstoried and is never 'told' or expressed" (White & Epston, 1990, pp. 11-12).

As noted, the goal of the therapeutic process is to loosen the hold of the dominant story by externalizing the problem from the individual. The conversation that might begin with "Jim is depressed" is reframed to "When the depression takes hold of Jim . . ." By viewing the problem as an external entity, the system is freed to challenge its influence on the members' lives. After externalizing the problem, the system members are asked to identify unique outcomes and times that they successfully fought off the influence of the problem. Using what are known as "landscape of action" questions that enable systems members to situate unique outcomes within their past stories and "landscape of experience" questions that promote reflection of the meaning of this new story in their lives, the system can heal (White, 1993). A client described her therapist, saying, "When she kept asking us how we would know when the crisis was over, we were all puzzled. I had no idea what she meant. As we continued to have conversations, I began to understand that she was interested in what we could learn from the crisis, step-by-step, as we moved through it. Once I began to see the crisis in a different way, I began to feel like I was more in charge of how I was living."

Narrative therapy holds a constructivist approach to change, which states there is no objective reality beyond the individual's personal experience or through social discourse. The centrality of subjective structures, also known as schemas, is crucial to the way the individual adapts to and understands various environmental realities. The acquisition of these personal representations of reality is seen as occurring through a social process of interaction with the environment. In this way, what is operatively and pragmatically true for each individual is based on constructive processes performed with significant others in their world. From a clinical perspective, this implies that these constructs are amenable to change through a social process.

COGNITIVE AND COGNITIVE-BEHAVIORAL THERAPY

Cognitive and cognitive-behavioral therapy intervene to reduce distress by changing maladaptive beliefs and providing new information-processing skills, based on the notion that thinking plays a role in the etiology and maintenance of disorder. The theory rests on the fundamental notion that all cognitive interventions attempt to produce change by influencing thinking (Mahoney, 1977). A cognitive perspective does not ignore the contribution of innate propensities or prior experience, although it does suggest that the way in which an individual interprets an event plays a significant role in determining how he or she responds. According to this perspective, thinking is central to determining subsequent affect and behavior and is itself influenced by existing moods and the consequences of prior actions (Bandura, 1986). The theory dovetails with the narrative/constructivist approach that suggests reality is a product of the personal meanings that people create (Michenbaum & Fitzpatrick, 1993).

Short-term cognitive therapy makes seven assumptions (Young, 1994) about individuals and their capacity to change:

1. Individuals have access to their feelings.
2. Individuals have access to thoughts, images, and visual memory.
3. Individuals have identifiable problems on which to focus.
4. Individuals have the motivation to do homework and to learn self-control strategies in order to return to a preferred level of functioning.
5. Individuals can quickly engage in collaborative relationships with others.
6. Difficulties in the therapeutic relationship are not a major problem focus.
7. All cognition and behavior patterns can be changed through empirical analysis, logical discourse, experimentation, gradual steps, and practice.

Cognitivists see people as both acting on the environment and affected by their understanding of it. They are proactive and self-regulating. Cognitive processes and self-reflection are central to human behavior and promote the belief that people are not reactive organisms or conditioned by the environment. Instead, they plan and predict the consequences of their actions. When the plan does not meet the prediction, there is disruption.

Cognitive theory proposes the existence of a set of processes regulating and regulated by environmental input. The self-system, as theorist Albert Bandura preferred to call these internal processes, is interdependent with the person's social and physical environment (Bandura, 1978). In this school of thought, several elements interact to give meaning to experience. The person's awareness and thinking, ongoing behavior, and the environment affect and in turn are affected by each other. The process is continuous. As the person's behavior affects the environment, the environment in turns affects the person's behavior, and the person's awareness and thinking about these interdependencies affects behavior, environment, and changed expectations. Bandura (1982) described the process in this way:

> By their actions, individuals contribute to the nature of their situations. People are therefore at least partial creators of their own history. Moreover, memory representations of the past involve constructive rather than reproductive processes in which events are filtered through personal meanings and biases and cognitively transformed. People thus serve as partial authors not only of their past experiences but of their memory of them as well. (p. 123)

In cognitive theory, there are three self-regulatory processes in the self-system. The first involves self-observation of behavioral quality. Concepts such as originality, authenticity, and ethicalness are applied as evaluative standards to one's own behavior. The second set of processes are the judgments of excellence and goodness of personal behavior relative to the behavior of others and the individual's past performance. Included among these judgments is the individual style of attributing responsibility for action to self or external causes. The last of the processes in the self-system are call self-reaction processes but would be better termed self-reward and punishment.

Cognitivists place focus on the sense of self-efficacy, or personal competence, as underlying a great many behavioral phenomena, including persistence in the face of obstacles. Self-efficacy has four sources. The first and most powerful is performance accomplishment. A person's own efforts either succeed or fail, and the outcome is instructive in planning future efforts. The second, termed vicarious experience, is derived from watching another's efforts succeed or fail. Such observations provide the individual with a basis of comparison to estimate personal competency in similar situations. Third, verbal persuasion is the least powerful regulator of self-efficacy because being told that task accomplishment can or cannot be mastered is far removed from the actual performance and does not strongly engage the individual's conviction. Finally, the level of emotional arousal, that is, the degree of apprehension and anxiety that an individual experiences in a situation, will test competence.

Cognitivists rely on this notion of self-efficacy as a predictor of the individual's capacity to deal with threat and crisis. A threatening perception is related to the degree of subjective danger that the individual experiences. The more the person believes that it is possible to cope with a potentially noxious experience, the less threatening the experience will seem. The person will also be less scared by quieting anxious and unrealistic fantasies about the experience. The individual will dwell less on unpleasant body arousal and will be more likely to transform the meaning of the threat into one believed to be managed effectively. Efficacy is seen as enabling, rather than protective. Efficacy equips the individual to make realistic decisions, sustain intimate relationships, develop productive habits, and adapt to circumstances in order to stay in charge of difficult situations. In crisis, the sooner the individual can recover self-efficacy, the sooner there will be a return to a state of equilibrium and health.

The cognitive model of change proposes that distorted or dysfunctional thinking (which influences the individual's mood and behavior) is common to all psychological disturbances. If a realistic evaluation regarding modification of thinking can be facilitated, there will be an improvement in mood and behavior. Enduring improvement, though, results from modification of the individual's underlying dysfunctional beliefs. As noted earlier, this is the point where cognitive and narrative therapies intersect.

There is growing interest and belief that reality is a product of personal meanings created by the individual. Where the original theory of cognitive therapy emphasized rationality and empiricism, contemporary approaches focus on a modification of the belief system through intervention with thought. A typical course of treatment identifies a problem important to the individual. An associated dysfunctional idea is then identified and evaluated. A reasonable plan is devised that can be practiced, and, finally, the effectiveness of the intervention is then assessed. The theory is based on an ever-evolving formulation of the individual and problem in cognitive terms. Current thinking is evaluated in the context of problematic behaviors, precipitating factors, developmental events, and enduring patterns of interpretation. Emphasis is placed on the present, with an active collaboration and participation between the therapist and client. The process stays goal oriented and problem focused. It is seen as an educative process, aiming to teach the client to be his or her own best therapist, emphasizing relapse prevention. It is time oriented and structured. Ultimately, the therapy teaches the individual to identify, evaluate, and respond to internal dysfunctional thoughts and beliefs.

FAMILY SYSTEMS THEORY

General systems theory proposes that the living organism is an open system, characterized by the flow of information in and out of the system. Living systems experience continuous change as they advance toward higher levels of organization and wholeness. A system is defined as a complex of component parts that are in mutual interaction, with focus placed on the relationships between the parts rather than on how the parts contribute to the whole. Each component of the system is related to at least some other parts in a fairly stable way within a particular period of time. This highly developed interconnectedness and mutual causality of each part of the system forms the cornerstone of family therapy. It describes regularities and redundant patterns that can be observed between people and other phenomena, such as "work families" or groups of "best friends," as well as those family systems connected by a genetic lineage. By adopting a re-

lational frame of reference, family therapists pay simultaneous attention to the family's structure, that is, how it arranges, organizes, and
maintains itself at a particular juncture in time, and how it processes,
that is, the way it evolves, adapts, or changes over time. The system is
complexly organized and is seen as a durable, causal network of related parts that together constitute an entity larger than the simple
sum of its individual members. Systems are composed of units that
stand in consistent relationship to one another, which leads to the in-
ference that they are organized around those relationships. In a similar way, the elements of the system are combined to produce a unity
that is greater than the sum of its parts. A change in one part causes a
change in the other parts, changing meaning in the entire system. Family theorists argue that, if this is true, then adequate understanding of
a system requires study of the whole, rather than separate examination of each component part. No element within the system can ever
be understood in isolation, since elements never function separately.

Family systems theory emphasizes the nonverbal aspects of communication, called transactions, and articulates the relationships between participants. The process of communication is defined as the
way in which members of the system share meaning with each other.
Family therapists prefer to think in terms of circular causality of communication: reciprocal actions occur within a relationship network
by means of a set of interacting loops. From this perspective, any
cause is seen as an effect of a previous cause and in turn becomes the
cause of a later event. This implies that the attitudes and behaviors of
the system members are tied to one another in powerful ways in a
never-ending cycle. All forms of systems therapy believe that it is this
internal structure of the system, defined through communication
transactions, that determines its behavior and not the environment in
and of itself. This concept is known as structural determinism, where
the structure serves to maintain the organization of the system. Such
a stance connotes the belief that a counselor will be able to provide
instructional interactions to clients, but that such instructions will
only serve as guides, compelling the system to make internal changes
that the system itself can produce. This belief links systems theory to
narrative and cognitive theories through constructivism.

Constructivists view knowledge as actively constructed and built
by the individual; it is not passively received. Cognition then orga-

nizes the experiential world rather than seeking to discover alternative realities. In turn, cognitions produce the individual's adaptation with the environment. Although knowledge of others and importance of language is emphasized in the constructivist theory, its implication for family therapy is held in the consideration of the individual's subjective experiential world as presenting and maintaining the "frame" of reference for problems and problem resolution.

Family systems theory notes that there is a progression of the family unit through transition periods, called nodal events. Such developmental activities include, for example, the birth of a child, children leaving home, or death of a family member. Nodal events, which can escalate into crisis if not well-integrated in the systems life cycle, often require the family to rewrite or renegotiate family rules in order to remain functional. Family theorists will teach that these nodal events can be troublesome, since families develop homeostasis, defined by those recurring interactional patterns that maintain stability and balance, especially in times of stress. When a crisis occurs, system members will try to maintain or regain a stable environment by activating systems-learned mechanisms to decrease the stress and restore internal balance. Families that seek to maintain a normal range of behavior are seen as rule governed.

Normality is defined in a phenomenological context. Insight is developed through the continuous process of interpreting levels of contexts of meaning. The energy of the system has a marked tendency toward stability and dynamic equilibrium, particularly in the context of change. Consider a young couple as an example. Each mother spoke to the couple, saying, "We'll plan for you to be with us at the holidays." As the couple considered the dilemma of being in two places at once, they reached the decision to stay in their own home at the holiday time. Both families were horrified and were quite demanding that the couple come to each extended family celebration. Each parent said, "Christmas just won't be the same without you. We can't have it if you aren't with us."

Experiential family therapies challenge reductionistic tenets of the problem-focused school of thought. Sartre's (1946) classical philosophical assertion "Existence precedes essence" is basic to this practice. Thoughts and intellectualizations ("essence") are viewed as attempts to decipher meaning from experience ("existence"), but the

experience of living comes first. A person who lives only intellectually is not in touch with—or reflecting on—personal life experience.
Consequently, important nonrational experiential data are ignored.
This person would not know himself or herself and therefore would
have no authentic self to offer others in relationship. For the family
therapist, this asserts that there is more to life than what can be observed and measured. It implies that the counselor will be primarily
interested in the direct experience of the family and will seek to intervene to facilitate here-and-now experiences. During a conversation
with a family in crisis, the therapist directed the participants "not to
talk about what you wish might've happened. Let's talk about what
we have at hand."

Family theorists will focus on isolation and alienation of the family during crisis, believing that such alienation will make restoration
of intimacy difficult to achieve. Therapy emphasizes the process of
awareness, which is a "re-minding, a realization, a bringing into consciousness of the mind's own inherent mechanism for orienting"
(Kempler, 1973, p. 61). New awareness will lead to self-responsibil-
ity and growth. As one woman said, "Once I knew what it was that
I needed, I was able to go out and look for satisfaction." Awareness
leads to new experience, which is seen as the key to growth and re-
growth in the therapeutic process. As the individual, in the context of
the system, becomes more aware by exploring the present experience, there is movement into a position of recognizing choices and
responsibility for behavior. Theorists also believe that self-awareness
often brings about an integration of fragmented or "unfinished" aspects of the self that have been outside awareness. Ultimately, change
is noted to be integrated through an existential shift, or a "carrying
forward" (Gendlin, 1974) that occurs in the family when it experiences a moving, present-centered, full authentic encounter. Such a
powerful experience often goes beyond the ability for explanation
and results in a marked change in how the individual perceives and
how the system acts in the world.

Largely following the work of Minuchin (1974), family therapists
view families and related systems as comprising a number of co-
existing subsystems, in which members group together to carry out
certain systems functions or processes. Subsystems are organized
components within the overall system and can be determined through

their task function and the boundaries maintained between each component. A parent said to her young son, "Because I'm the mother, that's why. Why can't you act better when we're in public?" The boy answered, "Because I'm your kid, that's why." According to Minuchin, boundaries are invisible lines that separate a system, subsystem, or an individual from outside surroundings. In crisis, boundaries are damaged. Essentially, boundaries protect the system's integrity and distinguish between those members considered to be insiders and those viewed as outsiders. They allow the system to be sufficiently clear to allow information to flow between it and the environment. In terms of the system, the more flexible the boundaries, the better the information flow. The system is open to new experiences and is able to alter and discard unworkable or obsolete interactive patterns. When boundaries are not easily crossed, the system is closed to what is happening around it and is suspicious to the outside world.

While there is no unified theory of family therapy, most family theorists would agree that the approach to change views people as products of social connections and attempts to help all members of the system. Symptomatic behavior in an individual arises from a context of relationships, and interventions are directed to help that person alter faulty interactive patterns. They would continue saying that individual symptoms are maintained externally through contemporary transactions. Family therapists discard traditional diagnostic labels based on individual psychopathology and would say that such a labeling fails to provide an understanding of systems dysfunction and tends to pathologize individuals. The overarching goal of family therapy is to change maladaptive systems interactions, particularly by focusing on repetitive behavioral sequences between members that are self-perpetuating and self-defeating.

EXPERIENTIAL/EXISTENTIAL THERAPY

Existential philosophy asks deep questions about the nature of the human being and the nature of anxiety, despair, grief, loneliness, and isolation. It also deals with the questions of creativity and love. From understanding the meaning of these human experiences, existentially oriented therapists will devise methods of therapy that support clarifying humans in ways that are resolute and as free of distortion as possible. The approach focuses on the realization of one's being and its impact on the self. The philosophy rests on the notion that an individual will be victimized by circumstances and other people until he or she is able to realize, "I am the one living, experiencing, and choosing my own being." However, understanding this notion is not in and of itself a solution for the individual's problem. It is thought to be the precondition for the solution. To understand *being* also brings focus to the understanding of *not being,* or nothingness. Nonbeing is illustrated through the threat of death, or destructive hostility, severe incapacitating anxiety, or critical sickness. The threat of nonbeing is present in greater or lesser intensity at all times. Therefore, the "I am" experience, or the experience of being, is known in this school of thought as ontological, which translates from the original Greek to "the science of being."

In regard to crisis, a primary tenet of existential therapy is called being-in-the-world. The concept describes the phenomenological world in which the individual exists and participates. The belief rests on the notion that the human world is the structure of meaningful relationships in which a person exists and is composed of powerful, personal, and participative experiences. An individual's world includes the past events that condition existence and includes all of the variety of deterministic influences that operate on the person. It is how the individual operates on these influences, in terms of awareness, that molds and reforms belief and behavior. Awareness of the world means, at the same time, to be designing it. Crisis diminishes and distorts awareness of the world.

From the existential point of view, there are three modes of world. The first is the *unwelt,* meaning "world around," and refers to the biological world and the environment. The unwelt speaks to the world of objects and of the natural world. It includes biological needs, drives, desire, and relief, and the world of biological determinism and finiteness to which all must adjust. It is the reality of natural law. The second is the *mitwelt,* literally translated as the "with world," and speaks to the world of relationship with fellow human beings. It is the world of personal relations and love. The third is the *eigenwelt,* the "own world," and is the relationship with one's self. The eigenwelt is the least understood and theoretically presupposes self-awareness and self-relatedness. It involves grasping the what-something-in-the world personally means to the individual observer. It is a "for-me-ness" that gives personal meaning. As an example, an individual who would say, "What a tragedy," means, "For me, this is tragic."

In this theory, the individual is seen as existing, dynamic, and becoming at every moment. Existing involves a continual emerging, in the sense of evolution, and a transcending of the past and present in order to reach the future. Transcendence describes the process of every human being, every moment when he or she is not seriously ill or temporarily blocked by despair or anxiety. This capacity to transcend the immediate situation is not learned but is a given in the ontological nature of being human. To the degree to which a human being can be self-regulated allows for the capacity to objectify the world and to think and talk in symbols. Such a sense of imagination provides a heightened sense of reflection, which circularly leads to self-regulation and integration.

Existential therapy is concerned with people realizing their potential. It emphasizes working with the whole person and not losing that wholeness in concepts such as drives, conditioning, or archetypes. The process holds that, as people develop, they build self and world construct systems, based on the experience of themselves in the world. As they develop, each must confront the givens of existence, including the inevitability of death, the conflict between freedom and the limits of existence, existential isolation, and the meaninglessness of existence. How the individual confronts these concerns is based on his or her constructs. Revision of these constructs is figural in therapy. When the constructs are damaged as a result of crisis, the individual is thrown precipitously into an existential dilemma.

Experiential therapists work these dilemmas in a related sense to the existentialist school of thought. By helping the client access internal experience through attending to a bodily felt sense, the individual moves through different stages: from clearing a space to attending to and symbolizing this felt sense. The primary goal of the therapy is to help the individual integrate information from his or her emotional and cognitive systems, which facilitates a more satisfactory adjustment to the environment. The role of emotion is emphasized for personal development and higher-order functioning. According to this view, the growth tendency is based on adaptive emotional experience. Emotions are seen as being important to the individual's well-being to the extent that they enhance orientation and problem solving.

Change in experiential theory is viewed as occurring by the co-construction of new meaning in a dialogue between the client and therapist. The therapist plays an active role in confirming the client's emotional experience and in helping the client synthesize an identity based on strengths and possibilities. In this view, integration, defined as a synthesis of emotional schema and levels of processing that create new meaning, becomes the operative process. The principle of coherence emerges and can be viewed as facilitating healthy functioning. Coherence allows aspects of experience, as well as levels of processing, to be coordinated and fit together in an affiliative relationship with each other and integrated into a cogent whole that makes sense. It is identified as a part of the individual's self-organization. *Re-owning* disowned or lost parts of the self into coherent forms is the aspirational goal for treatment. This process involves awareness and meaning creation as well as identification with disclaimed action tendencies.

A keystone of the therapeutic process is that of responsibility, that is, the ability to effectively respond to a wide variety of personal, interpersonal, and environmental circumstances. Therapy helps individuals who are panicked when a decisional crisis mounts. Factors related to decision making are explored and then reexamined at progressively deeper levels. Once the deeper meanings are worked through, the decision generally glides easily into place. The aim of experiential/existential approaches is to "set clients free" (May, 1981, p. 19), with freedom understood as the capacity for choice within the natural and self-imposed limits of living. The freedom to do or act is probably the clearest freedom an individual can possess. May (1981) and his peers say that the freedom to be or to adopt attitudes toward situations is another less clear but even more fundamental freedom. Freedom *to do* is generally associated with external, physical decisions, where freedom *to be* is associated with internal, cognitive, and emotional stances. Within these freedoms individuals have a great capacity to create meaning, that is, to conceptualize, imagine, invent, communicate, and physically and psychologically enlarge the world.

Crisis diminishes an individual's capacity to live in the present and takes the person back to survivalistic strategies and instincts. Experiential theorists would say that this is a reduction of and a failure to acknowledge freedom and results in the dysfunctional identification of limits, leading to repressed living. This diminished identification forfeits the capacity to enliven, embolden, and enlarge personal perspective. Such a failure to acknowledge limits results in the sacrifice of the ability to discipline, discern, and prioritize life choices. The greater issue becomes how to emancipate from internal polarities and integrate freedom and limits. This question speaks to the issue of personal identity. Change processes are applied in four basic dimensions: the immediate, the kinesthetic, the active, and the profound. The goal of integration of crisis is to help the individual embody underlying fears and issues and, in doing so, to help attunement, at the deepest levels, to the nature of those issues. In doing so, this helps the person to respond to, rather than react against, those issues. The net result, according to the theory, is an enhanced capacity for intimacy, meaning, and spiritual connection in one's life.

MEMORY WORK AND TRAUMA

Recent research and writing affirms this perspective by identifying memory as the primary component of traumatic experience. Study of the neurological basis for trauma and crisis is in the early stages, but already the work of many researchers is contributing to our understanding of the biological and physiological bases for trauma. A small part of this work is briefly introduced to affirm the importance of this avenue of study. The difficulty in researching brain structure and function necessarily means that some of the work is still hypothetical, but nonetheless useful for consideration.

Daniel Siegel (1995), a noted psychiatrist and student of the functioning of the brain, hypothesizes that memory is the way the brain responds to experience and creates new brain connections. He suggests that memory is of two types, implicit and explicit.

Implicit memory, present from birth, encodes information on a nonverbal level, creating behavioral, emotional, perceptual, and bodily memory. Experiences that occur before the development of language are encoded on the implicit level. Conscious attention is not necessary for implicit memory to occur. When implicit memories are recalled, there is no sense of recollection. The individual is unaware that the response is generated from experience in the past. These memories are mental models. Mental models lead to generalizations from the repetition of experiences and affect emotional response and behavioral patterns. For example, if the significant caregiver in the life of the baby is loving and nurturing, the baby will grow into an individual who expects others in similar positions to also be loving and nurturing. This expectation occurs without the conscious consideration of the child. Object relations theory identifies early attachments as critical for the individual's more mature relationships. If the children grow into adults that expect positive relationships, they will naturally be trusting and accepting of friends and loved ones. If they have experienced neglect or abuse, they will naturally expect that relationships are dangerous. They may find themselves paranoid and distrusting without reason. Individual perceptions are filtered through these mental models, defining the way the individual understands and responds to experience.

The second type of memory, known as explicit memory, begins to develop after the first year of life. Explicit memory utilizes basic implicit memory encoding mechanisms but also processes experience through the integrative region of the brain, the hippocampus. This region of the brain develops after the first year and a half of life and establishes the brain structure necessary for explicit memory to occur. Explicit memory unfolds in two types, factual and autobiographical memory. Factual memory develops around the age of eighteen months, autobiographical around the age of two. As the hippocampus develops, the mind is able to make connections between elements of implicit memory and to create connections between dimensions of explicit memory. The sense of understanding as the individual recognized similarities between current and previous experiences develops as an individual recounts the experience of crisis or trauma. When explicit memory is recalled, the individual experiences the internal sensation of recollection. Unlike the case of implicit memory, for explicit memory to occur, the individual must actively attend to the experience at hand.

Autobiographical memory occurs in the prefrontal cortex, that part of the brain involved with higher-level functioning, including self-awareness, response flexibility, and the regulation of emotion. These processes are profoundly shaped by the attachments in a person's life. Therefore, the prefrontal cortex is shaped by interpersonal relationships. These relationships are particularly important during early childhood as the brain is rapidly developing, but continued development occurs throughout the life cycle.

In this manner, experience shapes the brain. Each new experience is embedded into old memories, both implicit and explicit, creating the unique response of the individual in the context of the common experience of the crisis event. All aspects of experience can be linked with a myriad of previous learning to create new connections. For example, on an afternoon walk, a four-year-old was confronted with a large, unfamiliar dog. The dog, eager to make contact, playfully jumped on the boy, throwing him onto the ground. The child screamed and scared away the surprised dog. While the boy was not hurt in any physical sense, he had been deeply frightened by the experience. He quickly became hypervigilant on outings, looking for threatening, unexpected animals. His anxiety became greater and greater to such a degree that he began to find reasons to avoid walks with his mother. This fear was diminished with the purchase of a small, loving dog. With age and experience, the child mastered his fear, recognizing those times he did and did not need to be afraid. Only then did the child lose his fear of strange dogs. In this example, the association of the dog and fear generalized to all dogs. Resolution of the trauma occurred as age and understanding and new linkages occurred.

The psychiatrist-neurologist Eric Kandel (1998) was the recipient of the Nobel Prize for discovering the underlying brain chemistry that leads to this response. He demonstrated that when neurons are repeatedly activated, the genetic material inside these neurons' nuclei is "turned on" so that new proteins are synthesized, enabling the creation of new neuronal synaptic connections. In this way, experience leads to memory. As the Canadian physician-psychologist Donald Hebb said, "neurons which fire together, wire together"(1995, p. 34).

Severe stress is stored differently in memory. An overwhelming experience blocks normal encoding by inhibiting the hippocampus from processing input, which enables implicit memory but blocks explicit memory. This occurs as a result of excessive discharge of either neurotransmitters or stress hormones that block the work of the hippocampus. This prevents the individual from using past experience to bring understanding to present circumstance. A second process involves the dividing of attention in the face of trauma. When confronted with overwhelming stimuli, consciousness will be directed at the less disturbing components of the event as self-protection. The recollections of an abused child characterize this process. The child can quickly relate details, such as colors or pictures on walls, sounds from the outside environment, smells from the kitchen, but cannot identify his or her assailant. The event is stored in implicit memory without the mediating processing from explicit memory needed to impose understanding and acceptance.

The process of remembering allows the brain to make these important connections with previous experience as a way of bringing insight and a sense of control. It also allows implicit memories the advantage of connections with explicit memory so that understanding and meaning can be imposed on traumatic experience. The importance of this process cannot be overstated.

Remembering allows the individual to *re-member,* to gain "new legs" from "those that were cut out from under me," as one fellow described. Purposely bringing into consciousness repressed, buried, or overwhelming material transforms the toxicity of the crisis into a direction for growth. This re-membering is sustained through the combined work of the individual and the affected social system(s). Michael White, a noted narrative therapist, believes to take on meaning, the stories of our lives need to be told in the presence of an audience (White and Epston, 1990). The therapist and social system become crucial parts of this audience as witness to the individual's pain, paradoxically creating an environment for healing.

The therapist and crisis victim may, in a self-protective way, seek either consciously or unconsciously to avoid this process. The natural inclination of human nature is to retreat in the face of danger or distress. In crisis, individuals finding themselves in the presence of conflict express a desire to escape or even deny the existence of the impact of the trauma. So, too, the therapist, feeling the affective power of the trauma, may collude with the client to avoid painful or frightening material. However, if the victim is to recover, examination of the length and breadth of the crisis must be "the road less traveled." Without this process, the victim is sentenced to carry the burden of grief and suffering alone, allowing the trauma to define the future in increasingly destructive ways. In the initial phase of the crisis model, the therapist creates a safe space for this work to be done. Continuing research on brain functioning will help therapists to understand and enhance the process of storytelling and remembering in resolving crisis.

Chapter 5

Remembering the Crisis

PHASE I: REMEMBER

1. Share the story
2. Validate the emotional impact
3. Evaluate the context of the crisis
4. Protect vulnerable family members
5. Negotiate a solvable problem
6. Network with relevant resources

INTRODUCTION

Using the systemic model for crisis intervention, resting firmly on the tenets of the four theoretical persuasions discussed, the goal emerges for the client and system to move toward equilibrium, returning to a sense of efficacy, increased self-reliance, and a broadening of individual mastery. The process is grounded in immediacy and is action oriented. It has limited goals, for resolution of the crisis, with resolution defined by clarity and focus, and for integration of the lessons held in the crisis into the fabric of daily living. The model instills hope and relies on the utility of support from self and others as a means of facilitating change.

Many may view the first stage of crisis counseling simply as a time to assess the nature and severity of the crisis event. As such, the focus is on identifying symptoms of distress and developing a plan of intervention that addresses discrete and observable symptoms. Once this

Crisis Counseling and Therapy
© 2007 by The Haworth Press, Inc. All rights reserved.
doi:10.1300/5953_05

task is accomplished, the work of applying psychotherapeutic change strategies can occur. The beginning therapist is particularly likely to minimize the importance of this phase by prematurely ending the initial steps, as soon as the type of crisis has been identified and placed in relationship to the individual's prominent symptomatology. This is not helpful to the client. In fact, the first steps of this crisis model may be the most powerful avenue of the entire model for healing and bringing lasting, integrated change.

As the crisis victim journeys to interior places where the event is lodged, the therapist helps the client to integrate the implicit and explicit dimensions of memory, to recover parts of the story easily repressed but important for healing, and to finally create meaning out of suffering. This is accomplished by anchoring the crisis event to previous learning, which creates new linkages to new learning.

STEP I.1. SHARE THE STORY

The first step of crisis work is directed toward the telling of the story. Storytelling is a powerful tool for making sense out of the events of life. This can be understood on a neurological as well as a psychological level. The experience of a crisis is lodged in the left and right hemispheres of the brain. Each processes the crisis in important and unique ways. The right hemisphere has a nonlinear, holistic manner of processing information. This part of the brain is specialized for taking in and processing visual and spatial information. Mental models, autobiographical data, nonverbal information, intense emotions, and social understanding are functions of the right hemisphere.

The left hemisphere involves linear, logical, language-based processing. This left mode of thinking includes the search for cause-and-effect relationships in order to relate the crisis experience to past learning and searches for right versus wrong thinking. Making sense of a crisis event requires utilization and connection of modes of thinking. The crisis victim often feels confused, disjointed, and unbalanced. Personal storytelling begins with an incoherent, unfocused, emotionally charged representation of the event. As the story is told, the right and left modes of thinking are integrated so that the reflective, insightful, purposeful parts of the brain are engaged. A sense of time and pattern connects the present circumstance with the past and an anticipated future.

Research supports the importance of the story from diverse disciplines of anthropology, psychology, and sociology. Siegle (1995) points to recent findings from neurological studies that contribute to the understanding of why these stories are as important. The results tell us this:

- Stories are universal.
- Stories are found throughout the human life span, playing an important role in intergenerational relationships.
- Stories most likely are unique to humans—no other animals appear to have the narrative instinct and storytelling drive.
- Stories involve logical sequencing of events but also play a powerful role in regulating emotions (in this way, stories are a good examples of how emotional and analytical thinking are intertwined).
- Stories play a role in everyday communication as well as in the internal sense of the self. This blend of the interpersonal and the personal characteristic of the human mind reveals the importance of social interaction.
- Stories play a vital role in memory processes.
- Stories have been correlated with brain function, particularly since the left hemisphere is driven to make logical sense while the right hemisphere supplies the emotional context and autobiographical data needed for a personal story to make sense.

The telling of a coherent story comes from the bilateral, interhemispheric integration of the mind. It allows the storyteller to make sense out of personal experience and the listener to engage in empathetic understanding. As other members of the family listen to the crisis victim tell the story, they also relate it to their own experience and understanding of self and world. A similar process occurs within the therapist. The therapist's maturity is valued in this complex perception of self, other, and experience. The skill of the therapist lies in the ability to create an atmosphere for a true telling ("truth telling") of the story within the safe, supportive context of the significant relationships of the victim.

The victim, in this sense, is not just the individual who is directly affected by the crisis event but includes any and all who are touched by the experience. The unique and shared experiences of the crisis can be collectively held. For example, a family's home burned to the ground in a terrible house fire. Each family member suffered different losses in response to the tragedy. The father of the family said, "I've got to provide a roof for my brood." The mother said, "Our history is damaged. Our priorities are lost. I don't know what to do. There are things that I will never be able to replace." One of their children became increasingly anxious at night and began to fear the dark, losing a fundamental sense of safety and security. The entire family lost its sense of familiarity of surrounding and, more relevant, their healthy sense of insulation from the ephemeral nature of daily life.

Consider another, more personal incident. A young adult woman, attending graduate school while living at home with her parents, was raped in a campus parking lot. She certainly was the direct victim of the physical assault. She needed immediate crisis intervention to deal with the trauma, including the physical and emotional impact of the attack. Her family would become indirect victims. The young student's father was enraged when he learned of her rape and did not have clear trajectories to discharge anger, scattering his wrath like buckshot fired into the wind. "I'm furious," he said. "How dare some jerk hurt my daughter? I've been telling her all year long that parking lot was dark and unsafe. This is going to break her mother's heart. How will we ever get over it?" His broad blasts of fury and pain reflect feelings leaving him as helpless and victimized as his daughter. The young woman's mother sank into a deep depression, resulting from a triggering of her memories of childhood molestation. The victim's younger brother implored his sister and parents to keep the crime secret from the community. "If people find out about this, I'll be humiliated," he cried. "Nobody wants to think about this. I sure don't want to talk about it, and that's all people will want to do when they find out. I can just hear it now: 'What happened?' That's all they'll want to know—'What happened?'" The student's brother stood on the edge of the abyss of humiliation. The school, fearing negative publicity, discouraged legal involvement and prosecution. The investigating officer became another indirect victim; his righteousness stemmed from memories of his younger sister's assault years before.

The experience of a crisis will always elicit a knot of painful and distressing symptoms. A powerful element to begin the healing process is to invite all members of the system—direct and indirect victims, and caregivers—to share their individual and collective stories. Simply telling the story, recounted in a safe and secure environment, gives victims the experiential sense of being held in their distress. The storytelling allows painful and powerful thoughts and feelings to be externalized in a way that rapidly reduces the power and pain of the trauma. A collective sharing of the story, with participation from all involved in the crisis, validates individual experience and sensitizes each participant to the unique experience of other members in the system. For example, a small southern town's idyllic facade was shattered as the news was told that a beloved mental health worker had committed suicide. As the story was recounted, the town learned that he died following a painful exchange with a peer in the agency where he worked, with whom he was romantically involved. The man's brother, a minister, struggled with his moral convictions and the lack of an adequate answer about the nature of suicide. The mental health agency workers talked of their guilt about missing the seriousness of their colleague's depression. His clients were confused and angry, particularly those who had self-destructive concerns of their own. Alone, these individuals were likely to be stuck in the pain of their own grief.

The role of the clinician is to facilitate the storytelling and sharing in such a way as to progressively bring more of the details of the experience to light. The goal of this step encourages each system member's progressive feeling of being understood and heard, which develops and deepens understanding and works to restore systemic integrity.

This storytelling process may be repeated numerous times as the victims search for ways to integrate experience that has no place in current functioning. One therapist explained it this way: "It is like an old-fashioned flour sifter. To get the flour to the right consistency, you have to turn the sifter over and over and over until it eventually is all sifted through." In telling the story, the crisis client gradually incorporates an alien experience into consciousness. One client said, descriptively, "I felt a little stupid, but I needed to tell every detail of the accident over and over again before I could really begin to figure out what to do. Telling it over and over I finally 'heard' what I had to say. What was outside of me finally got in."

Successfully facilitating this step of the model requires the therapist to be skilled at listening, encouraging, summarizing, and questioning. Questioning is purposefully placed last in this order. The use of questions is likely to distract the storyteller. Reflecting phrases or themes is a much more effective strategy, assisting the speaker to recount important details of the crisis event. Adequate time should be invested so that this step of the model maximizes its benefit. The power and importance of telling the story not only begins the healing process; it *is* the healing process.

STEP I.2. VALIDATE THE EMOTIONAL IMPACT

Joining with the client around powerful emotions is crucial to the experience of empathic understanding. Emotions are the primary means of building relationships with others. The capacity to label and articulate emotion is a unique human capacity and is crucial for the development of social relationships. Too often, the defining of emotionality in relationships is reduced to the labeling of feelings by name, such as fear, joy, sadness, or depression. Emotions are much more complex and consist not only of an internal experience but, in a broader sense, of the perception of the environment, the internal dialogue related to the nature of the environmental stimulus, the feelings resulting from a positive, negative, or neutral evaluation, and the behavioral response demanding approach or avoidance. These dimensions of emotion foster the physiological reactions common to the fight-or-flight response.

Nonverbal cues provide keys in the recognition of affective experience. Eye contact, facial expression, tone of voice, body posture and movement, gestures, timing, and intensity of responses reveal underlying emotion. As the client shares emotion, the therapist experiences a resonant connection. Mutual memories, feelings, and sensations are triggered. Scientifically stated, humans have mirror neurons in the brain that cause the perception of emotion in another to automatically and unconsciously be experienced in the observer (Seigel, 1995, p. 94). To keep this process helpful, this empathetic understanding and relating requires the therapist to remain keenly attuned to both the client's and his or her own affective experience. The therapist's internal affective state acutely impacts the emotional dimension of the client's experience.

Without emotional contact, it is virtually impossible to accomplish crisis work. With authentic connection, the client feels safe, understood, and held. When this is not present, the potential rises for the client to feel judged, isolated, and alone. Siegle's description of integrative communication exquisitely describes the nature of the interaction between client and therapist when this step works well. Though it is presented as an application to parent-child relationships, it is an accurate description and translates well into the crisis counseling relationship.

1. *Awareness.* The therapist must be mindful of personal feelings and bodily responses and be equally as aware of others' nonverbal signals.
2. *Attunement.* The therapist must allow his or her mind to align with that of the client.
3. *Empathy.* The therapist must open his mind to sense another's experience and point of view.
4. *Expression.* The therapist must communicate internal responses with respect; the internal must become external.
5. *Joining.* The therapist must participate in give-and-take communication on both a verbal and a nonverbal level.
6. *Clarification.* The therapist must help the client to make sense out of personal experience.
7. *Sovereignty.* The therapist must respect the dignity and separateness of each individual's mind.

Practicing these guidelines as the affective experience of the client is externalized, clarified, and integrated will open intrapsychic and interpersonal channels of communications and avenues of insight and learning.

The logistics of this process ideally require that all system members impacted by the crisis be present and involved. Following the immediate impact of the crisis, all individuals are asked to share their stories. This gives the clinician insight on the content and process dimensions of the family. Some may emphasize the cognitive dimensions of the crisis, while others may hold particular relevance to emotional or behavioral memories. There is an old joke about a blind arts patron who touches the sculpture of an elephant with varying degrees of delight and disgust. The same metaphor applies to crisis work. Individual "views" of the crisis will give the clinician an opportunity to form a gestalt regarding the impact of the crisis upon the individual and the system. The clinician can then share a therapeutic perspective in an effort to encourage clients' clarity and attention to pieces of the crisis that may have been disowned.

The actual telling of the crisis story focuses on the experience in a cognitive, linear fashion. Identification and expression of feelings in a safe environment allows for a clearer understanding of emotional impact as the individual's affective world is explored. One woman, in a session with her therapist, recalled the automobile accident of a friend. She said, "I told the story to the police several times, and I thought about the tragedy, but I wasn't able to cry for my friend until we got together and realized how the accident had changed her, and my, life. I've got lots more tears coming."

Expression of feeling is idiosyncratic according to personality style, gender, and cultural background. Individuals and systems will respond to crisis in character. If it is outside of a family's personality style to be emotionally demonstrative, they will stay reserved in the presence of crisis. The system will seek to self-preserve, by doing what is most familiar, even if it may be seen by others as dysfunctional. A teenaged boy survived a boating accident. He came to the crisis counselor and said, "Would you please tell my mother that I won't feel better if I 'just have a good cry,' as she says? Everybody keeps waiting for me to cry. Give me a break! I just survived a near-death experience. Doesn't that qualify me to decide how I feel about it? The more they say, 'have a good cry,' the less likely it is that will ever happen." The wise counselor asked the young man about his expression of feeling and found other, more personally appropriate avenues for demonstration and discharge of feelings. Clinicians should be attentive to cultural and gender-socialized responses for feelings. Many men feel more comfortable with anger than with fear and depression. Women may feel comfortable expressing fear and depression but ill at ease in the presence of anger and disgust. Once the client has found overt expression of immediate and surface levels of feelings, the clinician can guide and assist in the excavation of unrecognized, unconscious feelings. The clinician may also listen for recurrent personal themes and life-scripts that will facilitate exploration of the personal "blind spots" the client has in his or her life.

From a systemic perspective, the skilled crisis therapist must be sensitive to expression of emotionality from those less dominant in the system. Body language, such as the way a wife is unable to look at her husband, or a son's grimace as his father speaks, gives voice to emotions unspoken, but present. Courage is often needed to risk the raw display of emotions exchanged by people in crisis. One teenager, whose brother died of a drug overdose, met his estranged father at the funeral. After they reconnected, he said, "I didn't know what to say. We were glad to see each other, but it was pretty awful under the circumstances." In the months that followed, the son and father reunited and received coaching by a therapist to help deal with the pain and tension of the circumstances that led to the distance between the two, as well as the agony of the death that brought them together. The therapist who worked with the family described the reconciliation: "The father was a 'hot reactor' and was pretty volatile emotionally. His son stayed detached and ill at ease. He was a 'cool reactor.' It was my job to keep both in the room, accepting and encouraging each one's emotional expression as normal. It took a fair amount of skill, though, to keep the lid on and protect the damaged system from more harm."

The clinician's own experiential anchoring and acceptance of personal limits and emotionality is self-protective. In crisis work, the clinician is susceptible to entering the system as another hidden victim who can be overwhelmed by the crisis. The task evolves to allow personal impact without "falling headfirst into the quagmire," as one clinician admitted. A graduate student working with a regional hospice made the courageous decision with input from her supervisor to discontinue her training program as she realized, with each shared story and particularly in the presence of anger, that she began to resonate to early experiences of abuse and neglect at the hands of her alcoholic father. She found an inability to hold her own pain, much less that of others. She became progressively resentful and projected much of her anger toward her supervising therapist, to whom she attributed an uncaring attitude. As she distanced and explored the experience, she realized that "it was a reflection of my own feelings. I felt like I had been abandoned by the professional community years ago."

By necessity, good crisis work needs to be performed in the context of the therapist's own nurturing community. The clinician should have a professional support system and an intimate circle of loved ones. Exposure to crisis will elicit reconnection with enduring hurts, which is difficult for all engaged in the work. With a strong supervisory relationship, the counselor can move toward insight and integration of emotional wounds. Just as the client feels less alone and isolated, more capable of externalizing emotion for insight and integration in the counseling relationship, so does the clinician. The affective component of the model strengthens the therapeutic bond, allowing the emergence of understanding, and creating space for recovery.

STEP I.3. EVALUATE THE CONTEXT OF THE CRISIS

In high school physics, students are taught that for every action there is an equal and opposite reaction. Crisis clinicians are similarly taught that every action will have impact on the larger system. There can be no independent movement within a system which is, by definition, interdependent. A crisis will affect the entire functioning of the system, with its most profound influence reverberating throughout the family. The clinician dealing in crisis work is also obligated to understand the transgenerational flow of unfinished business. One clinician put it this way: "I've learned a good bit about family therapy from my plumber. He says that you watch the flow of water to see where it starts, and where it pools. He says that water flows downhill. There's a lot of application of that truth in crisis work. Whatever unfinished family business is lurking in the system rears its ugly head in the presence of systemic stress. A crisis puts stress on the system, and the baggage rolls out and follows a flow of anxiety. If I can stay aware of the family history, the influence of members in the family of origin, of those who support the system, and with all of their functional roles that support homeostatic balance, I can quickly understand the context of the impact of the crisis."

The genogram is the best assessment tool available to explore the meaning of the crisis in the context of the life of the family. Generational patterns, family secrets, systemic strengths and weaknesses, and significant historical markers provide important clues to individual and family response to crisis. The genogram (McGoldrick & Gerson, 1985) is constructed with the help of all involved in the crisis. Using this format, the participating members can increase their comfort level and share information that may be painful, embarrassing, or secret, or that may threaten the system—all of which is important for the clinician to glean in order to be able to shore up the system's resilience. As in the telling of the story, using the genogram to externalize the emotions to illustrate the family constellation decreases the emotional impact of the crisis. It has the potential to decrease the power of the family history and whatever unfinished business may tumble out in response to the crisis, which may threaten resolution and integration of the trauma.

A gentleman named Thomas suffered a life-threatening accident. His wife, Lynn, came to see a clinician shortly after the accident, while her husband was still hospitalized. She said, "He's got to have me by his bedside all of the time. He's getting stronger and I'm getting weaker. He's feeling better and I'm getting depressed. I feel like I've held the family together through the crisis and now I'm starting to crumble." The marriage, destabilized by the accident, was threatened until the shared experience of constructing a genogram demystified Thomas's need for Lynn's constant presence. The early death of his father left deep-seated fears of abandonment. Before the accident, he was an independent, self-sufficient man who was accustomed to wielding his power at work and home. After the accident, he fell into an unconscious panic each time his wife left him physically or retreated emotionally. Lynn's lifelong struggle with a controlling father was revisited and irritated by Thomas's ever-increasing demands. The genogram powerfully informed both marital partners about the sources of their frustrations and anger, clearing new space for humor and compromise as the troubling patterns diminished.

As the therapist researches the historical, familial, and systemic significance of the crisis, equal attention must be given to positive traits that have helped the client to weather similar storms. Asking the client about these conditions and strengths encourages connection with previous learning. Even simple, seemingly insignificant events that have been mastered in the past will give the therapist insight into the nature of the client's resiliency. The client will often have an "ah hah!" experience as he or she realizes strengths from similar incidents. For example, Doris, a college senior, was devastated by the breakup with her fiancé. When questioned about similar experiences, she initially said, "No, it's not happened to me before. I've never had anyone choose to end a relationship with me." With further questioning regarding the premature endings in her life, she remembered having moved from one city to another in the fifth grade. Searching for strategies in that memory, she found that getting involved in new activities, talking with intimates about her feelings, and learning horseback riding have been sources of comfort. Translating those coping mechanisms into the present, Doris self-prescribed a healthy course of action.

Other more enduring strengths recognized by the therapist in the ways that clients cope with everyday as well as crisis events allow insight into those natural strengths that each client possesses that can be most easily mobilized in the face of crisis. For example, a couple facing the loss of their expected retirement income assessed their strengths using Seligman's positive psychology assessment tools. They each discovered their unique strengths, looking at ways they might address their financial needs differently. The creativity of the wife coupled with the determination of the husband helped to create a real estate team that earned them the Outstanding Rookie of the Year Award for most sales. Their crisis led not only to a very lucrative job but also enhanced and enlivened the relationship between the couple.

STEP I.4. PROTECT
VULNERABLE FAMILY MEMBERS

The nature of protection of direct and indirect victims of crisis can involve a variety of interventions: physical, emotional, social, and spiritual. The most important and pressing needs for protection arise out of thoughts or actions toward suicide or homicide. The assessment of danger and lethality is critical. Overlearning the exact steps of a comprehensive suicide assessment enables clinicians to overcome their own feelings of panic in the presence of destructive clients and provide a supportive structure to assess the degree of threat.

In the face of great loss, those in crisis may suffer feelings of isolation or depression. Psychological pain may intensify to the degree that suicide or homicide might seem a viable alternative or solution.

Lacking a long-term history with a system in crisis, the therapist must, in an intentional and direct manner, assess the possibility that self- or other-destructive acts might occur. The willingness to ask questions that explore taboo topics creates a comfort zone for the client to explore internal dangerous thoughts and feelings. Oftentimes, admitting to such dark feelings neutralizes the potential for action and can open avenues for family members to hold each other securely so that thoughts do not emerge as action. One client said it best: "As soon as I admitted I had thoughts of killing myself, I no longer felt such a powerful urge to act on something I really didn't want to do."

The therapist adopts a triage approach. Questions are asked in a manner that invites the client to respond in an open and honest fashion. Clinicians must be cautioned to monitor hidden personal anxiety that quickly joins with the denial of the individual and the system that such thoughts could occur. After summarizing the nature of the crisis, simply asking, "Have you had any thoughts of hurting yourself or someone else?" opens the door for a forthright discussion of self-destructive ideation. Should the client respond in the negative, the clinician repeats the question, then follows up by asking, "Can you promise that, should you have such thoughts in the future, we would be able to talk openly about them?" This question establishes groundwork that lethal thoughts are benchmark topics to be discussed in a therapeutic setting. The client is to be reassured that the clinician is invested in safety. Even the need for hospitalization is explained as a protective rather than a punishing option.

The client's admission to suicidal or homicidal feelings constitutes an emergency refocus of the therapeutic relationship. At this point, the therapist completes a thorough suicide assessment.

Assessing and Managing the Suicidal Client

The rate of suicide in the United States has remained relatively constant at approximately 12 per 100,000 for the last decade. With the present population, this amounts to 30,000 deaths per year. Over 90 percent of completed suicides are associated with a mental disorder. Although the rate is highest among older adults (sixty-five or older, and especially Caucasian males), this subpopulation has declined over the past thirty years while the rate among the young (under age twenty-five) has dramatically increased. The latter finding has been linked to the increase in substance abuse and depression in young people, both known as risk factors.

It is generally believed that those who attempt suicide (ten to twenty times the number of completed suicides) represent a different population from completers. Attempters are mainly female, suffer from a high rate of personality disorders, and make repeated attempts; completers are mostly male, they suffer from a major mental disorder, and over 60 percent make only a single but most often successful attempt. Anyone who attempts suicide, however, is at high risk for eventual completion.

The assessment of suicidal ideation proceeds along a gradient, from least severe to most, with a specific line of inquiry as part of the assessment of mental status. Beginning with general questions about the consideration of self-harm, the interviewer asks whether thoughts of death or suicide have occurred, and, if so, how often and how persistently do they come to mind. These thoughts should be characterized as passive or active. The individual who states, "I would be better off dead," is at lower risk than the one who says, "Sometimes when I'm driving my car, I get an impulse to drive headfirst into other cars." Questions then follow regarding suicidal impulses, current intent, and any plan. Details of a plan, including method, time, and place, should be reviewed and noted, and the individual should be interviewed for any rehearsal behavior, either through thought or past action. Past history of similar thoughts, wishes, impulses, plans, or attempts should be obtained. The individual with a plan should be asked about lethal means that could be used to enact the thought, or if there is a plan to obtain them, such as the purchase of a gun.

As a part of the evaluation, the clinician should make a determination about the individual's attitude toward suicide, which may range from its inevitability or desirability to ambivalence and rejection of the idea. The individual should be asked about barriers to suicide. Reasons for living and reasons for dying are fertile ground for exploration. Those factors that have kept the individual alive are informative. Changes in the present or anticipated in the future also give the clinician direction and thought regarding the lethality of the individual's motivation. As one woman said, "The only reason that I stay alive is for my children. I know they couldn't understand my emotional pain and why I would want to leave them. So, I hang on for them. I don't have any reason to believe that things will ever change for the better, so I just hang on. I just hang on."

Finally, the assessment includes a discussion revolving around who has been told about the suicidal ideation. The clinician will find help in the collateral system when significant others are involved. Such collaboration works most effectively with the individual's permission and is included as part of an overall safety plan. The aforementioned woman was willing for the clinician to involve her husband and best friend in the course of treatment. Each was horrified with her hopelessness and feeling of worthlessness. She had described this time in her life, minimizing it as "difficult." Once the depth of her despair was known, help could be mobilized and resources improved for support and care.

There is no certain way of predicting who will commit suicide. The assessment and weighing of risk factors alerts the clinician to those individuals who should be monitored. The determination that an individual is at risk, whether or not the ideation is present, shapes the course of treatment by introducing the objective of risk reduction.

The most telling risk factor is the presence of an existing mental disorder. Over 90 percent of completed suicides are associated with the presence of such a disorder. Factors that may increase the risk for an individual with a current mental disorder include recent hospitalization (within the past year), recent or impending loss (of job or interpersonal relationship), a history of impulsive or dangerous behavior, previous suicide attempts, a family history of suicide, social isolation, and the presence of a concurrent medical disorder which is characterized by chronicity, poor prognosis, or persistent pain. The common use of substances at the time of suicide suggests that acute disinhibition may be an important contributing element. The presence of multiple risk factors in the individual raises the significance of the clinician's attention.

Four diagnoses have been associated in particular with the risk of completing suicide: depression, substance abuse and dependence, schizophrenia, and borderline personality disorder. While crisis counseling does not require the clinician to be a diagnostician in the traditional sense, it is incumbent on the professional to be aware of the risk factors that contribute to completed suicide.

The most commonly associated diagnosis is depression, present in over 60 percent of completed suicides, most likely an underestimation of frequency. The concurrent presence of anxiety raises the risk, especially when the individual's coping skills and defensive styles begin to break down. Substance abuse leads to a disinhibiting of impulsive acts and can undermine judgment and restraint. Command hallucinations, found in individuals suffering from a psychotic state, may signal the individual to self-harm. Irritability or anger associated with impulsivity may indicate an individual who is especially prone to taking self-destructive action.

Finally, the importance of determining the presence or absence of a gun cannot be overstated. If a gun is present or easily accessible, steps to limit access during the course of treatment are warranted. Many suicides are impulsive. National statistics indicate that over half of all suicides are committed with guns, especially handguns. Guns are especially likely to be associated with the very young (adolescents) and the elderly.

There are three steps the clinician should take in order to manage an individual who is suicidal. The first is to take steps to mitigate or eliminate risk factors. This includes limiting access to weapons, addressing the abuse of substances in order to restore normal restraint and inhibition, and treating the anxiety or agitation associated with depression. The second step revolves around the strengthening of barriers to suicide, including increasing intimate and interpersonal contact, and creating a clear safety plan. Taking steps to stabilize the environment—through the crisis work—should lower risk, as will identifying and addressing dangerous behaviors that may represent suicidal intent. The clinician should make lethality an acknowledged and targeted issue. The third and final step involves treating the associated disorder, either through continued crisis intervention or more intensive treatment, including psychotherapy, medication consultation, or hospitalization.

STEP I.5. NEGOTIATE A SOLVABLE PROBLEM

Central to the impact of crisis is the feeling of loss of control over life and environment. One man said, "After my home burned down, I didn't know which way to turn. Nothing felt safe; nothing was predictable. I was scared of everything. My family went to hell in a hand basket and I was the one supposedly in charge. What a joke!" A crisis disrupts the individual's normal coping mechanisms. By definition in systems theory, families seek to maintain homeostatic equilibrium, particularly when under stressful circumstances (Rainer, 1998). The system will seek what is most familiar, even if it is not the most functional route toward optimum resolution of distress. Therefore, it is a crucial therapeutic step to start immediately working to reestablish the system's balance through a regaining of the sense of control. The aforementioned father said, "I had to have something I could do. I just couldn't sit around twiddling my thumbs."

Identifying one concrete goal that can be accomplished in the system will facilitate positive movement. The goal must be immediate and simple to pursue. The clinician should negotiate with sufficient confidence that the goal can be met and achieved. As one clinician said, "I am less interested in what the goal is and more interested that the client can accomplish it. Oftentimes, I have to be a cheerleader just to get the client moving. There have been many times that I feel like the therapist in the movie *What About Bob?* 'Baby steps,' I say, 'just take baby steps.' This is what it takes to get the client moving, though, and that is the object of crisis work—to get the system moving in a positive direction again."

The more remote, abstract, and complex the goal, the less likely the individual and system will be able to mobilize the resources needed to ensure success. It is best if the problem requires a cognitive function, such as deciding funeral plans, or a behavioral action, such as calling a reputable funeral home director following a death. Problems requiring strong affect or that tap into the individual's belief system may be problematic for rapid and observable accomplishment. The clinician is obligated to look at the system, particularly in the extended family, to assess the degree of existing chaos or disorganization. Crisis does not resolve existing problems. Whatever prodromal dysfunction is found in the system will only be underscored by the disruption of the crisis event. The more distress found in the family and the situation, the less likely it will be to identify a solvable problem. One family member reported, when such an intervention went awry, "The therapist told us something to do. I don't remember what it was. We all went in different ways like the Keystone Cops, then got into a fight with each other like we did when we were children. It was not a great idea." No matter how direct the clinician is in suggesting the task, the individual and the system must be fully invested in working to complete the task function through to resolution, or the results will fail akin to the earlier example. Any hesitancy or ambivalence should be construed as a lack of commitment to the task. The individual who says, "I'll try . . ." or the family who says, "I guess we could do that . . ." indicates an inability or an unwillingness to take the step into problem solving. One client said it best: "It took me a little while to get up my courage, and I really didn't trust myself. Fortunately, the therapist didn't give up on me, and kept pushing me to begin to do things for myself. Once I was able to realize that I could solve problems and take care of myself, I began to feel stronger."

When clients fail to follow through on task completion and resolution, the therapist must protect the system from further erosion. Verbal or nonverbal signs of disappointment will diminish rather than build self-efficacy. Even through the eyes of an astute clinician, it is possible to mistake the degree to which a client is able to function. James, for example, was a high-powered executive of a local bank. A major embezzlement scheme had been unearthed, causing a significant crisis in the workplace. James presented to the crisis counselor as only mildly disturbed by the event and turned all of his attention toward his employees. The counselor asked James to take a lead role in working to restore a sense of safety in the bank by having the locks on the accounting doors changed. He did not accomplish this task. His embarrassment at having "forgotten" to do this was countered by the counselor with, "Of course. I'm so sorry. I should have realized that you had 'people' rather than 'place' concerns uppermost on your mind. Let's figure out who might give us some help with this task." This intervention allowed the man to save face and reframe his forgetfulness in a positive direction. The transaction allowed the counselor to recognize a deeper need for support than James initially presented.

It may also be helpful to guide the crisis client through the assignment. Such a directive stance allows the client to claim a sense of ownership of the solution while feeling the increased security of clinical support. For example, a young woman named Jayda discovered that her husband had been sexually abusing their daughter. She tearfully reported this to her crisis counselor. Rather than making telephone calls to the authorities herself, the counselor walked Jayda through the process, then sat with her as she made the proper reports.

The therapist's support encouraged the young woman as she followed through with a very difficult assignment.

Problem selection is helpful to the therapeutic process. Most clients are stuck in a state reflective of "I don't know what to think," "I don't know how to feel," or "I don't know what to do." Giving assignments that help the individual move in the direction of self-discovery of the answers to these questions helps to restore a more balanced perspective of the crisis event. Listening for descriptive and metaphoric language helps the clinician to identify strengths and deficiencies in these realms of experience.

The formulation of the problem becomes figural at this point. The problem resolution should be within the behavioral repertoire of the client, developmentally appropriate, and framed in the language consistent with the worldview of the person. If a child is having difficulty with a crisis, comparing the crisis to his or her schoolwork or homework gives an air of familiarity. In a similar light, a physician can understand taking an individual's emotional temperature. An engineer can relate to developing a plan of action. A pilot recognizes the value of charting a course. This is a tender and powerful way the clinician communicates understanding and acceptance of the client.

STEP I.6. NETWORK WITH RELEVANT RESOURCES

The crisis clinician becomes a resource broker for the client. A counselor said, "A woman whose husband asks for a divorce needs a lawyer. A family whose house has been flooded may need the housing authority. A man diagnosed with cancer needs help accessing his community medical resources. I've got to be able to identify them all!" The crisis clinician will find significant disorganization in the system following the critical event. A rise in anxiety is also noted as a typical reaction to the initial impact of a hazardous event. Anxiety seems to fit a curvilinear model; too much or too little leaves a person in a state of inertia or with undirected or disintegrative energy (Janosik, 1984). Manageable anxiety may motivate the clients toward action; overwhelming anxiety may impair the ability to do even the most simple problem solving.

Working with crisis puts the clinician in an active, direct, and involved role. Knowledge of community resources is critical, and the clinician is enjoined into the role of advice giver/social worker, whose job is to help the client manipulate the external environment and to access secondary and tertiary resources. One woman talked about the process: "I got a cancer diagnosis. It came out of the blue and I was completely at odds about how to find an oncologist. At the time, I didn't even know what the medical specialty for cancer treatment was called. I had to have help and my doctor wasn't a great resource. Fortunately, he knew someone who was a good therapist and not afraid of my illness, and I was able to get good referrals, ask the questions I didn't even know how to ask, and to get actively involved in dealing with my disease."

The clinician is also obligated to attend to the interpersonal assets that are available to the client and the surrounding system. A discussion of the significant people within the individual's environment will yield this information. Finding those who are available and willing to help supports containment of the systemic disorganization. One woman said, "If I heard 'if there's anything I can do to help . . .' one more time, I thought I'd scream. Then I started assigning people tasks. I was amazed to see that there were those who were just talking because they didn't have anything to say, and others who were really interested in helping and who were willing to be resourceful. Those were the people I needed in my life during a critical time. The rest moved on, and I let them go." Though anxiety, fear, and discomfort may be rampant, rarely are all emotions out of control (Korner, 1973). Accessing and mobilizing resources, both internal and environmental, helps facilitate adaptive responses and heightens coping responses to the crisis.

Networking with community resources usually means working with groups that have a strong identity and can be readily organized for action. Accessing such small formal and informal groups helps the individual live more effectively, provides remediation and amelioration of the crisis, and potentially serves to prevent future problems caused by a similar crisis. These resources may provide ongoing support for the client after the crisis has passed and the crisis counselor is no longer involved. They provide a wider "net" to support and catch the client should conditions for crisis return.

Chapter 6

Reorganizing the System After Crisis

PHASE II: REORGANIZE

1. Formulate a plan for change
2. Identify developmental issues
3. Engage therapeutic tools
4. Assign homework
5. Support systemic rules, roles, and rituals

INTRODUCTION

Consider a tornado that rips through a community, destroying all in its path that is not deeply anchored in the earth. Crisis and trauma work in similar ways. They "flatten" the individual's space, leaving only foundational roots to rest upon. The first phase of the systemic model described these anchors; the existing foundation is recovered and reclaimed. The second phase reframes what is left, actively adding to the social, emotional, and behavioral repertoire. This phase works to move the client toward a renewed sense of control and feeling of being in charge. Most frequently, the crisis client is burdened with irrational thoughts, a diminished support system, or inadequate coping skills needed to rebuild ordinary functioning. The second phase of the model addresses part or all of these needs.

STEP II.1. FORMULATE A PLAN FOR CHANGE

In this step, three interconnected and interactive regulatory systems are at work. They are the external stimulus events of the crisis,

Crisis Counseling and Therapy
© 2007 by The Haworth Press, Inc. All rights reserved.
doi:10.1300/5953_06

external reinforcements, and cognitive mediational processes. The impact of environmental events on behavior is largely determined by cognitive processes governing how these external influences are perceived and how the individual interprets them. Psychological functioning involves a reciprocal interaction among three interlocking sets of influences: behavior, cognitive processes, and environmental factors. As the parent of social cognitive theory, Albert Bandura described the process in this way:

> Personal and environmental factors do not function as independent determinants; rather, they determine each other. Nor can "persons" be considered causes independent of their behavior. It is largely through their actions that people produce the environmental conditions that affect their behavior in a reciprocal fashion. The experiences generated by behavior also partly determine what individuals think, expect, and can do, which in turn affect their subsequent behavior. (1977, p. 345)

Essentially, the person is considered the agent of change. Emphasis is placed on the human capacity for self-directed behavior change. A basic assumption of this step is to change individual cognitive processes. It is not so much the experience of the crisis itself, but rather the person's interpretation of that experience that produces psychological disturbance.

In formulating a plan for change, the crisis is constructed as a nonpathological "problem of living." Any abnormal behavior that emerges as a result of the crisis is assumed to be acquired and maintained in the same manner as normal behavior. Behavioral assessment focuses on the current determinants of behavior rather than an analysis of possible historical antecedents. Specificity is the hallmark of this step, and it is assumed that the person is best understood and described by what that person does in a particular situation.

The clinician adopts a scientific approach to helping at this stage. This includes approaching the problem and resolution from an explicit, testable framework. Therapeutic techniques should have measurable outcomes that can be personally replicated in other circumstances that may present in the individual's life. With the help of the clinician, the traumatized individual seeks to identify goals that must be reached in order to resolve the crisis and feel safe again in the world. Strength-oriented models of intervention are useful in this context. One therapist says, "I always ask my clients how they will know when things are better and they no longer need my help. Sometimes I'll ask what the individuals will be doing differently when the crisis is resolved." Another counselor varied this theme, saying, "I want to know what my client's goals are. If we aren't clear on that up front, we're going to miss meeting their needs."

Contracts

Many crisis clinicians report utility in generating a written contract that outlines the responsibilities of the client and the counselor. Putting a concrete "face" to the work has the potential for offering assurance and structure to a vulnerable system. The contract allows for an increased sense of collaboration on a plan for change.

Negotiating contracts for change has become widespread in counseling and psychotherapy and is useful in crisis intervention (Kanfer, 1980). Contingency contracts are agreements between individuals who desire behavior change and those whose behavior needs changing. All contracts specify the positive consequences of adhering to the contract and the negative consequences of noncompliance. Such contracts have been effective with a variety of problems arising out of crisis, including academic problems, delinquent behaviors, marital distress, and issues surrounding loss (Dowd & Olsen, 1985). Based on Dowd and Olsen's recommendations, the following guidelines for effective contracts are suggested:

1. All aspects of the contract should be understood and agreed to by all parties affected in the system.
2. The contract should be in a written form with a solemn signing indicating commitment to the agreement.
3. The contract should stress rewarding accomplishment rather than reinforcing obedience.
4. The contract should be considered the first of a series of steps if the behavior to be changed is complex.
5. The contract is not a legal document and can be renegotiated at any time by any of the signers.

6. The behaviors to be achieved should be clearly and objectively defined. They should be relatively short-term goals.
7. If possible, behavioral goals should be quantified and specified (who, what, when, where, and how often) so that it is clear when the contract is being honored.
8. The contract should not contain goals that parties to the document are incapable of reaching. Success should be simple and easy to achieve.
9. The reward should be timed to be delivered as soon as possible after the new behavior is displayed.

Counselors may prefer verbal contracts with their clients. Verbally contracting follows the same set of steps included with the written system noted previously. Included in the verbal contract are expectations for all participants in the system, including resources and any anticipated stumbling blocks to recovery. A therapist said, "It is important for me to ask what might 'gum up the works' of my client's recovery. I'm sometimes surprised at how accurately my clients can tell me things that might prove troublesome. Knowing those and adding them into the contracting process can give us concrete and workable symptoms to address, leading to a much more successful outcome. I want to work in a stepwise, linear fashion as much as possible. I also want to build in recognition that small changes are effective and cumulatively lead to lasting change."

When a system is traumatized, it is expected that some sense of regression will occur. Regression is a return to responses indicative of earlier, more "childish" forms of action. Such response is expected, since the individual loses the sense of option and choice of response sets during the acute crisis. According to Jerome Frank (Frank & Frank, 1991), those who seek help will be feeling demoralized. Demoralization is described by Frank as "a state of mind characterized by one or more of the following: subjective incompetence, loss of self-esteem, alienation, hopelessness (feeling that no one can help), or helplessness (feeling that other people could help but will not)" (p. 56). According to this view, when clients seek help in crisis, they are looking not only to alleviate problems and symptoms of distress, but also to decrease feelings of discouragement.

An assumption is made in the crisis model that the client is ready to change behavior patterns and will be responsive to outside help (Prochaska & Norcross, 1994). As one client said to her therapist, "Something has to change." Clients in this stage benefit from directives that involve experimenting with different behaviors.

STEP II.2. IDENTIFY DEVELOPMENTAL ISSUES

Emily Dickinson wrote:

> Growth of Man—like Growth of Nature—
> Gravitates within—
> Atmosphere, and Sun endorse it—
> But it stir—alone—

We all have assumptions about the nature of development. We commonly assume, for example, that a child's development is in the parents' hands; that is, children become what they are made. It is assumed that it is the parents' job to teach, to correct mistakes, to provide good models, and to motivate the child to learn. Such a view is reasonable and is shared by many theorists and practitioners. While scholars may use more scientific language, the foundation of this school of thought is that the child is a product of the social environment and that parental and authority figures structure the child's thought and behavior.

Other traditions of thought look at development from a different eye. These writers are less impressed by parental efforts that teach and influence children. They are more interested in how people grow and learn on their own. They will look to the individual's natural genetic tendencies and will look for spontaneous interests. For example, children at a certain age will develop an inner urge to stand and walk, just as they will develop a spontaneous need to find order in their environment. These writers think that humans have an inner need to seek out certain kinds of experiences and activities at certain times of life. While developmental theorists may disagree on varied points, most share the fundamental orientation that includes this interest in inner growth and spontaneous learning.

Regarding crisis intervention, the need to identify developmental issues is both practical and theoretically sound. Depending on the individual's age and stage of life, crisis will have a profound influence on recovery. By adopting a life span approach to crisis, context and perspective can be mustered, giving the clinician and client creative ways to view resolution of the event and its impact in ongoing activities of life. The successful mastery of developmental issues has long-term effects. At the same time, interruption of normative transitions will also increase the risk for further distress.

Understanding Development

The earliest writers on child psychology were philosophers, clergy, educators, and reformers. Their primary debate centered on nature versus nurture: To what extent were the behaviors of adults part of their inherited nature and to what extent the result of their experiences during childhood? Debate centered on how an infant learns and how much of an innate moral sense the infant holds. Rousseau, for example, spoke of the child as a "noble savage" having intuitive knowledge of right and wrong. Left alone, "the child will become increasingly fit to live in the world . . . because nature has endowed him with an order of development that ensures his healthy growth. More than that, the typical interventions of parents and teachers mar and distort the natural succession of the changes of childhood" (Kessen, 1965, p. 74).

Early theorists focused mostly on the development of the child. Not until later in history did theorists become concerned about the ongoing development of humans into later stages of life. Regarding adolescence, theoretical perspectives are quite divergent. Writers now agree that adolescence is a turbulent stage because of the dramatic physiological changes occurring during this time. Sexual and aggressive drives that help the child move into the larger world provide the teenager with tremendous amounts of energy that oftentimes overwhelm good judgment, primarily because of a lack of life experience.

Adolescents are typically confused by new social conflicts and demands. Most developmental theorists will agree with the fundamental thought that the task of adolescence is to develop an inner feeling of who one is and one's place in the larger social order. It is expected that the upsurge of instinctual drives will contribute to the adolescent's identity problems. At the same time, while teenagers may not be aware of it, they will identify with those others whom they perceive as appealing and therefore work toward becoming like them. It is believed that each person's identity is partly a synthesis of various partial identifications.

The same is true of accomplishments. The ability to stand up, walk, run, play ball, read, and write all contribute to the sense of self. Teenagers progressively come to see themselves as "ones who can do all of these things." Such accomplishments carry through into adulthood and become a part of a positive and lasting identity with importance for the larger community and culture.

As the individual moves into adult life, concerns for adjustment problems begin to shift and change. Life passages in adulthood have increasing personal and familial importance to the individual who must make major decisions regarding love and family, career, and the problems associated with aging. Erik Erikson (1959) talked about these tasks as the attainment of intimacy and of generativity. Intimacy, from the Latin word meaning "innermost," is achieved when an individual is sufficiently secure in personal identity to feel truly mutual with another. It is known as the experience of mature love and the capacity to be touched at a core level by those things that fit an individual's fundamental values. Generativity is a broad term and refers to the production of things and ideas. Generativity unfolds when individuals begin to give of themselves to others in ways that help create a better world for the next generation. It is a sense of nourishing the world through a giving back of wisdom learned through life experience.

The psychological literature typically views the period of old age as one of decline. The period involves a series of physical and social losses demanding attention. Most developmental theorists not only focus on the environmental losses of the elderly, but on the inner struggles associated with this period that hold the potential for growth and wisdom. The goal of this time of life revolves around integrity, defined as the sense of order to life and the acceptance of that one and only life cycle as something that "had to be" and permitted no substitutions. It is the individual's elasticity. One gentleman described it like this: "It is how far I can be bent out of shape and still snap back."

Integrity is a feeling that extends beyond the self and transcends social and political boundaries. It is this inner struggle that tends to make the older person something of a philosopher, out of which grows the strength of wisdom. Wisdom may be expressed in many ways, but it always reflects a thoughtful, hopeful effort to find the value and meaning of life in the face of death.

The concept of learning plays a major role in every developmental theory. Learning is the process by which behavior is modified as a result of experience. It refers to both acquisition of a new response or set of responses and the changes in frequency of an action already present in the individual's repertoire. Concepts basic in all developmental learning theories include stimulus and performance factors in learning, and outcomes and behavior associated with the learning process.

Stimuli provide information about a given situation. Those that allow the individual to predict the probable outcome of behavior teach discrimination. Crisis significantly disrupts this process. Discrimination is an adaptive process and extends throughout the developmental life span. New information constantly allows the individual to correct overgeneralizations and make more appropriate discriminations. For example, children who generalize to playmates the whiny, dependent responses they make to their parents soon discover that whiny behavior does not work as well with peers. When responses that had led to rewards in some situations lead to punishments or to no rewards in new, similar situations, the individual makes discriminations and learns to identify the discriminative stimuli that enable a prediction of the probable outcome of behavior.

Although there is an old saying that "you can't teach an old dog new tricks," people do learn quickly, so that in most new situations they are capable of making a variety of responses. This repertoire of responses involves a set of behaviors holding different strengths. Arranged from strongest to weakest, they form what psychologists call a response hierarchy. When presented a stimulus, an individual will "default" to his or her strongest response. Other responses will be available as the individual actively brings them to awareness. One of the chief advantages of thinking in terms of such a response hierarchy is that development can be considered as shifts in the hierarchy. As the individual learns new ways of behaving, some "childish" responses move down and more mature responses become probable. This is more functional than "either-or" demands on behavioral responses. Human beings function in more powerful ways in the presence of choice.

Ability and motivation also impact an individual's capacity to learn. Abilities lead to motivation. Discovering a capacity to be good "at something," an individual is much more likely to exercise these talents and to spend time improving personal facility.

In terms of outcomes, most human behavior is obviously intended to gain a reward or to avoid negative consequences. This suggests that outcome is among the most important factors in learning and performance. A crisis disrupts this sense of how reinforcement will be delivered. A positive reinforcement generally means that the behavior it follows will become more frequent. If the behavior learned with positive reinforcement suddenly brings no reward, the behavior will ordinarily become less and less likely until it either disappears or returns to some baseline level.

Rarely though, in real life, do people receive a reward every time they make a response. Usually the rewards are intermittent and come now and then. Laboratory studies with both animals and humans indicate that behavior that is intermittently reinforced persists for a long time without reinforcement; in contrast, behavior learned with constant reinforcement extinguishes quickly when it is no longer rewarded. Intermittent reinforcement explains why some old habits, even bad ones, are oftentimes so hard to break.

Practicing from a Developmental Perspective

Much of the practice of crisis intervention from a systems approach rests on the view that psychological problems will present differently not only because of the individual's present environment, but also because of his or her developmental stage of life and the impact the crisis has had on the intergenerational family system. An assumption of the systems approach states that change in any one part of the system affects all parts of that system.

A family in crisis illustrates this point graphically. The family came and requested help following their teenage son's arrest for burglary of a local business. The upscale, middle-class family was horrified with the son's behavior, particularly when he tested positive for marijuana and Ecstasy in his system. They reported having worked "all [his] life" trying to help him "toe the line," as the father said.

Eventually, the young man left the family home. The couple had no more control over the son's actions and began to fight with each other. Within a year, they filed for separation because of their differences. The mother reported to a friend, "I had no idea that the problems with our son would affect our whole relationship. Our marriage fell apart in the wake of our failure to deal with him."

Another systems principle states that each individual will reflect a piece of the whole system; as noted earlier, the most powerful system to which an individual belongs is the family. A crisis will affect all members of the system. As the old Zen saying goes, "Drop a rock into a pond and both rock and pond are forever changed." This is definitely true in crisis.

To understand the developmental life phase of the individual, the crisis is best viewed through the lens of the family's interactions. Symptoms are understood as an expression of dysfunction in the family; the greater the impact of the crisis, the more pronounced the symptomatology. In the presence of crisis, it can be assumed that the individual will retreat to a state of familiarity and that problems present before the crisis will be underlined and illuminated after the critical event. This perspective is grounded on the assumption that if symptoms following the crisis do not rapidly remit, then problematic behavior might begin to serve a secondary function or purpose for the family. This may be due to the family's inability to operate productively, especially during developmental transitions, or it may result from dysfunctional patterns handed down transgenerationally.

One of the more useful developmental models of the stages of human growth and development belongs to Erik Erikson (1963). Erikson's psychosocial perspective described human development over the entire life span in eight stages, each marked by a particular crisis to be resolved. For Erikson, crisis means a "turning point in life, a moment of transition characterized by the potential to move either forward or backward in development. These moments point to both dangers and opportunities" (Corey & Corey, 1998, p. 288). From a positive perspective, crises can be viewed as challenges to be met rather than catastrophic events based on an external locus of control. In Erikson's view, to a large extent, an individual's contemporary life is the result of earlier choices. Early failures lead to later vulnerabilities; successes lead to family strengths. Life has continuity.

STEP II.3. ENGAGE THERAPEUTIC TOOLS

Researcher John Norcross provides a definition of psychotherapy that is theoretically neutral and relatively concrete:

> Psychotherapy is the informed and intentional application of clinical methods and interpersonal stances derived from established psychological principles for the purpose of assisting people to modify their behaviors, cognitions, emotions, and/or other personal characteristics in directions that the participants deem desirable. (Norcross, 1990, p. 218)

Processes of change are the covert and overt activities that people engage in to alter affect, thinking, behavior, or relationships related to a particular problem or to more general patterns of living. There are several factors of change that are seen as encouraging, regardless of the counselor's theoretical stance. Identifying these factors allows the counselor to optimize chances for therapeutic success.

All clinicians believe that any therapeutic endeavor is oriented to helping people change. Tactics of intervention are differentially employed to bring about lasting change. Such "tactics," or therapeutic tools, are drawn from the clinician's repertoire of methods learned from training and practice. The engagement of therapeutic tools should be well rooted in theory, the clinician's personal style, and the clinician's personal philosophy (Mosak & Maniacci, 1998). The task of crisis intervention work is to keep the system in therapeutic motion.

As has been stated, a crisis will upset the system's balance. What may have been predictably potent as a therapeutic intervention at one point may lose its effectiveness at another. The clinician is obligated to be creative, because if one tactic does not work, the counselor must find another to use in an attempt to facilitate change. The creative clinician will be enjoined to find those interventions that have a solid therapeutic rationale. Using tools as an end in themselves, rather than a means to an end, will make the clinician appear gimmicky. Techniques must not be rooted in therapeutic intention. Instead, the issue of what works best, for what type of problem, and under what circumstances must be maintained as the figural therapeutic rubric. The clinician should also remember that whatever the range of application of a specific therapeutic tool, again the task is to facilitate movement. As one clinician said, "I've thrown out 'If at first you don't succeed, try, try, try again.' Now it's 'If at first you don't succeed, do something different.'"

This being said, all interventional tools should be framed in regard to those therapeutic commonalities known to favorably influence outcome. These are the core features of any therapeutic maneuver known to be "curative," that is, those that are responsible for therapeutic success. To the extent that clinicians can arrive at a philosophical and technical mind-set of strategies based on these commonalities, they will transcend distractions and distortions imposed by different theoretical biases.

Positive Expectations

Most contemporary research reports that treatment is enhanced to the degree that clients expect the treatment to be effective. Positive expectations are seen as a critical variable for therapy to continue. If the individual begins to feel relief and acknowledge change, that person will invest more time and sense of self into the process. It is a working assumption that therapists consciously strive to cultivate hope and enhance positive expectancies. Expectancy designates a client's expectation with regard to positive outcome with a particular therapist; in other instances, it refers to a client's expectation about procedures in therapy, such as the length of treatment, the role of the therapist, and the like (Garfield, 1986; Tinsley, Bowman, & Ray, 1988).

Therapeutic Relationship

All counseling, including crisis intervention, is at root an interpersonal relationship. The single greatest convergence of thought among theorists is that the strong therapeutic alliance is paramount to a successful outcome. There is a great deal of support that people improve in the process of crisis counseling as a result of the relationship between counselor and client. The largest variation in outcome is accounted for by preexisting client factors, such as expectation for change and severity of the problem at hand. The desirable type and relative importance of the relationship are still areas of theoretical controversy. At one end of the continuum, some systems, such as behavior therapies, view the relationship between client and counselor of little importance; the processes and content that must occur in therapy could just as readily occur with a programmed computer, without the therapist's presence. For these theorists, the therapist is included for practical reasons, because technology is not sufficiently advanced for therapy to proceed without the therapist present.

Toward the middle of the continuum, some schools, such as those of cognitive theories, view the relationship as one of the preconditions necessary for therapy to proceed. From this point of view, the client must trust and collaborate with the therapist before being able to participate in the process of change.

At the other end of the continuum, some humanistic theories see the relationship as the absolute and essential process that produces change. They support four "necessary and sufficient conditions" for a therapeutic relationship:

1. Of the two people in the relationship, the therapist must be more congruent or emotionally healthy than the client.
2. The therapist must relate in a genuine manner.
3. The therapist must relate with unconditional positive regard.
4. The therapist must relate with accurate empathy.

Placebo or Hawthorne Effect

Psychologists have known for years that many people can improve solely as a result of having special attention paid to them (Prochaska & Norcross, 1999). Usually such improvement is assumed to be due to the increase in morale and esteem the people experience from having others' attention. At the conclusion of crisis counseling, one woman stated, "I really needed a shoulder to lean on. In my heart of hearts, I knew that, with time, I had the resources that I needed to truly recover. I just didn't have the energy and strength right then to go on. I truly appreciate the time I got from my therapist. I'll forever be grateful that such a competent person gave me her undivided attention. This, more than anything, helped me to chart a successful course."

Applications of therapeutic tools are always designed to facilitate the process of favorable change. Change processes are engaged and used within the therapy sessions and between meetings. Several points regarding the positive nature of change have been theoretically developed from a comparative analysis of the leading systems of therapy

(Prochaska, 1979). Regardless of theoretical persuasion, the crisis counselor will find that the following processes will facilitate positive change: consciousness raising, catharsis, choice, contingency control, coping, and meaning making.

Consciousness Raising

Traditionally, increasing an individual's consciousness has been one of the prime processes of change in counseling and therapy. Crisis is prone to immobilize an individual. Therapeutic technique that involves increasing consciousness is assumed to increase the information available to individuals so that they can make the most effective responses to the stimuli impinging on them. Consciousness can be raised either at the level of the individual's experience or at the level of the individual's environment. When the information given by the client is contained in the stimulation generated by the individual's own actions and experiences, the process is called feedback. In crisis, many individuals lose the capacity to see themselves. The woman who was planning social events following the funeral of her husband was told by her crisis counselor, "You seem to be moving very quickly and need to have many people around you at all times." She was able to respond, "I'm so afraid of being lonely."

Consciousness raising focuses on information processing. Information in therapy is usually very personal and likely to produce as strong an affective reaction as a cognitive response. Consciousness raising allows the therapist to shine a metaphoric beam of light on the darkness of the client's experience. In the darkness, clients are prone to have difficulty finding their way. The therapist provides light to guide the individual effectively through a challenging course.

Catharsis

Historically, evoking emotions has been one of the tried-and-true ways of providing personal relief and behavioral improvement. Catharsis has been based on a hydraulic model of emotions, in which unacceptable affects, such as anger, guilt, or anxiety, are blocked from direct expression. The damming off of such emotions results in pressure from affects seeking some form of release. If emotions can be released more directly, then their reservoir of energy is discharged, and the person is freed from a source of symptoms.

Choice

The role of choice in producing individual change has been a hallmark of many systems of therapy. Clients in crisis will believe that their choices are limited or completely eliminated. In truth, there are many conditions that limit choice. However, the freedom to choose has traditionally been viewed as a uniquely human response made possible by the acquisition of consciousness. The easiest choices follow from accurate information processing that entails an awareness of the consequences of a particular alternative. At an experiential level, an increase in choosing involves the individual's awareness of new alternatives, including the conscious creation of new alternatives for living. This process also involves the individual's experiencing the anxiety inherent in being responsible for whatever alternative is followed.

A client came to see a counselor regarding the crisis of an unplanned pregnancy. As she explored all available options, her counselor facilitated informed thought regarding the consequences of each alternative. The client said, "I am so stuck. Everywhere I turn, there is no right answer here for me. I can't raise a child. I have no job, no husband, and no money. I don't want an abortion, but I can't imagine myself giving a baby up for adoption. Each choice makes me anxious; I'm tied up in knots. I wish I had been a lot more careful with birth control before I got pregnant."

Contingency Control

In crisis, an individual feels that choice has been taken away. The loss of control of the consequences impacts the individual's direction to where the choice leads. If reinforcement is made contingent on a particular response, then the probability is increased that the individual will make that response. On the other hand, if a punishment is made contingent on a particular response, then the individual is less likely to emit that response. Crisis changes contingencies that govern behavior. Change efforts, then, are related to which particular consequences control which variables. The individual's valuing of particular consequences is an important variable affecting contingency control, either personally or environmentally.

During crisis work, it is not unusual to find that individuals modify their experience or response to anticipated consequences without changing the consequences themselves. Such a reevaluation oftentimes provides relief. As one woman said, "After my caregiving responsibilities were finished when my mother died, I sat down and came up with a list of what I wanted. I completely surprised myself with what was and what was not important to me. I'm not sure how much other people liked how I began to act on my new priorities, but I know that I was satisfied and began to feel better and better. That was my goal."

Meaning Making and Coping

In crisis, individuals will attempt to cope with stressful events through meaning making. Certainly the frontline response to resolution of crisis will be found through cognitive activities and problem solving. In circumstances that are not amenable to problem-solving strategies, the stressful impact of the problem may be buffered by responses that control the meaning of the problem. Changes in philosophical and religious beliefs are frequently reported following major life crises. People who have come to terms with crisis are oftentimes described as being "sadder but wiser," suggesting that their positive beliefs about the world have been tempered. Such a sense of coping through meaning making has the potential to change outcome in a progressively integrated fashion.

STEP II.4. ASSIGN HOMEWORK

The individual's completion of homework assigned by the therapist is a clear way to facilitate collaborative involvement. Completion of homework has been positively associated with reduction of symptoms (Worthington, 1986). Discussing homework assignments increases compliance and enhances the flow of process toward a favorable outcome. Wachtel (1977) says in his research that the integration of psychoanalytic and behavior therapy is accomplished through the assignment of tasks or exercises in which clients can then associate, respond, and describe their fantasies and fears. As one woman said, "I was afraid that I wasn't going to be able to do all the things that

I had agreed to do. Following the accident, my therapist and I discussed ways that I would feel comfortable driving again. Each step gave me more information about what I was afraid of. I didn't realize until I started the practice that, the more I practiced, the more I would find out about my fears. As I got better and better with my driving, the fears began to reduce and I felt more confident."

In crisis counseling, homework tasks should be individualized and be pointedly client and situation specific, depending on the demands of the situation. The clinician should be willing to discuss both the outcome and the client's expectations and fears of the homework assignment. The homework tasks should be oriented toward performance outside of the crisis situation in the "real world." Relearning the safety of the world and incorporating new adaptive and coping strategies is key to the resolution of crisis. The tasks should be kept relatively simple and should be at a level where the client is able to succeed.

A significant body of research has been devoted to the enhancement and maintenance of treatment effects. A major factor in maintaining treatment gains seems to be the degree to which the individual recognizes that changes are partially the result of individual effort. Homework seems to be a factor. When the individual is able to engage in a process of cognitive appraisal of past performances in a situation, this cues an efficacy judgment that determines a further course of action. It is common theory that the most powerful method of changing cognitions is through performance-based activities. As one client said, "I can talk about this until I am blue in the face. I've got to get out and just do it for me to feel like they are mine." Homework assignments that focus on having the client engaged in the performance of alternative coping responses (to the crisis) lower the risk for future problems and distress. The expectation holds that if an individual successfully implements alterative behaviors in high-risk situations, appraisal of personal coping abilities will improve and increases in judgment of self-efficacy will result. Behavioral application strategies through homework also help the crisis client to see that change and its maintenance are consequences of their own efforts. The client, through successful completion of homework assignments, is helped to anticipate future life crises/stresses and his or her reactions to them. Individual attribution style and strengths should always be emphasized in homework assignment.

Practice through experiential learning can provide vivid in vivo experiences. As stated, the tasks should be kept relatively simple and should be at a level where the client is able to succeed. One client described the process this way: "My counselor kept giving me homework tasks that made me feel like I was in rehab following an automobile accident. Each step led to another. I was grateful—most of the time—that she was able to be prescriptive. It helped me to regain strength and to take those necessary steps that I was so afraid of in the beginning."

As homework is prescribed and therapeutic tasks achieved, the client regains the personal authority to self-manage. Homework allows the individual a safe and predictable opportunity to gather information needed to self-monitor. Self-monitoring is not only necessary for self-management but also must be sustained to maintain effective self-management and to avoid a return to self-regulatory failures that occur in the presence of crisis (Kirschenbaum, 1987). Successful task accomplishment allows for the opportunity to judge personal behavior in the context of the changed environment. Crisis robs an individual of the ability to perform adequately in a given situation. A restoration of the ability for efficacious behavior increases confidence and competence.

STEP II.5. SUPPORT SYSTEMIC RULES, ROLES, AND RITUALS

In a very intentional way, addressing the roles, rules, and rituals of the individual in the context of the family helps to restore a sense of safety and security within the system. The rules, roles, and rituals of the family system define its shape and structure. They create the sense of continuity that gives history and meaning to the family's ongoing and immediate functioning.

Loss of Role Functioning

In crisis, existing rules and roles can become insufficient, inappropriate, or unrealistic. Members of the system will need to revisit these rules and roles in order to accommodate the new demands emerging from the crisis. The crisis counselor serves an important function by helping the family to understand the insecurity and instability that unfolds when roles are unclear and rules become inadequate to define the structure of the system.

Consider a family whose matriarch is dying. In her final days, she worries about her family's continuity. "I have been the family's connector. My adult children call me the telephone of the family, since I keep everyone up to date with important information about everyone else. I don't know who, if anyone, will pick up this job when I'm gone. Everybody's been totally reliant on me to do this, particularly since they've all been grown." Further exploration revealed this woman to be the keeper of family tradition. She defined who, when, and how holidays and all rites of passage would be celebrated. Her adult daughter said, as she reflected on her mother's role, "Mother makes almost all of our family decisions. We don't let anyone else tell us what to do like she can. She had a way of making things work. Now that she is no longer able to take on such a monumental task, I'm afraid most of our traditions will drift away." When asked if another family member might "step up" to the task, she said, "I don't think so. We all live far apart from each other and don't have the interest in our extended family like she did. My brothers and I have been talking about this. We didn't realize how much of a job this is. We are just now trying to prepare for her funeral. Even with her help and input to plan her own funeral, we are having difficulty coordinating all of the different aspects of how this will all work out."

If the family is to remain intact, roles will have to be accommodated with the majority in the system willing to accept the shift. Otherwise, the family system will significantly change. In a more immediate framework, the daughter of the dying matriarch continued: "We've all gathered at Mom's house and there is no one in charge of cooking, cleaning, or transportation. We are running over each other in the most uncomfortable ways. Even though we are all adults, we still need a mother to help keep us all together and in the right place at the right time." Failure to address role disruption may contribute unnecessarily to system chaos. The effective counseling strategy actively evaluates and assesses current and historical role functioning and the rules and responsibilities of each member in the system. Identifying areas of loss and promoting problem solving and generation of solutions becomes a collaborative therapeutic task.

Use of the Genogram

The genogram is an excellent tool for discovering precrisis roles and responsibilities. It is assumed that the crisis counselor will have at least a rudimentary understanding of genogram construction, which is beyond the scope of this text. Using the techniques of the construction of a family-of-origin "tree," questions can be directed toward the communication and dissemination of information within the extended system. More questions can be built around the nature of the loss associated with the crisis, including how the family handles financial crises and how issues related to the holidays and transitions will be addressed.

The degree of disruption of traditional and routine family rhythms is of prime importance for exploration. The variable most relevant for the counselor revolves around individual family members' ability to accommodate to the demand of the crisis to shift roles and rules while maintaining the thread of continuity to precrisis rhythms.

An example will prove helpful. Nathan was a powerful executive in a regional bank. A national firm bought out his bank and his job was outsourced. Despite a healthy financial situation, he was shattered by the loss of status and employment. His regular twelve-hour workday was disrupted; he found he had no place to go. Nathan was at home with nothing to do, since his role of "breadwinner" was abolished. His wife, as manager of the family in this stereotypically "traditional" household, began to feel angry with his demanding presence. His children, who had a distant relationship with Nathan, felt awkward as he sought them out for companionship. Sensing his loss of place and relevance in his family, he became depressed and withdrawn. "I'm a stranger in my own household!" he complained.

Rituals and Healing

Rituals are instrumental for healing the system. A ritual can give the family system the opportunity to create meaning of the crisis event. Consider the crisis of divorce as an example. Both parents must create a new rhythm for the child who will begin to establish a place in two residences. Divorcing parents John and Rachel wished to accomplish this task in a way that would communicate their commitment to caring for both of their children. Rachel, the custodial parent, took her children to the porch of their dad's new home on a bright Sunday afternoon. Both parents took turns and discussed plans for visitation, ways to stay in contact with the nonattending parent, and how the children's safety and happiness would be addressed by the adults. This transitioning ritual gave the children a clear message that their parents were working together to create new family demarcations. The ritual established fluid boundaries for the children and more firm limits for the adults in each other's lives. The following weekend, John sat on Rachel's porch with the children and the ritual was reenacted.

The importance of ritual establishes transition points in the lives of those ready to change. Its help in bringing order and continuity cannot be overstated. Rituals and traditions include all social behavior that is patterned, repetitive, and conventionalized. They can be as simple as a bedtime story told to a child or as complex as religious services associated with death. The ritual embodies the values of the system. It is culturally driven. The same activity may look quite different when enacted through the lens of multicultural systems. A Protestant funeral is different from a Catholic or Jewish service. Cultural traditions vary in regional and ethnic ways.

Often, it is through formal ritual activities that the system connects to the larger social community during times of loss. While rituals are private declarations of value, they are not secret. An example will illustrate. A young woman was sexually assaulted on her university campus. Because of the stigma associated with rape, she felt ashamed and carried the humiliation in secret for many months. Her isolation contributed to a deepening and distressing depression. Two semesters following her attack, the Women's Center at the university sponsored an event titled "Take Back the Night." Victims of rape were invited to share their stories in a public forum as a way of educating the public and healing personal wounds. The young woman found a place to participate in the event and felt a surge of support and sympathy for what had occurred months before. She reported a heightened sense of freedom for "letting go" of the traumatic event in a safe public place.

As stated, developing rituals is highly dependent on cultural and family tradition. The crisis counselor will need to be particularly attentive to family mores and folkways for a ritual to be successful. Looking into the family structure to find traditions that are held by the system is thought to be a more powerful approach than the counselor creating and applying any specific structure. Three different approaches are suggested in the development of rituals for the resolution of crisis.

Approaches to Ritual and Rites

The first approach is to actually enact a tradition that has been elevated to the place of a ritual in the life of the family. This allows the counselor and the family to evaluate the activity in regard to its value, meaning, and symbolic and historical significance. The bedtime story is a good example of this practice. In a family facing the death of a terminally ill mother, the crisis counselor helped the family not only to read but to write stories about their family life. This practice extended into stories about their future life without the physical presence of the mother. The children in the family settled on the symbol of a butterfly to communicate the mystery of the natural, but frightening progression of life coming to an end. The image of the butterfly strengthened the children's understanding of the mysterious progression of life from birth to death. Use of the bedtime story hour also helped to use the metaphor of sleep as a time of learning about the upcoming separation of physical death. By looking concretely at the members of the system, the emotions aroused by a particular tradition, and what symbols are included, the crisis counselor transforms habit and tradition into therapeutic ritual.

The second approach to ritual is to talk the activity through, imagining enactment in the mind's eye. Through conversation, the client can investigate and analyze, in a narrative form, the value of current rituals. This can clearly lead to the acknowledgment for change or the reassurance in the continuity of the ritual. A simple illustration is helpful. A child's difficulties in middle school escalated into a crisis when he made a lethal threat against his entire class. As the family dealt with the crisis, they talked about food preparation in the home. They discovered that all family members had a specific and clearly defined role in this routine activity except the troubled middle child. It became a family task to help him to find a place for himself during food and meal preparation. Such a seemingly small alteration in the family's rhythm opened new lines of communication and allowed for a generous emergence of support for the young fellow. Talking, as

opposed to enacting, the ritual allows for more analysis and creatively enhances the family's ability to accomplish systemic goals.

The third approach to ritual includes exercises that create an atmosphere where understanding is triggered by diverse activities. Consider the following suggestions as crisis counselor:

1. Clients are asked to describe a typical day outside of the presence of crisis. Habits and traditions for preparing for the day or night, for physical sustenance, and for arriving and leaving are examined for comforting and soothing patterns that can be reproduced.
2. Clients are invited to bring scrapbooks or to construct journals that tell stories about the system that shares important events in the life of the family.
3. The family is allowed to write shared stories about important life events and to focus on how the events were successfully managed.
4. Alternately, the counselor suggests that the family write similar stories with themes that match the family's struggles.
5. A family motto is constructed or articulated that is spoken in the family's colloquial language and repeated when a member is threatened, hurt, or challenged. One family described themselves in this way: "If you can't say something nice about someone, say it behind their back." Though a bit cynical, all family members agreed that this was a paramount rule in the life of the family.

Sources of family power become evident through these means. One mother, whose husband was tragically killed in an accident, shared a scrapbook of their life with her preschool-aged child. The activity encouraged and gave the child permission to talk openly about memories of her father. The activity helped to make the father a symbolic and ongoing presence in their family's daily lives. Another woman had framed a portion of fabric from her grandmother's traveling bag that was carried during her immigration into the country. She told the story of "Grandmother's travels to the new world. She was young, all alone, and was venturing into a new life. She did this because she loved her family enough to want them to have a better life." Another family shared the memory of a family elder. When any one of his grandchildren walked down a dark hall, he was remembered to say,

"God will watch you." The family continues the saying, even though all children are now grown with children of their own. When in uncertain territory, they will remember their grandfather's injunction, "God will watch you."

Each of the exercises opens the family in a benign way of discovering more of the traditions that help carry them through difficult transitions. The stories allow room for developing those traditions that have meaning to the family continuity. Asking important questions about the family rituals helps the crisis victim to reclaim meaning, even in mundane life circumstances.

The crisis counselor is obligated to help the client prepare for future times of difficulty. Establishing rituals and reinforcing traditions are effective ways of managing affective distress such as anxiety, depression, or feelings of rejection. Teaching a client meditative breathing before stressful encounters, encouraging an abuse survivor to repeat self-affirmations as a morning habit, or having a family "high sign" are examples of empowering the crisis victim to prepare and handle difficult times, and to feel centered and in charge.

In designing rituals, several key questions are suggested for the crisis counselor:

1. Does the ritual fit the client's personality and background?
2. Is the ritual appropriate for the issues that the client brings for work?
3. What must be structured and what left more flexible?
4. How easily can the client incorporate the ritual into his or her life?
5. What meaning will the ritual carry in the healing process of the client?

These questions serve as excellent guidelines for assessing the importance and value of a particular ritual in the life of the individual and family system. Investing the time to develop ritual activities is important in all crises, especially those with no societal routines readily available. Examples of these types of crises include failed pregnancy, suicide, adoption, gay and lesbian "coming out," and rape. Helping individuals and their families develop rituals that engage the participants in meaningful, supportive interaction with significant people, through symbolic action, invites transformation into personal growth.

Chapter 7

Restoration and Exiting the System

PHASE III: RESTORE

1. Track progress toward goals
2. Acknowledge indicators of the time to terminate
3. Address future sources of stress
4. Refer for continuing treatment
5. Exit the system

INTRODUCTION

As in any form of therapy, the crisis counseling relationship has a beginning, middle, and an end. Each phase is defined by the nature of the therapeutic relationship, goals for treatment, and the process by which these goals are attained. For most crisis counselors, the demands of the beginning and middle stages of treatment are more clearly defined than those at the end. Initial and midterm goals seem to be more easily accomplished than those required in the third phase. Counselors typically report more comfort developing a therapeutic relationship than with ending one. Setting goals is easier than determining that they have been met and integrated. Developing skills for change requires a mind-set that is different from the skills needed for termination and closure.

Historically, despite the ascribed importance to termination, theoretical and empirical literature has neglected discussions of the final stages of treatment (Quintana & Holahan, 1992; Martin & Schurtman,

Crisis Counseling and Therapy
© 2007 by The Haworth Press, Inc. All rights reserved.
doi:10.1300/5953_07

1985; Marx & Gelso, 1987). The effective termination of counseling has been identified as central to the maintenance of client therapeutic gains, for the consolidation of client progress, and is noted as the stage of therapy at which the most positive growth may occur. Understanding the nature of the termination process will aid the clinician's ability to make sense out of each progressive step the client makes. Monitoring markers of termination indicates when closure has been successfully achieved and helps both counselor and client become increasingly aware of barriers to resolution of the crisis. If the effects of termination are not used constructively, many of the gains made in treatment may be lost. The therapist may not only lose an educational opportunity with the client, but may suffer personal narcissistic wounds as well. The systemic crisis intervention model structures termination to enhance these opportunities for helpful and lasting outcome.

By nature, crisis involves loss. Termination is a unique type of loss for the counselor and the client. It is defined as the planned conclusion of productive therapy, not due to circumstances of arbitrary or unavoidable interruption. The counselor's mandate is to structure the restoration phase so that termination contains wholesome lessons in dealing with separation and individuation. This challenge was poignantly illustrated by a terminally ill mother who told her adult children, "I've taught you how to live, now I'll teach you how to die."

The first two phases of the crisis model teach clients to accept guidance and support. The third restoration phase teaches independence and self-reliance. This is no small or easy task. The ability to be independent of therapeutic support, the resumption of personal control over choices, and the integration of change are all crucial to a rebuilding of the client's sense of personal integrity.

Termination involves three distinct issues and activities: assessing progress toward treatment goals and ongoing needs for treatment, resolving remaining affective issues and bringing closure to the therapeutic relationship, and maximizing the ability of the client to generalize learning, leading to the integration of new skills with deeper understanding and facility.

Crisis counseling has a primary focus on helping the client restore precrisis goal equilibrium. If the relationship has been well-structured, behavioral evidence will be clear to both client and therapist when goals are met and equilibrium restored. If the counselor has over-functioned with advice and retention of control that should be naturally transferred to the client, resistance to termination will be more intense.

Those personal affective issues that are most tender to the client will be revisited in the termination process. Separation, the saying of goodbye, and feelings of confidence in purposeful living emerge as challenges for the client. Done well, the client can embrace the natural support system and experience a return of self-efficacy. Left unaddressed, the individual will feel incomplete and lost without ongoing therapeutic contact.

Even when these goals are attained, the formal end of a therapeutic relationship can be difficult. Crisis counseling oftentimes involves a close and intense relationship; it is not unusual that the personal characteristics of the client will mirror those of the counselor. One counselor described a termination event when his client grew a beard. The counselor, of course, was bearded. When pursued, the client spoke of liking "the look" and that it reminded him of his therapy. He spoke of this process and associated the presence of his therapist with a return to safety and security.

By nature, the process of termination can become a repetition of the crisis state. Clients will often experience a return of initial feelings of fear and insecurity. This issue becomes particularly relevant since the boundaries set in traditional psychotherapy are not always the same in crisis counseling. As one therapist said, "My best boundaries are my skin. I carry my office around on my feet." Counselors may find themselves in multiple roles. One therapist said of his role in crisis work, "I have been in clients' homes, hospital rooms, and met relatives. I have acted as advocate and coach as well as counselor and confessor. One time I helped a client to hire a caregiver for an elderly parent. I know that emergencies never happen on schedule, so I have to adjust." These types of activities are foreign to traditional psychotherapy and are likely to blur the role of the counselor in the eyes of the client.

A cautionary note is important at this point. Crisis counseling relies on the premise that the client is a "normal" person in an abnormal circumstance. It is not unusual that under other circumstances, these clients would be able to engage in more egalitarian interpersonal relationships with the counselor. As the crisis is resolved, clients oftentimes will unconsciously work to "level the playing field," as a counselor described the process. Clients may seek to create a more personal relationship as a way of "proving" a restoration of normality. Counselors may also find difficulty in giving up and letting go of the relationship. Current and past losses, countertransference issues, and poorly defined goals can create ambivalence and compromise the ability of the counselor to terminate effectively.

The last phase of the model is intentional in its design to mitigate the possibility of these and other negative reactions, optimizing the opportunity for shared celebration, significance, and restoration of optimal functioning. Step-by-step, the victim of the crisis resumes a sense of self-ownership and personal power. The therapist works to transfer and integrate the ownership for resolution, emphasizing the changes that have been made. Marking accomplishments, their value in future endeavors, and continuing needs can be actively addressed. Then, in a very intentional manner, the counselor removes his or her influence from the system. This restores integrity to the system and is the final "gift" of the crisis counselor. Issues of separation and individuation, autonomy, and control will be underlying themes determining the success of the restoration of the system.

STEP III.1. TRACK PROGRESS TOWARD GOALS

This step should be started during the first session with the client. Asking the question "How will you know when you no longer are in need of my help?" will, from the beginning, establish the idea that concrete indicators will mark the time of termination. This notion is communicated in positive language, with the idea established that the counselor is a temporal agent for facilitating change, not a permanent fixture in the life of the family. Such a process is best established through collaboratively set goals that are made as concrete as possible. One counselor said, "I want to make sure the whos, whats, whens, wheres, and hows are clearly spelled out." The mark of a good goal in crisis counseling is one that can be recognized as having been attained, or not, by all concerned members of the system. Even when some goals are abstract and focus on thoughts and affects, they should be made objective with behavioral indicators or should be measured using reliable results from objective assessment tools. For example, the measure of depression can be tracked with the Beck Depression Scale (Beck, 1990/1992). Similarly, the measure of anxiety can be assessed through the Burns Anxiety Inventory (Burns, 1989). Both scales provide a number rating indicating levels of emotionality.

Such collaboration allows the client a sense of ownership in the therapy process and gives berth for maximum power over the therapeutic encounter. One crisis counselor related a story: "After the devastation of a hurricane, a small, close-knit community gathered and I facilitated their early discussions for recovery. They first decided they needed to restore basic services and meet individual family needs for food, clothing, and shelter. Then they would be better able to talk about the loss they communally experienced. The group collectively decided that these fundamental activities would help restore a sense of safety and security. They were able to set goals for themselves, all with markers of success for each one." One of the townspeople discussed the counseling process: "Our counselor rolled up his sleeves and worked as hard as we did for getting back to normal. At that point, we were ready to take it from there. What we needed, and thankfully what we got, was a good coach."

Successful tracking notes usual signs for completion of tasks and improved symptomatology consistent with the client's larger goals. The presenting complaint will have disappeared, though this is not always the case. It may be sufficient for the client that symptoms are no longer blocks to daily life but become annoyances that can be used as markers for future progress.

Reframing Experience

Progress toward goals usually involves a reframing of the problem. To reframe means to change the conceptual and/or emotional setting or viewpoint in which a situation is experienced and place it in another frame which fits the "facts" of the same concrete situation equally well or even better, thereby changing its entire meaning. What changes as a result of reframing are the meanings attributed to the situation, and therefore the consequences, but not the concrete facts.

Tracking progress toward goals involves helping the client to shift experience. Reframing is such an effective tool of change because once an individual perceives an alternative class of membership for a given set of facts, it becomes difficult, if not impossible, to go back to the trap and anguish of the former view of the "reality" of the crisis.

A client described it this way. "I never would've thought that my son's death from AIDS could have any good in it. However, during his illness and subsequent death, I learned many valuable lessons about my life. I never knew that I could have tolerated as much pain. I have experienced the depth of intimacy in the midst of sorrow. I've given to others when I didn't think I had anything left to give. And I've been the recipient of some very loving acts of kindness when I felt so raw and vulnerable. Since my son's death, I've been back to these places many times. I wish there had been easier ways to learn all of this about myself, but you take what life gives you."

The shift of experience allows this parent an opportunity to view the crisis of the child's death through new eyes. While the "facts" of the death are not changed, his anguish over the reality is tempered with the lessons that have been gleaned from the tragedy. The parent continued his discussion, saying, "These lessons gave me a way out of the pain. They helped me to recover from the agony of my child's death. As I live again, I am different and changed." Such is the mark of a successful reframing of experience. It lifts the problem out of the symptom frame and into another frame that does not carry the implication of unchangeability.

Behaviorally Based Goals

Crisis counseling is a goal-driven type of therapy. Since restoration of equilibrium is noted as one overriding focus for time and attention in treatment, specific short-term goals are identified as markers for therapy work. Use of a step-by-step plan makes the process concrete and observable. A counselor calls this her "blueprint for change. It gives us a collaborative place from which to work." Often these changes are minimal, with little movement in affective states. One clinician described the process well: "A depressed client will stay depressed if you only ask them how they feel," she said, "but when I inquire about specific symptoms and changes, my client may describe sleeping better, having fewer self-destructive thoughts, and beginning to find pleasure being with other people. These are good markers for change and much easier for everyone to see."

Throughout the therapeutic relationship, the counselor should be intentional in tracking progress, pointing out what has been accomplished by the client to effect change. The language of change should be specifically oriented to accomplish this. "I can see you're feeling encouraged with your ability to set up interviews" accomplishes more and is significantly more effective than saying, "I'm proud that you were able to make those calls I assigned you." The second statement has a parental context that places the therapist in the role of directing and judging change; the first encourages autonomy and places the motivation and action toward change within the client.

The Client's Resistance

There will be times that the client may consciously or unconsciously sabotage change efforts. The crisis counselor is advised to understand this resistance from a benevolent perspective. Resistance has been described as present in every therapeutic situation (Brammer, Shostrum, & Abrego, 1989). Family therapists and systems theorists traditionally have viewed resistance as attempts by the family to maintain a homeostatic balance, even if it is dysfunctional. Most families will come to seek help as a result of change and are looking for a sense of security. Certainly, this is true in the presence of crisis. The system will seek stability rather than further disruption, so attempts toward further change, even as a result of therapeutic endeavors in the system, will be warily met. The crisis clinician should anticipate resistance.

Perhaps the most generous understanding of resistance in crisis work revolves around the viewpoint that resistance is perceived as unconscious communication between client and therapist regarding deeply felt defenses and coping patterns. Resistance signals the helper that the rhythm of the helping process is changing and may be headed for termination (Brammer et al., 1989). Some cognitive therapists see resistance as a natural reaction to a changing worldview. These therapists will speak to the shifting constructs the individual has about the world, which is seen as a progressive move toward the completion of crisis counseling.

No matter how dysfunctional or disrupted, the client will naturally cling to habitual ways of thinking about life. When a crisis disrupts these views, there will be a resonance of personal alarm sounded as the therapist invites further, albeit temporary, disruption needed to restore the system. The client will try at a deep level to hold onto core beliefs, which may bring more distress. This view suggests and sup-

scheduling an alternate time. The therapist noted her own distress and realized that the ambivalence over termination was at least as much hers as it was her client's. The departure of her own son for college had complicated her ability to terminate appropriately. "I couldn't believe it was me that was having trouble. Thank goodness for supervision. I was able to recover and end the relationship appropriately."

The clinician was experiencing separation anxiety, defined as "the signal of danger and reaction of distress upon isolation or separation from a needed person" (Burnham, 1965, p. 346). Not only was she experiencing guilt feelings because of the perceived abandonment of the client, she was also feeling abandoned by the client who in many ways became a symbolic representation of her son.

Counselor feelings of loss at termination can be seen as part of a normal mourning experience. The body of literature on the process and experience of loss provides a theoretical framework in which the effects of the ending of meaningful relationships can be examined, including the therapeutic relationship. Grief is considered an adaptive, healthy response to loss (Schneider, 1984). Loss is continually an issue for the counselor as clients move in and out of the counselor's professional life (Headington, 1981). Acknowledging the existence of grief at termination, Hurn (1971) describes a separation between two adults whose relationship has been in the nature of collaborative work as "a momentous enterprise. Reactions emotionally appropriate to each are expectable and have either a mourning-like character or one that predicts mourning" (p. 346). This statement reflects an acknowledgment that while counselor affective reactions are to an extent a normal response to termination, they become problematic for the effectiveness of counseling when they are not adequately acknowledged and processed by the clinician.

STEP III.3. ADDRESS FUTURE SOURCES OF STRESS

Crisis intervention, by definition, is short-term work. Just as the initial session sets the tone for the therapeutic relationship, the ending phase enables the client to maximize the benefits from the relationship. Clients are encouraged to consider and decide how the change process might be continued in a positive direction. With brief interventions, the goal is to teach clients, as quickly and efficiently as possible, the coping skills they will need to reclaim their lives and live in self-directed ways once the crisis is resolved. While all future challenges cannot be anticipated, the client and counselor can work in collaboration to prepare for expected and unexpected stress.

Three Outcomes

The results of crisis counseling focus on one of the three outcomes: adjustment as the same, adjustment as better, or adjustment as worse resulting from the crisis. The overarching goal of the crisis model points to effecting change in the direction of increased understanding, enhanced coping skills, broadening support systems, and deepening meaning and significance in life, despite its hardships. Whatever the outcome, the crisis client is not immune to future challenges. One client misunderstood the outcome and said, "I thought this was a trial by fire. I passed and thought, 'Well, nothing can hurt me now.' Was I ever wrong."

Life continues to bring challenges, which can be developmental, situational, or secondary to the original precipitant. Developmental crises occur as the individual moves through phases of life that require a revisiting of the meaning of the crisis in the person's life. Situational challenges emerge as demands outside of the client's control impact on personal adjustment. Secondary issues that unfold are oftentimes the most surprising and troubling. A man who fell during a skiing accident accepted the use of a wheelchair for his return to work. When his daughter wanted him to "walk" her down the aisle of her wedding, he found himself revisiting old issues of anger and resentment related to unconscious issues of dependence and frailty.

As noted, resolution of the crisis is time limited. For example, an eight-year-old girl was seen in therapy following her mother's death. She was helped to come to terms with the loss. Her counselor worked with her to normalize her feelings, connect to other loving adults, and restore age-appropriate involvement in outside activities. A primary focus of treatment was absolving her of the guilt of her mother's death. She felt like it was "all [my] fault." As resolution occurred, crisis counseling was ended. However, it is likely that this girl will experience the loss again, even at a crisis level, at those junctures when the mother-daughter connection is particularly powerful. Marriage, the birth of a child, and other family members' deaths present vulnerable points in this girl's development. These places are called transcrisis points in adjustment. Preparing for them makes their effect less powerful.

To prepare, the clients are encouraged to share with their counselor what they perceive to be these transcrisis times of challenge. Together, they construct a plan for responding. For example, a divorced father was able to use his therapy to think through his involvement in his daughter's future wedding. He described different scenarios, role-played interactions with his daughter and ex-wife, and identified resources for answering questions and thinking of alternatives to problems. When faced with the reality of the situation in future years, he felt he was now more likely to respond in a helpful, not harmful, manner. In this step of the restoration phase, the clinician is concrete, translating learning into active programs to meet contemporary and anticipated challenges of daily living.

A variation of this approach involves helping the client make an assessment of personal strengths (assets) and liabilities (weaknesses). In reviewing the work accomplished to resolve the crisis situation, clients may reflect on other critical points in their lives and will revisit significant decisions that were made at these turning points. Helping clients assess internal coping skills and environmental resources needed to meet the challenge of ending one stage of life and moving into the next stage of development "shores up" the strength of the system. One client said it best. "I thought I'd be done with my counseling and move on. As I got stronger, I realized that although this was the worst crisis of my life, it wasn't the only one. Lots of other choice points from my earlier life came back to me. Some haunted me, some tickled me. I was fortunate that my therapist predicted that I may have these types of memories and that they may be potential sources of stress. I guess everyone carries some type of baggage. I'm just glad to know what some of mine are right now." The wise counselor helped her client to predict future transition points in her life and to systematically apply newly learned coping skills from the crisis to potential stressors.

STEP III.4. REFER FOR CONTINUING TREATMENT

The role of the crisis counselor is to provide aid in coping so that the client can restore personal equilibrium. This role is well-defined by short-term, concrete, and measurable goals. At the time of termination, clients may have identified precrisis vulnerabilities they might wish to address or may speak to new issues more suitable for longer-term psychotherapy. Some crisis victims have mental disorders that become apparent. Others may wish to continue counseling out of their experience of the meaning and power of the therapeutic relationship.

If the client requests referral for continued treatment, the counselor can help to identify appropriate routes for help. Should the counselor believe the client will need further treatment, but the client does not request it, the counselor can diplomatically address the susceptibility to distress.

The client may wish to extend the relationship with the crisis counselor. If this is mutually agreed upon, the therapeutic relationship should be renegotiated. Since there is such a distinct difference between crisis work and other types of psychotherapy, a full and informed understanding should be provided by the counselor. The flexible, directive, and supportive stance of the crisis counselor may significantly differ from a more traditional psychotherapeutic relationship. Continuing with the same counselor or opting to accept a referral to a different clinician is an issue for discussion in terms of "fit" for longer-term work. The counselor must be aware of personal issues and consider who might be the best match for the client's longer-term needs. If a referral is needed, the counselor should know and be prepared to discuss practice orientation, fee arrangements, and scheduling flexibility of the clinician. Releases of information should be discussed and signed.

Crisis clinicians should be sensitive to the possibility that clients will seek to please them. They may agree to longer-term therapy despite a lack of motivation, if it is believed to be their clinicians' wishes. Of course, this is a poor predictor for long-term success in psychotherapy. If the client chooses not to follow up with recommendations, the counselor should take personal disappointments to supervision as a preventative for interference with the gains the client has indeed made.

Finally, the clinician should ensure that the crisis is, in fact, resolved before the referral for continued treatment is made. Crisis counseling seeks to reduce anxiety. Traditional counseling and psychotherapy, particularly in early stages of treatment, evokes anxiety.

Until the client has resolved crisis-related issues, it is unwise to begin longer-term therapy.

STEP III.5. EXIT THE SYSTEM

The system's boundaries cannot be reestablished until the clinician exits the system. Termination in the literature is usually described as having a major effect on the gains made during therapy and on the promotion of further growth. Termination must be initiated in a clear, intentional manner. Often, an exit ritual is helpful in accomplishing this step. One counselor invited members of the system to share what they had individually learned about resolving the crisis. They took turns and identified ways of helping each other should future difficulties arise. Finally, each shared his or her personal needs of each other in the ensuing weeks and months. The counselor began and ended the exercise by thanking the family for allowing her to be a part of a meaningful time. She ended the session by saying goodbye to each member, wishing them well, and reminding them of their strength as a family. Such a natural progression with the system facilitates understanding and integration of the crisis experience.

Termination, as has been clearly noted, is a two-way street. Some clinicians may drag their feet because of personal feelings of sadness or attachment. The therapist may feel anxiety over the literal loss of an intimate and meaningful relationship, especially if it means losing a relationship with a client in which the work was particularly rewarding. In addition, the clinician may treasure moments of professional growth within that relationship and "a place and time in which some of life's trust and most poignant moments occurred" (Yalom, 1970, p. 280). But, it cannot be said too clearly that the system's boundaries cannot be reestablished until the clinician leaves the system. All theories agree with the task of keeping the system in motion toward progressively independent action. If clients cannot find individual ways to solve problems, they will be unable to deal with future crisis issues. By exiting the system, the client and clinician can incorporate the bittersweet feelings of a job well done. Life experienced in the crisis as abnormal can return to normal.

Some clinicians find that discussing the end of counseling by formal termination is most easily accomplished at least two sessions before the end of the counseling relationship. The client is reminded at the end of each session of the time remaining in the relationship. In some cases, spacing meetings further apart allows the client the safety net of the relationship while experimenting with progressive independence. This creates a more natural ending. Each case will require clinical intuition and collaboration with the client.

Crisis counseling, like life itself, ends. The goals of therapy may be more fully realized in the termination process. To the degree the clinician can maintain the highest emotional availability during the process, the client learns the value of the relationship and has an opportunity to practice and master "future goodbyes" (Maholick & Turner, 1979). Termination gives both client and clinician an authentic moment to contact and connect to their mutual humanity. It teaches an awareness lesson by allowing the client to be sensitive to an ongoing genuine relationship and a shared behavioral experience, which must end. The client accepts that the therapeutic relationship exists in fact and that what is felt is real and not artificial or "just practice." By accepting the possibility of an ending to human relationships, the client may be encouraged to participate more fully in relationships with others. With successful termination, the client can remember the enriching experience of at least one relationship that was no less rewarding because it ended.

This last step completes the systemic crisis counseling model. The clinician has taken an active, directive approach, staying involved in the life of the individual and the system until the crisis is resolved and balance restored. The Chinese symbol for crisis is a combination of two elements: danger and opportunity. The presence of the crisis counselor becomes a source of opportunity for growth and meaningful development. The collaboration effort involves negotiating the process of the crisis away from destructive trauma, toward meaningful adaptive learning. A crisis survivor's words help illuminate the process: "I wouldn't have asked for this tragedy to occur, but I have to say, it has changed my life for the better. I'm grateful for the chance to see more, feel more, be more than I ever have before." This is a changed perspective.

Chapter 8

The Impact of Crisis in the Lives
of Children and Adolescents

INTRODUCTION

In times of crisis, children are a particularly vulnerable part of the family system. Physical, emotional, social, and psychological immaturity creates an almost total dependence on adults for help in managing the stress of crisis. For adults distress is communicated by talking about the problems they are experiencing. Children are less likely than adults to be able to articulate problems created by the crisis and the response of members of the family; they are more likely to send nonverbal messages communicating distress. Often adults preoccupied or impaired by their own problems fail to see the markers indicating a child's struggle to cope with crisis.

Because children's responses to crisis are so different from that of adults, problems go undetected and the power of early identification and intervention is lost. Educating families and those who serve families to identify high-risk symptoms and to intervene appropriately benefits the child at the time of the crisis and beyond. With support, children can weather the storms of crisis and show surprising resiliency in the face of trauma. Without support they may become like the adults who present at mental health agencies carrying the residual effects of unresolved crisis.

This chapter introduces relevant characteristics of children and adolescents in crisis, examining the types of crises that impact children in families, and exploring the role of resiliency in recovery. Examples will help identify how understanding can lead to action. It is beyond

Crisis Counseling and Therapy
© 2007 by The Haworth Press, Inc. All rights reserved.
doi:10.1300/5953_08

the scope of this book to do more than present an introduction to this work. However, if adults who are with children on a day-to-day basis are to create a caring community and find the ability to hold the youngster through negotiation of multiple challenges, a basic understanding of children in crisis is obligatory. Central to this understanding is an appreciation of the developmental characteristics of children as they relate to crisis and of the role of systems that support children, particularly the family and the school. Identifying examples of types of crisis that impact children enables adults in the child's life to be more astute in assessing and meeting individual needs. The crisis counselor serves a crucial role in helping adults at home and at school become effective supports.

DEVELOPMENTAL CHARACTERISTICS OF CHILDREN IN CRISIS

The impact of crisis on children is strongly influenced by age and developmental stage. Differences in physical, cognitive, emotional, social, and spiritual functioning at different developmental stages influence patterns of symptoms and suggest preferred interventions. Physical development, particularly in young children, can be important in assessing the child's capacity for self-help and self-soothing. The more independent the child and the broader his or her social support network, the less likelihood there will be of enduring problems. Physical changes or challenges predispose children to more vulnerability in the face of crisis situations. For example, at puberty children cope with hormonal changes that affect mood, social changes that affect relationships with parents and peers, and physical changes that affect appearance and self-esteem. The child at this stage who is already stressed can be overwhelmed in the face of crisis.

Cognitive development is another important influence. The ability to conceptualize the world based on concrete or abstract concepts, understood through sensory awareness or symbolic representation, influences the child's understanding of the crisis event. Piaget's (1983) model of cognitive development is a helpful tool for understanding this process and the differences in cognition, or thought, at different stages. Piaget organized thinking and reasoning in a sequential process from the sensory experience of the infant to the sophisticated formal reasoning of the adult. His five-stage theory of cognitive development helps the counselor identify appropriate language and cognitive tasks necessary for understanding the meaning of the events in the life of a child.

The changing cognitive skills of children also influence ways they express emotions and meet basic safety and security needs. Piaget's model of cognitive development helps explain the varying nature of emotional expression in children. Infants live in a sensory world, lacking the language needed to encode experience or express individual needs. Their language is nonverbal. In order to understand the child, adults must be able to interpret these nonverbal cues. This process is interactive. The infant's total dependence on caregivers for meeting basic needs bonds the child to the emotional and psychological nature of the caregiver. The world is interpreted by the child on a sensory level through the experience of the caregiver. The depressed adult will be experienced as distant. The anxious adult will communicate fear.

Preschoolers have significantly more vocabulary than infants but are still bound by the concrete world. They must talk of what they can see, smell, taste, hear, and feel. Speaking in abstract terms leads to confusion and fear in the young child. For example, consider a clinician's case involving a boy who was prepared, with therapeutic help, for his grandfather's funeral. The child's parents and the therapist were convinced of his readiness for the loss. Much to their surprise, the child, who had been complacent throughout the rites of passage associated with his "Poppy's" death, became hysterically terrified when asked if he wanted to "go view the body." After consultation with the therapist, the boy's parents discovered that their son believed that "viewing the body" meant looking at only the body, minus "Poppy's" head. The young boy was frightened to see his headless grandfather. While the story is now told in humor, it is sobering on another level to recognize that the accepted language of death may be inadequate for a child's understanding.

By school age, the child will begin to relate in abstract terms but will continue to think concretely in the here and now, with limited reference to self and a noted lack of understanding of process and pattern. The demand for this child to continue at "work," that is, to go to school despite the crisis, without the understanding and support of teachers or school counselors, sets a course of failure and may precipitate inappropriate mental health labels. For example, an eight-year-old boy was labeled as having attention-deficit/hyperactivity disorder because of symptoms of inattention, distractibility, difficulty finishing work, and irritability toward classmates. An overzealous, less than comprehensive evaluation led to the diagnosis, which in turn led to a referral from his teacher to the family's primary care physician. A request was made to medicate the child on a psycho-stimulant. Before prescribing the medication, the physician wisely asked for the child to be evaluated by a psychologist. The assessment revealed the family in early stages of rupture as the parents separated and moved toward divorce. Counseling was offered to the child rather than medication. His behavior was reflective of the insecurity and anger he was feeling, rather than of a diagnosable attention disorder.

At adolescence, the ability to be empathic, to recognize consequences of behavior, to identify with peers, and to seek support outside of family members creates a dimensional response to crisis that has similarities and differences with adults. Adolescents should be evaluated in terms of strengths and vulnerabilities. Crises such as divorce and death are likely to create shifts in family roles that may challenge relational proximity in teenagers. While adolescents aspire to maturity, their developmental maturation limits the capacity to shoulder adult responsibilities. Critical negotiations that change resources, particularly those that change the adolescent's financial status, cause eruptions of anger and anxiety. Caregivers often focus on lifestyle changes that misrepresent the adolescent's sense of loss. Teenagers act out if they behave according to the job description of adolescence. Understanding these concerns as normative allows adults to respond in a more supportive (rather than critical) way to teenage angst in the presence of the immediacy of crisis.

The ways in which an adolescent responds to crisis is formative in the development of the adult life. This indicates a crucial need for understanding and early intervention with the young person. This early intervention prevents the development of lifelong destructive coping patterns. As an example, a fifteen-year-old adolescent was referred for continuing problems in school and the community. His referral into therapy gave rise to a discussion and exploration of earlier life experiences. At age eleven, the boy begged his mother to take him to the grocery store to purchase a special cereal. After a great deal of struggle, the mother agreed to take the son to the store with his two younger siblings. On the way to the store, the family was involved in a tragic railroad accident. All in the family car were killed but the young boy. He received no counseling after the accident. There is no doubt that his self-destructive behavior could be viewed as a reflection of the emotionality surrounding the death of his mother and younger siblings. Early intervention may have mitigated or eliminated much of the negative outcomes. The decision of no treatment leads him into more, rather than fewer, problems.

A dimension of behavior requiring assessment and support is found in the social relationships of children. These social relationships can be understood using Eric Erikson's (1959) model of development. Erikson explores the developmental "tasks" of children at eight stages of development from infancy to old age. Early in the life of the child, parents and adult caregivers help young ones with task mastery, which supports the foundation of learning psychological resources necessary for integrating experience. Early successes build on each other, and future tasks can be more easily managed.

Emotional development mirrors cognitive development. As children mature, they are better able to understand and articulate their affective state. Spiritual development is also predicated on cognitive development. Fowler's (1991) model for understanding spiritual development helps the crisis counselor to understand questions children ask about the role of a universal spirit and the importance of meaning making in the context of crisis. Adolescents are prone to ask difficult faith questions; parents are well-advised to accept the tension and sometimes anger associated with feelings of injustice.

Social developmental characteristics determine the nature of attachments to parents and caregivers. The same characteristics also determine the ability to verbalize needs, wants, and fears and mark the repertoire of coping mechanisms developed from past experience. Infancy, preschool, school-age, preadolescent, and adolescent phases are clearly delineated by differences in each of these arenas. Infants are totally dependent on adults to meet all of their needs. The child mirrors the adult, reflecting the adult's moods and sensing safety and security. When crisis occurs, infants obviously lack the cognitive ability to understand and do not have the language skills to articulate experience. Calming the adult will calm the child.

Preschoolers, as they develop motor skills, self-help skills, and language begin to learn independence, though they still depend on parents for safety and security, basic needs, and interpretation of life events. Children's increased repertoire of words allows them to communicate to the extent that they are able to understand feelings. These feeling states communicate what they need in order to be helped. Often, however, feelings are translated into somatic complaints. The child will complain of an upset stomach or a headache or fatigue as a way to evidence distress. Using the language of feelings helps the child more effectively communicate the impact of a crisis event.

School-aged children have the advantage of the school system as a source of support for help. Teachers play a crucial role. In times of stress, the school can be a resource less affected than parents by the circumstances of the crisis. In school, if the family has not alerted the teacher to problems at home, the child's behavior may not be recognized as an emotional rather than academic problem. Failure to finish tasks, loss of interest in social events, increased aggression or withdrawal from peers, oppositionality, and anger may lead to incorrect diagnostic labels. Teachers are in an important position to recognize changes in behavior, signs of depression or anxiety, academic failure, and acting-out behavior as symptomatic of psychological problems. The drawings, stories, and play of children reveal life experience. Engaging parents in dialogue, using the school counseling staff, and opening conversations with children will help prevent incorrect diagnostic labeling and treatment.

The adolescent may be the most overlooked "child" of all. The pseudoadulthood of the adolescent and the seeming independence from parents is more apparent than real. Young people continue to need the help and guidance of parents who are obligated to provide stability during the rocky times of adolescence. Too much independence leaves the teenager feeling isolated and lonely, two emotions that are not helpful in crisis situations. Recognizing signs and symptoms of distress and risking engaging the adolescent in conversation about personal and family life open up communication and allow the adolescent needed support.

FAMILY CHARACTERISTICS AND CRISIS

The most relevant systemic factors relate to the family of origin. Defined as the kinship network of three generations, the family of origin is the most powerful system to which an individual belongs. It is the container for learning life structures and an individual worldview. By definition, children in the family of origin are vulnerable to the lessons and experiences of the system. Their dependence on caregivers to meet basic human needs makes any disruption or loss of relationship compellingly significant. Loss of a parent's or caregiver's capacity in crisis leaves the child in the presence of a basic fear of early life—that of abandonment. The initial fears related to abandonment originate with a lack of maturity of the perceptual skills of the infant. When the parent disappears, he or she no longer exists in the mind of the infant. Since the parent is the source of all things good, anxiety is triggered when the adult disappears, even for brief times. If the parent is, in fact, less than responsive to the infant's needs, his or her disappearance will cause the child extreme fright on finding himself or herself alone in the world. As children mature, they develop a set of objects relations that allows maintenance of a sense of security even when the parent "disappears." They know that the parent is not gone forever but will reappear, especially in response to cries of distress. When trauma and crisis take adult attention away from children, the original fear that the parent will somehow disappear is resurrected. This fear is reality based. Parents, preoccupied with their own losses, have little time or energy to devote to the child. If not physically, the child may suffer emotionally from the lack of connection with the parents or adult caregivers. When loss occurs at times of heightened sensitivity to separation, such as transitions due to developmental leaps, the loss is intensified. It is not unusual that a corresponding physiological shift occurs concurrently with the psychological sense of separation. Such a shift complicates the crisis state.

CLASSIFICATION OF CRISES

Kendall Johnson (1989) classifies the nature of trauma affecting children into three types: victimization, loss, and family pathology. Each of these will be explored as valuable aides to understanding children in crisis.

Victimization includes crises of assault, rape, abduction, and serious accidents. These events are brief but intense, robbing the child of a sense of safety and security. Bard and Sangrey's (1979) stage theory identifies victims' experiences as impact, recoil, and reorganization. During impact, the security of the child's world is disrupted. Early distress of children includes somatic symptomatology. They may experience headaches, upset stomachs, feelings of anxiety and depression, and problems with eating and sleeping. The thinking of the children may reflect feelings of blame and guilt. Their "magical thinking," a phenomenon describing children's irrational belief that they are responsible for everything that goes on around them, increases a felt sense of distress and anxiety. Adults have this type of thinking as well but usually recognize on some level the distortion this type of reasoning represents. Children rarely challenge their own thinking. They lack the cognitive skills to live within the rational worldview of adults.

The family is the primary and, except in rare instances, the most powerful system to which a person ever belongs. In the framework of this discussion, "family" consists of the entire kinship network of three generations, both as it currently exists and as it has evolved through time. The physical, social, and emotional functioning of family members is known to be profoundly interdependent, with changes in one part of the system reverberating in other parts of the system. Family therapists understand that the system's interactions and relationships have three properties and tend to be governed by the same rules as other biological systems: they tend to be highly reciprocal, patterned, and repetitive (Bateson, 1992; Hoffman, 1981). The reciprocity of the system allows for mutual relationships to be interchangeable and to move in correspondence with each other when stress is placed on the system. An outcome is seen, not as being caused by a triggering event, but rather in the interplay of responses that are governed by the structure of the family's relationships. By definition, the family is required to balance a sense of change with a sense of continuity and will work to stabilize itself with habitual and rhythmic mechanisms. The patterning of the family defines its personality and allows subsequent generations to understand the system's models of functioning. The repetitive and redundant nature of a family allows family therapists to make tentative predictions of the family's interactions based on its history. It is well known in family therapy that families repeat themselves (Rainer, 1998). What happened in one generation will often repeat itself in the next; that is, the same issues tend to be played out from one generation to the next, even though the actual behavior may take a variety of forms.

The rhythms of the family's approach to loss will vary with the degree of stress and discontinuity in the circumstances of death, the available support needed to balance the distress, the nature of the family's developmental history, and the availability of cultural rituals and grief practices. The greater the family's degree of stress and discontinuity prior to the death, the greater the family's risk for a loss of integrity in the presence of the loss. Families with a high degree of premorbid stress are prone to dissociate and distance from the overwhelming aspects of the grief experience and will, paradoxically, work to restrict the developmental tasks of accommodating to the loss, where bereavement is unconsciously viewed as a disequilibrating change, rather than a natural approach to balance.

Loss is a common experience of children. Throughout childhood they experience many different types of changes that involve loss. It can be apparent, part of developmental change, or can go unnoticed because of its insidious nature (Frears & Schneider, 1981). Apparent losses accompany crises such as a death of a family member, a friend, or even a pet, separation and divorce, illness, or injury. These losses are obvious; they usually impact the adults in the life of the child as well as the child. Loss is also experienced at times of developmental or situational transition. These losses and their effect on children are likely to be overlooked or minimized. Moving, changing schools, the birth of a sibling, sibling illness, and puberty serve as examples. Unnoticed losses include those that accompany events or experiences that on the surface are positive and beneficial but nonetheless involve loss. These might be acceptance into a special school for gifted and talented children, job promotions for parents, remarriage of a single parent, or recognition for special skills or talents in the school or community. Although they are valued events, they come with a price. The child may lose a special role in the family, may be separated from familiar support systems, experience loneliness as he or she leaves a comfortable setting or role, or may lose routines and rituals that have meant personal comfort and companionship.

Children respond idiosyncratically to crisis. While each child shares developmental traits with other children of the same age and stage, each has unique attributes. One may have an advanced IQ but may be less socially mature than peers. Another child may live in a nurturing, supportive family while a counterpart might live in an abusive, chaotic household. Gender, appearance, competencies, and skill sets all serve as parameters for children's response to crisis. This being said, the following examples examining the impact of death on children at various stages of development are intended to heighten clinical awareness and encourage the generation of therapeutic hypotheses, rather than to be taken as a guideline for how children "should" react.

DEATH: A CRISIS OF LOSS

Death is a crisis of loss many children encounter at some point in their lives. Tracking the experience of death for young children and adolescents and examining what the counselor, in concert with the parents, can do to help facilitate coping and adaptation presents a helpful structure for intervention.

Infants and Toddlers

Infants lacking language and self-help skills mirror the emotional lives of their primary caregivers. When crisis occurs, the infant's response is directly tied to the response of the affected parent or guardian. If routines are disrupted and caregiving becomes disorganized the infant responds to the loss of the security of repetition. If the adult is angry, irritable, restless, and anxious, the infant will respond in kind. For infants, disruptions of body functions, loss of appetite, sleep disruption, bowel and bladder distress, and an inability to be soothed, are indicators of distress. Immaturity in object relations leads to the belief that when people leave, they no longer exist. Death confirms this belief and becomes a primary cause of anxiety, particularly if strangers are brought in to assume caregiving roles for the infant and toddler.

Continuity and consistency of care, the two primary determinants of infant adjustment which are oftentime disrupted in crisis, become indicators of the system's efforts to intervene to protect the infant and toddler. Work to maintain these foundations in the presence of crisis helps to maintain the child's integrity. Knowledge that continuity is a crucial element for infant stability can help clinicians recognize and address multiple crisis resolution strategies until the natural caregiver can be restored.

Preschoolers

Preschoolers possess the cognitive skills to express thoughts and feelings. They are prone to ask many questions when confronted with the crisis of death. This curiosity about death and dying is difficult for many adults. Their questions are probing and abstract. Children will ask, "What happens to the body?" and "Where is heaven?" and "Why did Momma die?" Questions will reflect unresolved issues in the life of the child.

Children at this age, although they understand the concept of death as the absence of life functions, will believe that death is reversible. Toys of childhood allow a child to play out important psychological processes. The child's fascination with the jack-in-the-box reflects the need to understand that just because something is no longer in sight does not mean it is gone forever. This translates into belief that the person who has died will also magically reappear. Developmentally, the child is able to make the leap that although "jack" disappears, it still exists and can come back. In the crisis of death, the preschooler will have difficulty coming to terms with the notion that death is an object loss that does not return.

This belief in the reversibility of death engages the child in thoughts of joining the lost loved one. The importance of understanding this psychological phenomenon is demonstrated in the following case. A young child was brought to see a child psychologist for treatment. According to his parents, the child stated a wish to die. As the psychologist visited with the child, he learned that the girl's grandmother had died several months before. The child clearly stated that she missed her grandmother and wanted to visit her "in heaven . . . and you have to die to go to heaven." She did not want to permanently leave her parents but did want to vacation in heaven with her deceased grandmother. Teaching the girl's parents about the developmental level of the child's understanding of death alleviated a great deal of anxiety and opened the way for helping the child accept the permanence of death.

It is to be expected in the presence of stress and crisis that preschoolers, like infants, will have disruptions in somatic functions. Eating, sleeping, and eliminating may be affected. The child may become a picky eater or refuse to eat except in specified places. The child might regress to earlier stages of bowel and bladder control and may refuse to sleep alone. These problems frustrate parents who do not expect to have to respond to problems of childhood already mastered by their children. They need to understand that the somatization of psychological distress is a signal that the child is in a state of crisis. Resolution of the crisis state will restore previous levels of functioning.

Separation is a lifelong task of childhood and adulthood. In times of crisis separation may become a particularly painful issue, especially in crises involving loss. The child may refuse school or day care, even if there has been no previous adjustment problem. The preschooler can become clingy and may throw tantrums when asked to do anything out of the ordinary. Caregivers and clinicians understand such behavior as the child's means of longing for structure and security. When children feel out of control, they will seek creative ways to be in charge. The preschool child will deeply fear abandonment and will not be able to trust that the absence of a caregiver is temporary. Stuttering and regressing to "baby talk" are indicators of the child's pain and fear of loss.

To counter the pain, the parent or caregiver imposes structure. Structure reassures the child that the world is a safe, secure place. A familiar, repeated family tradition, such as a bedtime story, restores equilibrium. Preschoolers will also use transitional objects, such as security blankets, to regain a sense of the familiar and predictable world. Art projects give children creative ways to communicate needs, wants, and fears and to seek solutions. Drawing pictures, storytelling, and singing allow the internal struggles to be externalized. The intensity of the child's feelings will often be calmed through these outlets. Instituting good nutrition, exercise, and sleep allows for the child's natural healing processes to work in conjunction with psychological interventions.

Caregivers who answer questions with concrete facts help the child accept and integrate the reality of the situation. The child will seek many avenues for adjustment, including role-playing, the creation of imaginary friends, an increased need for physical comfort, and a reassurance of safety. "Listening" for the ways the child can seek solace and comfort occurs by observing behavior, listening to stories, and reading nonverbal cues, which allows caregivers to comfort and nurture the child through his or her grief. The work on the part of the adults in the child's life is to care for themselves, understanding the need for time and space to work through their own grief. The best predictor for child adjustment in response to the crisis is the primary caregiver's adjustment. Failure to respond with congruence that provides the child safety, security, and comfort can lead to problems such as failure to thrive and a loss of competency in the attainment of normative developmental benchmarks.

At this age, caregivers will want to use concrete terms when speaking of death. Euphemisms will confuse the preschooler. Plainspoken language is preferable. The child can be told that the deceased will no longer eat, walk, talk, or work. The child will need to know that the loss has occurred through no personal fault of the child. Specifically seeking signs of irrational guilt and allaying feelings of responsibility will help children direct their emotional energies toward constructive healing. Superstitions regarding death and characteristics of the loss will need to be addressed by allowing the child to talk as much or as little as the child musters energy. During the crisis of death, the child will not be his or her "usual self," but then, neither will the parent.

School-Aged Children

The school-aged child begins to develop social, emotional, and intellectual skills that will be progressively helpful in meeting the demands of the crisis of death. School-aged children develop a wider community than the younger child. Adults outside of the family can be employed to share difficulties, so that the child begins to recognize that other adults outside of the family may be able to respond to their needs. Teachers become figural to younger school-aged children as reference points for help. Individual and group therapy may be available in a school setting. Often school counselors offer group and individual work to teach children to understand their grief and reach out to peers for understanding. This supportive work diminishes the likelihood of the child feeling stigmatized by the crisis.

Developmentally, the child's primary need is a focus on mastery of academic, social, and emotional demands related to school. Death disrupts the primary demands of mastery functions and introduces the need to address the difficult psychological task of integration of loss. If problems in school can be linked to loss, patience and understanding with support to continue school-related activities help to ground the child in the familiar. Following the crisis of a devastating hurricane, the opening of school was the most important event contributing to the beginning of feelings of normalcy for the children.

During the crisis of death, school-aged children display unusual emotional responses. Typically, they regress to earlier stages, making irritable and whiny demands to the adults in their lives. Separation anxiety may reemerge, and the child may have multiple complaints, such as fear of the dark, demanding the immediate attention of adults. Angry outbursts are common, as is aggression in the home or school (particularly for boys who have been socialized for more physical demonstration of anger). It is not unusual for the child to lose interest in pleasurable activities, giving others the appearance of daydreaming or inattention. Some children become obsessed and ruminate with a threat of harm to self or others, particularly family members. Sleep may become disrupted and marked with nightmares or night terrors. As children seek reassurance through the parent's or caregiver's presence and concern, they may also become demanding and competitive with siblings for time and attention.

The goal of interventions for this age group is to reestablish a sense of safety and security, while enhancing the child's ability to understand the meaning of the loss in life. Allowing the child to question and to freely talk about the death helps adults continue ongoing assessment of the nature of the distress. At this age, patience and tolerance becomes paramount for the adult. The child will seek to bring a sense of mastery to a nondevelopmental task outside of normative experience. Providing help for the child through structure and a predictability of day-to-day occurrences aids in the restoration of security. Maintenance of routine normalizes the day as the child deals with the crisis.

School-aged children respond well to storytelling and play sessions. Unlike stories told by preschoolers, the older child uses language to express ideas about death. Stories reveal unconscious motives and unfinished business in the life of the family. Play sessions communicate the child's wants, needs, and fears in a benign environment. Bibliotherapy is useful for children at this age, since books can lead to more personal conversations about the crisis of death.

Children between five and eleven have the capacity to understand that death is final. However, as permanent as death might be, it is beyond the reasonable scope of the child to understand that death happens to everyone. Children will demonstrate superstitious beliefs to avoid reality, for example, the avoidance of stepping on sidewalk cracks. School-aged children are not as prone to ask as intense questions as the preschooler but will want answers to difficult questions. Adults will observe their attempt to use developmentally appropriate, but situationally inadequate, methods to understand and resolve the loss. There is a tendency for children to use magical thinking as a means of empowerment and feeling personal control while absolving themselves of the responsibility associated with legitimately potent actions.

A school-aged child in the midst of the crisis of death will typically exhibit signs of depression. Childhood depression appears in heightened emotionality, loss of previously mastered competencies, aggression toward peers, fear of personal harm, and loss of interest in school and home activities. Somatization is common, including gastric distress, headaches, and breathing difficulties. Relationships for depressed children may suffer as the child becomes competitive with peers for adult attention. As noted, regressive behavior is common in the age group, which may confuse adults who have experienced the child as more independent and capable of negotiating the demands of the outside environment.

The cognitive development of school-aged children equips them to use symbolic methods for resolution of the crisis of death. Games, creative arts play, and storytelling externalize distress into safe and acceptable channels for healing. Intentionality in making these opportunities available to children is important. Many hospice programs provide retreats that protect children while they explore the meaning of loss in their lives. Supportive and understanding adults shepherd the child through experiences that promote resolution of grief.

Preadolescence

Preadolescent children are particularly vulnerable to the crisis of death. They have yet to develop the skills that will be learned in adolescence to communicate distress. Even though peer pressure is most pronounced at this age, these children are the most prone to isolation in the presence of the crisis of death. They are unable to accurately measure their responses against those of others. The experience of internal psychological upheaval and situational disruption only adds fuel to the emotional fire. Developmental distance from parents, combined with vulnerable peer relationships, heightens the child's sense of being unique in the crisis, which illuminates the feeling of being misunderstood. Symptoms of this group also include somatic complaints. Relationships in the home may deteriorate through rebellious behavior, refusal to participate in family activities and chores, and anger and anxiety over separation. School-related difficulties with peers and loss of academic standing is common. Oppositionality, fighting, negative attention-seeking behaviors, and withdrawal from peers are symptomatic markers of crisis response. However, this age group tends to deny any and all problems while displaying irresponsible behavior. Such denial makes intervention with this age group all the more difficult for counselors. Preadolescent children are so afraid "not be to like everyone else," as one parent described it, that they are unwilling to test personal assumptions or perspectives with those who might be of help.

Children at this stage of development view death as possible and probable. They are aware that it can happen to them, their family, and friends. Helpful interventions vary. Most preadolescent children respond well to interventions marked by active interpersonal involvement. Cognitive-behavioral approaches have value to help the child separate belief from behavior and are useful to ease stress and anxiety. This age group will respond favorably in group counseling, if time is spent by leaders to build rapport and trust. A combination of psychoeducation and psychotherapy works effectively. Preadolescents have the capacity to understand process. They can speak to personal feelings of self and others, what helps them to feel better, how unreasonable guilt and responsibility can be put aside, and how loving relationships can be built and maintained. Activities that promote self-reliance are encouraging, as are activities that promote competency and self-esteem. Children at this age can learn techniques for stress management, relaxation, conflict resolution, assertiveness, and prosocial communication to help cope with the challenges of the crisis of death.

Adolescence

Adolescents, like children, have developmental characteristics that significantly affect their response to crisis. In the face of a crisis, most adolescents will retreat from primary caregivers in favor of seeking the comfort and security of peers. This may confuse the family, which sees this behavior as indicative of the teenager's lack of concern for the family's pain. However, such a retreat is normative behavior for this age and stage of life. For example, a teenager named John talked of his father's sudden death during his senior year of high school. His relationship with his dad had been characterized by tension and conflict. While both father and son had a great deal in common, at adolescence the father became increasingly critical of the son and resentful of John's demands to be treated in adult ways. John admitted that he wanted privilege without responsibility. Unknown to John, his father had chronic depression, which compromised his ability to enjoy activities with his son, such as tennis. It was not until after the man's death did John recognize that his father had been in compromised physical and mental health. This realization became a place of anguish for John; he felt like his struggles contributed to his father's early death. In truth, John was involved with a normative and developmental struggle for independence and autonomy. The process of maturation was overlaid with guilt and regret because of the father's death. John needed the wisdom of a counselor to understand the relationship with his father and recognize his conflicts were typical in parent-teenager relationships.

In distress, younger adolescents will focus primarily on the here-and-now impact of the crisis on their environment. Questions are asked relative to the crisis and day-to-day functioning. One practitioner calls these the "What about my trip to the beach?" questions. Older adolescents have developed formal operational thinking skills. These individuals can think in the past and present and anticipate the future. They have the ability to reflect on feeling and thinking states, can see consequences of behavior, and can develop long-term plans for coping with problems. These teenagers' ability to experience empathy for others allows them to integrate the crisis from personal, interpersonal, and social perspectives.

Such abstract thinking ability is not without problems for the adolescent. The ability to empathize without life experience may burden the teenager with unwieldy feelings of responsibility. Some teenagers may deny or repress their own developmental needs for independence and separation in favor of caring for others. A young man poignantly illustrates this dilemma. As a freshman in college, his father was seriously injured in an automobile accident. The young man wanted to drop out of the semester in order to care for his father, even though there was no intrinsic value to the act. The adults in the young man's life exerted considerable influence on him not to assume the role of "the man of the family." The fellow's struggle with his identity of masculinity and independence created quite a challenge due to the crisis found in his father's accident. The father eventually did die from injuries sustained in the accident. The son gave up extracurricular activities and suspended his college career in favor of caring for his family. Believing his activity would make his mother happy, the steps only compounded the tragedy held in the loss.

Recognizing adolescents in distress and encouraging them to seek proactive help is a daunting task. As with other developmental groups, teenagers are also prone to develop stress-related physical problems. Headaches, low back pain, gastrointestinal upset, and skin-related disorders all have somatic components that are responsive to stress. Teenagers are also prone to an edgy anxiety and depression that others will observe as moodiness, irritability, withdrawal, and aggressive acting out. Performance in school and extracurricular activities may be compromised. Pleasure appetites change in adolescents during crisis times. One teenager reported liking all sports and was a high school hero on his baseball team. After the death of a younger sibling, he dropped off his team. He said, "I don't think it's right that I should be having fun. This is what I'm doing in memory of my sister, and people who don't like my decision can take a flying leap." Other students may find that grades drop and overall interest in school will decline. Long-term aspirations for academic work diminish. It is characteristic of adolescents to be confused about their behavior in the context of the family.

The most difficult task for the clinician working with an adolescent in crisis is to come to a mutual admission of the need for help. The teenager's desire to fit in and withdraw from the state of crisis can override the need for help. Normalizing responses and facilitating an understanding of thoughts and feelings may open the door for help. Caregivers must be more intrusive in the teenager's life than they might wish. One clinician said, "When I work with teenagers, I just invite myself in and give them many opportunities to accept help. I wait for a teenager to invite me out, though I'm not as prone to leave as soon as the kid might want me to." Fortunately, adolescents have the capacity to speak in abstract terms of their life experience. They can speak openly about feelings and the impact of loss.

Creating meaning from loss is important in the life of the adolescent. Finding life lessons is a major part of teenage angst and can be relied on as healing energy. For example, a group of adolescents were helped in their response to the vehicular death of their classmate by creating a scrapbook for the parents of the deceased adolescent. They created a collective story of their life with the young girl and included pictures, letters, and newspaper articles related to the accident and subsequent changes in their community. In a formal gathering, the teenagers presented the scrapbook to the parents. An intimate bond was created between the surviving family members and the girl's peer group. Healing was facilitated by the concrete opportunity the scrapbook offered for emotional expression and points of connection.

Adults become quite concerned with drops in teenagers' academic performance. The response to such concern must be moderated by balancing understanding and encouragement. It is quite unhelpful for an adolescent to experience failure or isolation in response to crisis. School failure simply adds insult to injury. Support can be increased by helping the adolescent place boundaries around affective distress while temporarily reducing expectation of performance. This allows the process of healing to occur without creating vulnerability and exposure of a newly identified role, that is, the depressed one, in the family or peerage system.

The risk of destructive responses to a crisis is quite valid. A counselor remembered a young girl from a loving family whose mother died when the girl was fifteen. In the years preceding the death, the girl felt more contention than peace in her family. A baby was adopted, which robbed the girl of her favored position as "the baby of the family." She felt misunderstood by both parents. Her anger was expressed loudly and regularly within the context of the family home. After her mother's death, the counselor said, "Her behavior changed. She started drinking and that led to experimentation with marijuana. She was much more openly defiant and made more and more choices that were contradictory to her family's values. She became sexually active, said it made her feel nurtured, and turned up with an unwanted, unplanned pregnancy. With time and a great deal of support from her extended family, she was able to make decisions that were more prosocial. Eventually, she was able to settle down enough to address the guilt and self-hatred she felt in response to her mother's death."

Death at any age is difficult to understand and more difficult to accept. Working to help children and adolescents integrate the losses created by the crisis of death of a loved one can alleviate emotional, psychological, social, and spiritual vulnerabilities that may set the stage for later life problems.

In any crisis response with children and adolescents, prevention is key. Families, schools, churches, and community groups must partner and become a healing context for the child in crisis. Not only must adults facilitate understanding and acceptance, they must attend to the developmental shifts of the child as they normally move to "grow up."

CRISIS RELATED TO FAMILY PATHOLOGY

Family pathology is the third and last category defined by Johnson's (1989) model for understanding crisis in families. This category can be understood better as a context for crisis rather than a crisis event. For example, families with an addictive parent are at increased risk for crisis. From a systems perspective, the family exists in a state of equilibrium with each family member playing his or her role protective of family functioning. Unlike other crises, the role of the counselor may be to precipitate emergency by focusing attention on the family secret, or pushing the addictive parent toward treatment. Other types of family pathology include those marked by violence, physical and/or sexual abuse, poverty, social alienation, and mental illness.

The child's dependence on the family for need fulfillment troubles the family system in light of disturbed relationships, mental illness, or social dysfunction. Adults in key positions to recognize high-risk signals of family pathology can intervene to ameliorate the child's vulnerability to crisis. The recent emphasis on the study of resiliency is an attempt to identify means and mechanisms for helping children cope with crisis and trauma, freeing them from a life sentence of playing out the family pathology in their own families. Two examples of family pathology, the high-risk indicators of problems, the role of the counselor in intervention, and the community resources for supporting continuing change will be illustrated. Then, a closer look at the current study of resilience will close the chapter.

Family Pathology: Children in Addictive Families

Children in addictive families become locked in roles that support family dysfunction. Each role plays a part in protecting the addictive parent and the social image of the family. The oldest child is often the hero of the family. The hero plays the part of the responsible child, often taking on adult responsibilities in the family. At school and in extracurricular activities the hero may be found in a leadership or starring role. Outwardly this child appears to be mature, self-confident, and self-reliant. On the inside, this is a child who is robbed of childhood. The pseudoadult demeanor obscures anxiety and shame. Perfectionism, overfunctioning, and caretaking personalities help protect the family from being "found out." The second child may play the role of scapegoat. The scapegoat is the child in the family who displaces attention from the addict by acting out in ways that distract attention from the primary problem in the family, the addict. This child is more likely to come to the attention of adults in the school and the community. Through anger and rebellion, these attention-seeking children are troubled by low self-esteem, anxiety, and shame. The youngest child, known colloquially as the family mascot, is shouldered with the responsibility of providing comic relief and making the family laugh at its frailties. This child appears carefree, fun loving, and comfortable. In fact, this child's need to alleviate the suffering of others hides feelings of self-blame, guilt, and shame. By distracting the family through silliness, the emotional pain is ignored. The lost child is a role independent of birth order and plays out as a daydreamer who lives in fantasy, demanding little, receiving less. This child may live in a world created by imaginative desires rather than one determined by reality. The family is protected because this child places little pressure on it for need satisfaction. Outwardly the child may appear to be flexible, spontaneous, and often artistic; inside the child struggles, like the other children, with shame and guilt.

The rules in the addictive family create structure, that protects the addict as well: don't trust, don't feel, and don't talk; don't behave differently, don't blame the addict, and don't have fun. Trust is as important for children as for adults. Because the problems of the addict are denied or ignored, the child does not trust his or her own perception of reality. The child does not rely on the addict to provide parental support or guidance. More energy is spent in caring for the addict than in meeting his or her own needs. The children do not talk with each other, so they do not have an opportunity to test their assumptions or clarify their confusion. Messages that the addict is "sick" or "tired" or "frustrated" deflect attention and rob the child of the truth. Many children of addicts are adults before they realize their parent was a substance abuser. The focus on the needs of the adult children of alcoholics has made us painfully aware of the price paid by these children. They tend to have relationship problems, develop addictive lifestyles themselves, are at risk for marrying someone who will continue the addictive family patterns, and have difficulty with play. Only with psychoeducation and treatment do many escape the consequences of growing up in an addictive family.

To read the signals that suggest children are caught in the web of an addictive family, the personalities of these types of children, the social and emotional indicators of family dysfunction, and the patterns of functioning in school and social relationships must be understood.

Crisis of Family Pathology: Violence

Thousands of children are affected by living with an abusive parent or witnessing violence in their home. These children are at risk for the continuing cycle of violence later in their lives. Intervention is designed to protect these children. Spousal abuse provides children with a model for treating loved ones in destructive ways. Children may observe the abuse or may hear the sounds of violence in the home. They may be conflicted about how to respond, identifying with the abuser or feeling protective toward the victim. If the victim escapes the perpetrator of violence, it may mean that the child will be forced to leave the familiar and live in a shelter away from the child's school and neighborhood. The presence of other family members who are willing to provide shelter and security is helpful.

Child abuse is defined by four types: neglect and physical, emotional, and sexual abuse. All four are destructive, causing emotional, social, and physical damage. Neglect occurs when the basic needs of children are unmet. This may be intentional or cultural. Children who are neglected often show poor hygiene, wearing clothes that are out of season, and will go hungry, lacking basic self-help skills. Passivity and hypervigilence characterize their relationships. Children who are physically abused will often wear clothing that hides marks, cuts, or bruises. They may be very aggressive or extremely passive. Children who are emotionally abused show signs of self-hatred, low self-esteem, and anger. Sexually abused children may exhibit pseudosexual behavior. They may avoid situations that are physically revealing. Adolescents may run away or be suicidal. These are just a few of the high-risk indicators for abuse. Becoming aware of the presence and the number of high-risk indicators places the concerned adult in a position to help.

Family pathology can also include a significant lack of the ability to meet basic needs for food, shelter, security, and nurturance. Children in these homes may not suffer abuse but lack for those basic needs that allow age-appropriate development. Those children who show resilience in such homes have become the focus of research. Learning what protects children in these circumstances helps identify prevention techniques important for school and community.

RESILIENCE

Children faced with similar stressors show variations in their ability to adapt and change despite challenging and threatening circumstances. This ability to cope with the potentially damaging effects of crisis and trauma protects the child from present danger and, in some cases, creates those skills necessary to cope with future challenges. It is becoming clear in the literature that this resilience is much more prevalent than believed. Many young people are surprisingly hardy even under extreme conditions of poverty, family violence, institutional settings, and disasters. Identifying those factors that are correlated with this resiliency has become an important topic of study and research in the treatment and care of children and adolescents. This resilience, defined as the capacity to "bounce back" from adversity, becomes increasingly important in a world where it is virtually impossible to shield and shelter children from exposure to the horrors of terrorism and violence.

Potential factors contributing to resilience include individual psychological characteristics, social and economic factors, and access to quality educational and recreational opportunities (Cove, Eiseman, & Popkin, 2005). Individual psychological characteristics include "belief in one's own self-efficacy, the ability to deal with change, and a repertoire of social problem solving skills" (Rutter, 1985, p. 598). Social and economic factors include socioeconomic status, family dynamics, parenting skills, quality of relationships with teachers and other adults, neighborhood supports, and exposure to violence (Werner, 1993). Schools, sports clubs, churches, and other community resources can provide the access to quality educational and recreational opportunities (Smokowski, 1998) important in the development of resilience.

Models for explaining resiliency fall into three categories: compensatory models which identify factors that neutralize the effects of exposure to risk, challenge models that treat stressors as opportunities to develop coping mechanisms helpful in future stressful situations, and protective factor models which test how protective factors moderate the effects of risk factors and modify the child's future response to risk factors. The last model combines the previous two and is the one most widely supported. For example, assertiveness may neutralize the effect of parental conflict. The child may learn methods of stating needs and wants in a nonaggressive manner both in the home and the community.

Werner and Smith (1989) identify risk factors that are fairly constant from stressors that are more short term. Potential crises such as the birth of siblings, change in residence, family instability, or death of a relative are considered stressors. Researcher Lawrence Shapiro (2002) outlines the ten emotional skills that he believes will help children to cope with any type of stress. These would be considered to be internal protective factors as opposed to external protective factors. They are as follows:

1. Recognition of feelings
2. Communication of feelings
3. Learning to create happiness out of upset
4. Learning to feel safe and secure
5. Calming techniques in the presence of anxiety and anger
6. Understanding and reacting appropriately to the feelings of others
7. Helping others as a part of everyday life
8. Maintaining a positive attitude, even when bad things happen
9. Asking for help
10. Making good and responsible friends

Shapiro's template can serve as a model for building resiliency in children. Translating the skills into developmentally appropriate activities equips the child to endure and grow during crisis. A teenager who survived the loss of her family home was asked to describe how she "made it through" the crisis. She said, "I guess it boiled down to several things. I realized that I have friends and still needed to be a friend. I learned to really believe in myself and got practice in knowing what I could and could not do. This helped me be in charge of my behavior and actions. I still look at the bright side and just set new goals. I always make a plan to reach them."

This child references multiple internal and external skills. These skills include sources of support and structure in the child's life, such as parental warmth, presence of nonparental caretakers, informal sources of support, peer relationships, supportive rules in the household, shared values, and access to services. The child's community can contribute to these resources through parent training classes, child and adolescent interest groups, such as sports, drama, or art classes, opportunities for the development of positive peer relationships, and resources for families to cope with caretaking demands.

In the presence of crisis the effective clinician will search for strengths and competencies, evidence of previous coping mechanisms, and sources of support outside of the home. The expectation of resilience mitigates the helplessness experienced by the crisis therapist searching for effective intervention on behalf of children and adolescents.

Chapter 9

Application

INTRODUCTION

The three examples presented in this chapter represent three different types of crisis. Each is introduced with background for understanding the nature and dynamics of the crisis event. Intervention is tracked step-by-step through the three phases of the model.

NATURAL DISASTER

Disaster is an overwhelming event. The extensive destruction can arouse powerful feelings of anxiety, anger, grief, and guilt. Those directly affected and those who experience vicarious trauma because of repeated exposure to media coverage share common symptoms of individual trauma; the community affected reports collective trauma as the underlying securities of social life and community are disrupted or destroyed. The response to the crisis of natural disaster occurs in three phases: first, impact; second, accommodation; and, third, integration of loss and change exacted by the event. During each phase mental health support is crucial for the treatment of immediate problems and prevention of future problems.

The initial impact of the first phase produces shock. Normal physical and social supports are disrupted. Victims experience a psychological state described as a natural numbing and disconnection. This disassociation from the devastation of the disaster is in some ways protective. Victims will struggle with a good deal of confusion and despair. As one survivor of an earthquake said, "I had never been in an earthquake before. Who had? I simply couldn't believe that the ground under my feet had given away. Once the quake stopped, I felt like I was walking around in a movie, but I didn't have a script. The more I walked, the more awful I felt. I really didn't know where to turn or what to do."

The second phase, accommodation to a natural disaster, occurs two to three days following the event. At this point victims begin to show signs of anxiety and depression. As one man said, "I began to thaw out." With a wry smile, he added, "I wish I had stayed frozen a little longer." Normal biological functioning, including eating, sleeping, and focused cognitions, is disrupted. Attentional problems emerge, and individuals will find it increasingly difficult to concentrate. Most will find an upset of mood and will complain of helplessness and hopelessness. Many will show signs of survivor guilt and will openly struggle with the purpose and meaning of their survival when others have suffered injury or death. Some report "feeling like [I] was in a trance," and withdraw into fantasy. As individuals in the crisis "come to," each will want to tell a personal story and recount their experience of the disaster in an effort to find some sense of control in daily living. A survivalistic mentality emerges as family members seek to reclaim personal safety and security. Crisis counseling typically begins during this time.

The third phase, integration of the trauma, is the longest stage. Individuals must move from feeling like a victim to a state of feeling whole and intact. In this stage, children will initially regress to younger developmental stages and will experience separation anxiety, somatic distress, and mood disturbance. Adults will experience psychosomatic upset, as well. It is not unusual for adults to have difficulties making sense out of the realities of the disaster, which will intrude in recurring nightmares, daydreams, or flashbacks. Depression and disruption of mood may affect the individual's ability to feel productive in any activity. Interpersonal relationships become strained and are marked by guilt, irritability, and disappointment. Those who were spared the impact of the disaster may be viewed as lacking understanding and compassion.

Clinicians can rely on the systemic crisis model to structure their responses to individuals in the presence of a natural disaster. Suggestions for each step and examples of interventions follow.

Phase I: Remember

Step I.1. Share the Story

The individual who has encountered a natural disaster typically feels victimized by nature. Most individuals report this as a sensual experience, full of sights, sounds, and smells they would rather forget. One woman described her experience in a house fire. "I came home while the fire department was putting the fire out. Our house was totaled. I learned later that it started because of lightning. Fortunately, the smoke detectors went off, but between the fire, smoke, and water, everything we had was damaged beyond repair. I couldn't get into the house until the next day. What I remember most now is the smell. How can you describe the smell of your life being burned right in front of you? When we finally walked through the rubble, everything was wet, charred, or scorched beyond recognition. I remember finding the pair of shoes I had worn to work earlier in the week. The soles were melted and the leather curled. That's when I sat down and cried. Up to that point, I hadn't felt much of anything. Those shoes, those shoes. Something so small and ordinary brought me to my knees in pain."

It is helpful for the counselor to encourage the victims to tell their story in as much detail as possible. This will deepen their understanding and move them from numbness to sensitivity. The primary tools of the counselor are reflective listening and open-ended questions. Normalization of feelings, regardless of trajectory, is critical. Where one person may feel anguish, another may feel anger in response to the same environmental circumstance. Particularly with a natural disaster, the counselor should listen for the sensuality in the account of the crisis and invite the speaker to explore the experience through all five senses.

Telling the story in the presence of others allows the speaker to have a witness to his or her pain. Many will experience a sense of self-loathing early in the process and need to have a strong support system to neutralize and hold their distress. The woman's husband spoke to his family during this phase, saying, "It is all my fault. If I had called an electrician to install the lightning rods instead of trying to be Mr. Fix-It, this would've never happened. Now I've ruined this family." The systemic counseling strategy is to allow a full exploration of the distress and to encourage the system to hold and detoxify any unrealistic guilt. The counselor moves into helping the system, emphasizing its competencies rather than its deficits and inadequacies.

Step I.2. Validate the Emotional Impact

"I still can't believe that I was caught in a hurricane," the young client said. "We sort of knew that there was a storm coming and organized a hurricane party at our fraternity house. Those folks who lived in South Florida knew better about getting to higher ground. They left. We went out to a convenience store and filled up our coolers. When the storm finally came, we were having a good old time. Classes at the university had been canceled. The evacuation was voluntary, but recommended. The hurricane came, tore through windows, and blew the front door right off of its hinges. When the eye of the storm passed over, I was so anxious that I threw up. The second blast of the storm was terrifying beyond belief. It finally passed. Three of us were in a closet, holding onto each other for dear life, literally trembling in each other's arms. Rescue workers found us in the closet. I don't even remember moving until they came and got us."

Such is the stress of a natural disaster. In this instance, there were many school and community officials who were angry with the university students who remained during the storm. They felt valuable time and energy could have been directed toward some of the townspeople who had been injured or, in some cases, killed in the storm. The crisis counselor sought to listen and validate the young fellow's story while others railed against him and his cohorts. The counselor found the man in great distress and unable to care for himself with any degree of effectiveness. When questioned by law authorities, the young man began to sob in an uncontrolled way. The more he spoke of his impaired judgment, the more he wept, until he vomited again. He asked for "a way out," which is not an unusual response. Victims of a natural disaster will continue to feel the presence of the threat even after the event is over.

Reflection of feeling is paramount for the crisis counselor at this juncture. As one clinician said, "I'm ready to hear the good, the bad, and the ugly." Such a validation lessens psychological isolation and allows for a more solid channel of positive communication. Empathy is crucial, even if the expression of emotionality is difficult to engage. One of the young man's fraternity brothers was quite restless immediately after his rescue and felt like he literally needed to run. He went jogging and returned even further traumatized by actually seeing the devastation caused by the storm. He and another victim argued with each other and became physically combative. The clinician taught all of the fraternity brothers ways of talking, rather than acting on feelings, and encouraged the expression of emotion in less provocative ways. While others in the rescue thought the men needed to "lie in the bed they made for themselves," the crisis counselor found a less judgmental place from which to work and was able to accept, reflect, and channel strong emotion in prosocial ways. Encouraging them to volunteer their efforts in the cleanup helped focus their guilt and anguish toward constructive contributions.

Step I.3. Evaluate the Context of the Crisis

Evaluation of the context of a natural disaster is difficult. While the environmental impact may seem obvious, the internal need state of the individual may be more difficult to assess. Most individuals who find themselves in the presence of a natural disaster will report having multiple pressing and immediate needs. They may have difficulty talking about anything else. As one woman who survived a flood said, "I just don't know where to start."

For the crisis counselor, a mind-set that focuses on priorities is useful. Knowing the precrisis state of the individual will help to assess and judge these priorities. One counselor said, "It is useful for me to know what was important to these folks before the crisis. Natural disasters are so completely overwhelming that most people completely lose their sense of perspective. That's where I can be the most helpful. I can aid in helping the person in the crisis state to know what is most important and where to look first."

The counselor should use simple questions and gather a brief medical and social history. Any ongoing treatment needs should be assessed. A counselor related a troubling story in this regard: "I learned early on to assess medical and social histories. I worked with a community that was ruined by a tornado. One family in the town had an uncle who was on regular kidney dialysis. The tornado ripped through the outpatient clinic he attended. The immediacy of the need for his medical care overrode everything else." Knowledge of regular medications, urgent medical treatment needs, chronic mental or physical illness of family members, and need for medical aids should be assessed immediately. Familial or social changes, such as recent deaths or divorces, enlarge the context from which to work. History, whether it be medical, social, emotional, or spiritual, becomes relevant to current crisis needs.

Step I.4. Protect Vulnerable Family Members

Natural disasters, like other crisis states, will leave individuals in the presence of irrational thought and action. It is to be expected that individuals within the system will not know whether they are "coming or going." In addition to assessing the medical needs of any vulnerable members in the system, those emotionally overwhelmed also need immediate attention. Suicidal ideation is common after a natural disaster. Listening for the presence of lethality can help the clinician to provide necessary aid and assistance.

The counselor who learned of the family uncle on kidney dialysis continued: "I learned that this older fellow was despised by his family. They had always thought that he was mean and ungrateful for any help that came his way. He was a burned-out alcoholic who ended up on dialysis because he refused treatment for a kidney infection. He was afraid to die, but too mean to allow anyone to take care of him. Knowledge of what a difficult individual he was helped me decide to hospitalize him in another community while the family recovered from the tornado's destruction. Ultimately, they were able to make some better decisions regarding his care and he was institutionalized. The family found a fair amount of relief and began to say out loud that the tornado 'blew the uncle out of their lives.'"

Step I.5. Negotiate a Solvable Problem

With natural disaster, the counselor may have to take a much more active role in this step than might be true of other crises. The sense of loss of control will be paramount. This step facilitates the system's sense of being more in charge than they may immediately experience.

Well-being is increased in the presence of choice, and a feeling of balance can begin to be restored when the system addresses concrete demands.

The counselor continued the story of the uncle: "Once we knew that the uncle was at the most risk in the system and was likely to be most disruptive to their recovery, our first task was obvious: How would the family provide the care for him while minimizing his destructive influence on their progress to restore basic functioning? Three family members found telephones and contacted treatment facilities. One learned about the Medicare rules and regulations that governed the subsidization of his medical care. They put their heads together and came up with a suitable hospital for him. There was one family member who got along with the crotchety old fellow. He was willing to keep the uncle company and gave him the news of the family's plan to move him to a safer facility. Two of the family members, with the help of the state patrol, transported the fellow to the nearby hospital. The emergency services in the hospital were able to receive the fellow with minimal disruption in his dialysis, and the family felt an incredible sense of relief with their actions and competencies." The system in concert moved from paralysis to action, confirming their ability to regain control.

Step I.6. Network with Relevant Resources

The previous example supports the need for community resources in the presence of a natural disaster. This may be one of the most important components for the counselor who responds to victims of a natural disaster. Needs are oftentimes basic—shelter and safety. When needs are fundamental and pervasive, individuals may need assistance beyond the established support system. Community resources should be employed to regain the sense of control and mastery.

The family in the earlier example relied on the state patrol to transport their uncle to the hospital. Their personal vehicles had all been destroyed in the tornado. The counselor continued his story: "This was a proud and private family. They took care of themselves and didn't want others intruding in their business. Somehow, it seemed appropriate and they were able to accept the help of the police before they would allow the Red Cross or other social service agencies to help get the uncle to safety."

The crisis therapist who works with natural disasters will need to be familiar with emergency services. Many systems, such as schools and communities, have emergency crisis plans that will be implemented if disaster occurs. The clinician will be much more effective with knowledge of the structure of the crisis plan and with the resources that are available for help.

Phase II: Reorganize

Step II.1. Formulate a Plan for Change

Once the immediacy of the impact of the disaster has been addressed, the therapist working with the system will seek to formulate a plan for restoring life "as it was before." This process is individualized according to the narrative shared by the client. The stated goal is to help restore the system to its precrisis functioning.

The clinician helps to identify issues and concerns for the family or the individual that will be the focus of time and attention in crisis treatment. Since crisis work is brief treatment, the normative response for this stage is to help the system find its own homeostatic balance. Asking the questions "How do you see yourself coming out on the other side of this disaster?" and "How will you know when you no longer need help?" begins to give definition to the direction for change. These questions provide fundamental building blocks for change and help establish a plan for action. If the counselor assesses that components to the process are absent or unrealistic, progressively pointed questions can be employed to shape manageable goals. One therapist reported that a fellow, following a house fire in his South Georgia home, said, "I think I'm just going to close up shop here and start over somewhere else. I've always wanted to live in Oregon. I think I'll go there." Through reflection and discussion, the man decided that he would be able to make the move much more successfully if he would do some exploration regarding the viability of a life in the Pacific Northwest. In preparation for such a move, he decided to rent an apartment in Oregon rather than rebuild his Georgia home and to look for job possibilities that would transfer to different geographic regions. He further decided to give himself "a year to make the move. I'm not making good decisions right now, so I'd better take my time," he told his counselor. With time he discovered it was easier to repair his life in Georgia than to create one in Oregon.

The concept of mastery comes into play in this step. Natural disasters rob the individual of a sense of control and competence. The circumstance of a natural disaster reminds the individual of the temporary, fickle nature of life and how much the sense of control is an illusion. For those who do hold the illusion of complete control over life, a natural disaster can be humbling. Without intervention, such an event can take the individual into hopelessness, helplessness, and anger. This is the formula for depression. The counselor can intervene by guiding and supporting a realistic plan for action and an attribution of meaning to the experience, which will promote a sense of healing and health.

One fellow described his experience: "After the earthquake, I just had a long temper tantrum. We knew that we lived on a geographic fault but had always laughed at the possibility of a real earthquake. I couldn't believe that it actually happened to me. I'm an arrogant fellow, as you might be able to tell. This brought me to my knees, and I had to have someone else help me to make plans to recover. I'm a bit more humble now than I was before this whole thing happened."

Having a concrete and realistic plan for change communicates individual and systemic strengths and competencies. Working in a stepwise fashion allows for the eventual return of a life that the individual will recognize as "normal."

Step II.2. Identify Developmental Issues

All systems—families, groups, and communities—go through developmental stages similar to those of individuals. The phase of life of the system frames the perspective for the individuals to view their place in relationship to the larger whole. In truth, the phase of life, in a large measure, will determine the system's response to the disaster.

For example, consider the "normative" life cycle of a family. A couple marries and establish themselves as a separate entity from the families of origin. Two people come from different systems bringing varying histories, values, and styles of relating into the marriage. They may or may not understand the stress of the initial formulation of the coupling process. Each partner is prone to bring a particular viewpoint into the relationship and will be strongly invested in convincing the other to acquiesce. The stress of the struggle creates a tensile and solid container for the marriage. The sense of romance in the early stages of the relationship gives the couple energy and verve to continue the formulation process of coupling. Most young couples will say "for better or worse" but naturally focus on the "for better" sense of the relationship.

A natural disaster brings the "for worse" into full force in the relationship. Each member may respond to the disaster in a way that the partner has not previously witnessed. If the behavior is unseemly, the individual will feel a natural sense of embarrassment. Without discussion between the couple, a sense of shame may develop. If the spouse is unfavorably responsive, the partner may feel humiliated. Such shame and humiliation can lead each member of the couple to retreat and isolate, which creates more stress than the relationship can tolerate.

One young couple described their response to a tree that fell on their home during a rainstorm: "This is our first house. We were so proud of it and had it decorated in a way that suited us just perfectly. When the tree fell, it went right through the living and dining rooms. We never knew that something like this could happen. The insurance paid for the rebuilding of the house, but we couldn't replace the wedding gifts, the pictures, the memories. . . . We had worked so hard to get our home settled, and then something as harmless and beautiful as a tree destroyed our joy. We just felt despair. We had to rely on our parents again to help us make it through the rebuilding, and that was almost as difficult as the tree falling. Our parents didn't mind helping, but there was a price to pay."

The wife continued: "My mother wasn't much in favor of me getting married to begin with. She found several opportunities to let us know that we couldn't get along without them. It was a bad time to take cheap shots." Counseling helped the young couple to reestablish their coupling boundaries and minimize the distress.

Natural disasters occurring at different developmental stages will have different impact. While this statement seems simplistic, it is imperative that the counselor account for the normative developmental expectations of the system.

Consider the impact of a middle-aged couple who experienced the same disaster as the young couple. Living across the street from the young couple, the middle-aged couple had a massive oak tree fall on their home during the same rainstorm. This couple owned and lived in their home for many years. They had a long marriage, in which they had established a sound coupling system. The husband and wife had seen each other in "better and worse" times, and each responded in a predictable fashion to the disaster. The crisis therapist helped this couple with their loss of emotional safety. While the first couple needed help with continuing emancipation from their families of origin, the older couple needed assistance accessing and accepting help from their adult children. The first couple felt the loss of basic necessities as primary threats. The second couple found the loss of their treasures symbolic of previous life transitions, and marked with loving memories, as the fundamental disturbance.

The greater the physical impact of the natural disaster, the more symptomatic the system will respond. Community response through preventive counseling is a helpful and useful intervention for the crisis counselor. Working with individuals, families, and groups in the presence of a natural disaster will allow the larger system to begin to attribute meaning to the devastation of the experience. Common experience can open channels of communication and camaraderie that transcends economic and social boundaries. The crisis counselor can hold the essence of the system during the therapy process, which allows a greater opportunity for healing to emerge.

In the face of disaster, individual developmental issues are best understood through personal need states and symptom presentation. Children will be most likely to respond to the impact of disaster through the experience of psychosomatic symptoms and school disturbance. Adults are more prone to be troubled by anxiety and depression. They will have additional urgency to restore the order to life. It is to be expected that the adult will need to find a way to accept help. Children will find the resourceful adults in their lives and will expect help.

Step II.3. Engage Therapeutic Tools

In the presence of a natural disaster, the most important therapeutic tools the clinician has are the abilities to listen and to negotiate satisfaction of needs by larger systems. The counselor will need excellent triage and prioritization skills. Equanimity, the ability to stay calm in stressful situations, is a prime therapeutic asset at this point. Cognitive-behavioral interventions, particularly focused on the manifestation of irrational beliefs, are helpful. This is not the time to engage in intense, psychodynamic work. As one counselor said, "When I work with natural disasters, I feel more like a traffic cop than a crisis counselor. There are so many needs to attend to with my clients. I remember one woman was absolutely terrified that another disaster would occur. We had to discuss the probability of such an occurrence and look at the irrationality of the likelihood that a second disaster would strike. She had experienced a good deal of trauma in her early life. While I certainly was interested and took her history into account, there were behaviors and actions that she needed to take for contemporary safety and security. That was my primary focus with her in order to prevent a recurrence of earlier trauma."

Step II.4. Assign Homework

The counselor continued: "As we talked, it became clear that as my client had specific tasks to accomplish, she felt better and was more effective at managing her anxiety." Homework does indeed help to overcome the sense of helplessness many individuals feel after living through a natural disaster. Manageable tasks and activities make them a collaborative partner in reclaiming an effective daily life. Clinicians should note the degree of initiative the individual is able to muster. The more activation and effort, the more likely the individual is recovering to a precrisis level of functioning. Teaching the individual how to access and receive help following the experience of a natural disaster builds competencies.

Homework also provides a helpful cognitive shift in the brief framework of crisis counseling. Rather than moving from one session to the next, homework shapes the individual's thoughts to move from one task to the next. The counselor and client can work strategically in ways that allow the individual to think in a task-oriented framework. In strategic thought, this can be viewed as reclamation of the process of effective daily living.

Step II.5. Support Systemic Rules, Roles, and Rituals

Members of the system who have experienced a natural disaster will need to discuss their roles in the life of the family, and the role of the disaster as well. Role shifts and changes must be accommodated.

For example, the breadwinner of a family was injured in an accident attempting to repair his roof. He broke his leg and pelvis, and the ensuing treatment was disruptive to the family's financial standing. Family members were required to find ways to ensure their economic viability during the breadwinner's incapacity. The counselor described it this way: "The family was economically poor before the accident. When the father was hurt and incapacitated, the family had no cushion to fall back on. There were two teenagers living in the family. They were able to take jobs and put some money into the family coffers. They complained and were unhappy about the course of events but saw the necessity of the task at hand. Their father was quite upset that they had to work. In his culture, it was his job—only—to provide for his family. He was humiliated that the children had to provide the family's financial support. Counseling offered a place to discuss and debate the need for his children to work and to neutralize his humiliation."

Rituals help restore a sense of order and purpose to the system. Once the crisis is resolved, the members of the system may want to write and orchestrate a ritual that marks the transition of the family from one life cycle to another. The counselor must listen in a creative and active way to help the family to mark change.

A lovely example was told by a clinician: "A middle-aged couple lost electricity in an ice storm and was without power for several days. At the end of the third day, the couple, who were tired, irritated, and aggravated, restocked the fireplace and huddled around the hearth for warmth. The husband found a battery-operated radio, turned on some music, and moved two rocking chairs from the porch to the living room. He warmed some wine at the fireplace and invited his wife to join him in a romantic escape from the impact of the storm. As the music played she began to dance for him. The ritual helped the couple to tolerate and transcend their suffering for a brief time."

The counselor's role in this stage is to listen for the flow of the system's energy, and to look for moments where psychological punctuation may be helpful. These are the points where a ritual is useful and can be prescribed. Such activity elevates the mundane into the sacred and alleviates much of the pain of the crisis.

Phase III: Restore

Step III.1. Track Progress Toward Goals

Throughout the process of crisis counseling individuals who have lived through a natural disaster, the counselor must underline and point to those activities that restore a precrisis level of functioning. Framing comments in positive and encouraging statements builds a sense of confidence and mastery for more difficult tasks. Having developed a plan for reaching goals and marking each step for attainment of those goals gives members of the system a sense of movement and motion.

Step III.2. Acknowledge Indicators of the Time to Terminate

A client said it best: "I began to feel like my family got their life back. After the accident, I never thought that we'd be able to regain any semblance of functioning again. After awhile, we were able to look back. In a paradoxical way, this helped us to look forward, as well. The counselor said this would happen. We got our 'basics' back together again, and made sure that everyone was okay. I was so grateful that we had a plan. I always need a plan, so that I can know what I must do."

The counselor spoke from her perspective: "All the members of the system began to function with a greater sense of comfort. There was a lessening sense of anxiety and their depression began to lift. Folks began to laugh with a bit more ease, and they started to talk to each other about how the accident was a part of their lives. They started talking about the disaster in the past tense."

For the system, there should be a restoration of precrisis functioning. The system's pleasure appetite will resurface, and markers of esteem and self-efficacy will emerge. As one member of the family said, "I began to feel like myself again." The tentative sense of confidence in self is the indicator for the counselor that termination is appropriate.

Step III.3. Address Future Sources of Stress

In a natural disaster, future sources of stress will be related to the restoration of services and the individual's and system's sense of trust in living in the presence of the world's uncertainty. Role shifts and changes will need to be accommodated.

One individual spoke to his counselor about his fear of living with the possibility of a disaster recurrence. He said, "Every time there is a rainstorm, I get afraid that another tree will topple down on my house. I'm really having to work not to go overboard in those emotional places that remind me of the disaster. I know that any sign of a storm is a problem to me, and I believe that time will help ease my mind, as long as I know what is real and what is not. I have to learn not to project my fears into the worst-case scenario." The counselor responded by teaching his client anxiety management skills and relaxation response exercises. The client, who was quite appreciative of the help, told the counselor, "I think I'm better prepared now for a disaster of any type. You can't live through something like this and not be changed by it. I keep my flashlight batteries fresh. I know where extra sets of keys are. I know how I'll hit the ground running if another disaster comes my way. I don't want to repeat the experience, but I have a plan now how I'll respond. I didn't have that before."

Step III.4. Refer for Continuing Treatment

The aftermath of a natural disaster may leave a trail of ongoing problems for individuals. Losses must be grieved, and material possessions reassessed and, in some cases, replaced.

There will be members of the system who will have complications as a result of the disaster that cannot be addressed in the brief context of crisis counseling. Those individuals who continue to have higher levels of anxiety or depression than are the "new normal" for the system's functioning should be referred for continuing treatment. Individuals who have a damaged sense of self, a loss of resilience, or a deeply rooted sense of ambivalence regarding the ongoing nature of life will also need further help and assistance.

Having established the boundaries of crisis counseling as a brief and restorative service, the clinicians can collaboratively address their perceptions of ongoing problems with members of the system.

Finding appropriate psychotherapeutic help or social service resources is a useful task at this phase of recovery. Members of the system are more likely to trust the judgment of the counselor in this process, enhancing the likelihood of follow-through.

Step III.5. Exit the System

Once equilibrium has been restored, the counselor is obligated to take formal leave of the system. Appreciations, resentments, and regrets can be spoken with integrity and authenticity. Termination communicates the counselor's trust of the system's capacity to care for itself.

One counselor described the experience in this way: "We began to talk about the symbolic nature of the storm. As I prepared to terminate, the family decided that they wanted a weather vane as a symbolic marker of the passage they were making in their lives. It was an interesting process to be with them as they marked the 'way' for past and future storms. My job was done and I was able to depart with a sense of completion for me and a sense of ongoing process for them."

Crisis counselors may need to find a way to metaphorically "exit the system." Long hours, substandard housing, poor diet, lack of rest, and sheer numbers of victims needing help can overwhelm the physical and emotional resources of the counselor. Often the counselor "lives" with the victims physically and metaphorically. Being witness to devastating losses can take its toll. Taking time to rest and relax, limiting clinical demands, and finding ways to give meaning to the experience will counter the likelihood the counselor will become a hidden victim.

A counselor for the Columbine shooting shared her experience: "I worked from the time of the shooting until the school and community regained a sense of stability. I was amazed at my capacity to hold the suffering of others. When I left I resumed my normal practice, giving little thought to my own need to recover. Six months later I was asked to share my experience at a professional meeting. I had my notes all ready but when I started to talk I experienced shortness of breath, an inability to talk, and feelings of anxiety and dread. Fortunately the group recognized I was experiencing transcrisis. They were amazingly concerned and caring. I was humbled with the need to do my own work."

THE CRISIS OF SEXUAL ASSAULT

Sexual assault, more commonly referred to as rape, can occur to anyone, at any age, of any ethnic, economic, or cultural background. More so than most types of crisis, sexual assault is surrounded by a mythology that promotes silence and shame. Healing is often complicated for the victim of sexual assault because of the stigma associated with the crisis. Most rape victims are women, though this is not a gender-exclusive crisis. If women are silent about their experience, men are mute. The psychological cost of this silence is a life spent accommodating the damage and distress. Personality disorder, sexual dysfunction, depression, and anxiety can all be markers of an individual's life scarred by sexual assault.

Between 15 and 25 percent of women report being victims of rape at some point in their lives. Most victims know their perpetrators. The mythology of rape creates a mind-set that imposes a sense of responsibility on the victim for the attack. Loss of confidence and a diminished sense of self, including worth, esteem, and blame, often result.

Families and members of the intimate system of the rape victim are also affected. Spouses, for example, will find an increased amount of irrational responsibility for the rape. Identifying the needs of the indirect victims becomes crucial for treatment of the direct victim. The response to rape is significantly affected by the support system's ability to nurture and hold its members in the presence of violence.

Rape Trauma Syndrome

Burgess and Holmestrom (1985) have described the reaction of rape victims in two distinct phases: the immediate phase following the attack, which lasts several weeks, and the long-term reorganization phase, which will last for an indefinite period of time, from several weeks to several years. Under ideal circumstances, a crisis counselor will be able to respond to the rape victim as soon as is possible after the assault. Immediate help is required to negotiate the multiple demands of the attack and mitigate the possibility for secondary trauma from community resources. There are two common responses to a rape: a passive response or an expressive response. The passive individual finds herself calm following the attack. She may appear to be untouched emotionally and will demonstrate a cold, distant attitude, a calm demeanor, with an ability to make rational responses. The expressive individual fits the more commonly held stereotype of the rape victim. She may be emotionally labile, unable to focus, verbalizing unconnected thoughts and issues, and may appear hysterical. As point of fact, the passive individual is the more traumatized victim. She is unable to connect with the emotions created by the attack and must compartmentalize her feelings to the point of repression and denial.

Assessment of the individual who has been raped includes both a physical and a psychological evaluation. It is clear that a rape is seen as an emergency that demands rapid intervention that can be used to evaluate physical damage and to gather information important in a legal defense. The crisis counselor who will work with victims of sexual assault should know the local and state laws governing rape and should be familiar with the process of the physical assessment of the rape victim. The counselor will need to be well versed with all aspects of a rape kit and know the steps of evidence gathering in a health care setting. In this way, the counselor can work during the emergency to prepare the individual for the continued intrusion of the physical and psychological examinations that follow a rape. Suggestions for each step in crisis counseling and examples of interventions follow.

Phase I: Remember

Step I.1. Share the Story

The rape victim will want to share her experience. The crime of sexual assault is too much for an individual to hold; she will have a natural inclination to disclose details of the attack. A supportive, encouraging clinician will allow this natural flow to occur at an organic pace, allowing the narrative to unfold in a highly personal and idiosyncratic fashion. The counselor's goal in listening is to help the individual begin the sorting process, through the narrative, which helps define the attack in a more manageable way.

It is useful for the counselor to assess the response of the support system as quickly as possible as the narrative emerges. Interviews with intimates apart from the assaulted individual will allow the counselor to assess for secondary victimization and for the degree to which rape fallacies and myths have been activated. If the counselor assesses that intimates hold a "blame the victim" mentality or have other beliefs that may add humiliation to the narrative, the counselor can meet separately with the support system and work to neutralize the irrationality. The clinician can help "set the stage" for providing appropriate nurturance and support, based on the expressed need of the rape victim.

It is useful for the counselor to seek out primary supports of the same gender of the victim. Females will need other females to help in the early stage of telling their story. Males will need males. The gender-specific support, if available, should come from the intimate system of the victim, that is, the family or close social kinship network. Having a supportive other in the process of the unfolding of the narrative gives a needed set of eyes and ears to the process of healing. The counselor will want to listen for signs of guilt, self-blame, and magical thinking ("If only I had . . .") that will mark the victim's own irrationality related to myths about rape. The goal of the telling of the story is to alleviate a sense of responsibility that the victim "caused" the attack.

Step I.2. Validate the Emotional Impact

Rape victims have multiple symptoms. The crime of sexual assault registers physical, emotional, psychological, and social symptoms that will demand attention. Many victims will experience residual emotions that are sensually congruent with their experience during the attack. As one woman said, "I imagined that I was made out of stainless steel and that I wouldn't let him touch my insides. Now, it's like the attack has imprinted this image in my head: that I am made of stainless steel and that nothing can touch me. I want to feel differently, but I just can't right now."

One man reported that he had been bound by ropes during the attack. He said, "I fought every step of the way. When I was tied up, I knew that I could only fight so much, but I was unwilling to give in. I'm still feeling like I'm fighting. I feel revengeful, angry, and I want to fight back. These are feelings that I have against anyone who wants to get close to me. I know this isn't healthy. There are people that are wanting to help me. I'm so rageful that I just can't let anyone get close to me yet."

The emotionality of the attack may present in a variety of physical symptoms. Once the extent of the physical trauma has been established and treated, the individual may begin to experience symptoms meta-phorically related to the emotional response created from the attack.

For example, an elderly woman was raped following a day's work as a museum volunteer. She told the clinician, "I didn't mind the sex-ual part so much. I'm an old woman, you see. The sexual attack is something that I can understand and deal with. What is so troubling is that the rapist stole my youth, or at least my illusion of it." In the work that followed, the counselor listened and responded to the woman's physical limitations and the constraints of age and emotionality.

In this process, individuals will need help to contain the over-whelming emotionality of the rape experience. Oftentimes, feeling states will emerge that are overpowering. The counselor will need a repertoire of relaxation and calming exercises to pace the client through expression of feeling. Thought-stopping techniques and be-havior management strategies will be helpful to keep the individual from feeling intrusion at every turn. When the individual feels most vulnerable, the counselor should listen and intervene.

One counselor gave this example: "The woman said that every time she entered a dark room she felt violently ill. An image of the rape bubbled up in her mind and she was unable stop a graphic re-playing of the attack. The obvious first step was to place lights on timers in her home, so that she would not have to come into a dark house. The second step was oriented to helping her to interrupt her memory long enough that she could assess for realistic danger. In an interesting and creative way, she found that if she whistled, she was able to keep the thoughts at a suitable distance until she could reassure herself of being in a safe place." The simplicity of the intervention has elegance. When a rape victim feels too vulnerable to repeated intru-sion, the counselor seeks to find a way to attend to the emotionality in a realistic and accessible way.

Step I.3. Evaluate the Context of the Crisis

Other events in the life of the victim may cause feelings of anxiety and threat. The counselor should be aware that these feelings will be amplified and underlined following a sexual assault. Knowledge of the victim's role functioning within her intimate and vocational support systems will be helpful to assess the context of the crisis.

The elderly woman in the example earlier continued to tell her story to the crisis counselor: "I've lived in this little apartment for several years, and ride the bus to the museum three days a week. I'm a docent in a section of the gallery that holds my favorite art. I've always felt safe here since I grew up and have lived in this city all my life. My adult children trust my judgment and have never tried to get me to move out of my little nest. Now, they want me to consider something different. One wants me to live with her family, and the others are talking about an assisted-living facility. In so many ways, both options seem as frightening to me as the rape. Both choices tell me I'm old, just like the rape has brought my age and stage of life into full focus. I don't like either choice."

Consider this example in juxtaposition with the elderly woman's story. A young woman was raped at a fraternity party on a college campus. She told her story to the clinician: "I went to the party after a football game with a rival school. I was drinking; everybody was. I knew I was drinking too much, but I didn't care. It was the weekend and I had finished all my work, so I figured I could sleep off a hangover on Sunday and be good-to-go on Monday. Next thing I remember was waking up in the early morning hours on one of the sofas in the rec room. I felt like I had been kicked in the head, but figured it was just a hangover."

The young woman continued: "For the next couple of weeks, I knew that the brothers of the fraternity made all sorts of jokes about me, but I figured I deserved it. I was okay with all of it until I got a case of chlamydia. When the doctor examined me, he asked about sexual contact. I'm a virgin—or at least I was. He said that he could see evidence that I had recent sexual intercourse. That's when I knew that all of the talk and innuendo was true. Somebody slipped me a date rape drug at the party and I was attacked while I was unconscious."

The young woman was helped to move through the university channels to explore her options for legal and administrative actions. She found members of her support system who were able to provide emotional support and protection while the investigation unfolded.

Step I.4. Protect Vulnerable Family Members

Cases of rape and sexual assult include direct and indirect victims, including vulnerable family members, who may require protection. Rape is a crime of violence and, as such, can incite further violence. It is not unusual for rape victims to turn inward on themselves and manifest self-destructive thoughts and feelings. Indirect victims, such as parents, siblings, and spouses, may feel guilt or other angst, such as erroneous thinking, against the feeling of helplessness associated with sexual assault. The individual and system may feel shame, or even feel humiliated, by the assault and may be left feeling demeaned rather than supported in the community. It is also a reasonable possibility that the victim may retreat into silence and become socially withdrawn, which increases the likelihood for depression.

A lethality assessment for suicidality or homocidality of all victims invites the crisis worker into the presence of the shame and guilt and musters the potential for understanding, and a realistic joining of the system. By challenging the mythology held by the victims of the assault, self-blame and self-hatred can be minimized. Focus should be placed on safety and protection, not only from further assault, but from dangerous feelings and desires. Not only should such assessment be provided during the initial interview, but it should be frequently revisited as the impact of the assault and social repercussions become apparent. No-harm contracts offer concrete agreements and can be renegotiated as necessary. Mindful of the fact that the victim will need help channeling anger and possible acting out, the counselor can aid in channeling this energy from destructive hurting into active healing.

Step I.5. Negotiate a Solvable Problem

The rape victim will need to feel as though she is regaining control of her life as soon as is possible. From the first contact, the crisis counselor will look for ways to encourage choice and option, and to help the individual to reclaim a sense of being in charge and capable of making effective decisions. One counselor described the process in this way: "I ask lots of questions that contain choices—Would you like to wear the blue or the red coat? Would you rather have the interview in the morning or the afternoon? Which physician do you think will be able to help you in the best way? Choices give control."

Depending on the stylistic response of the individual, the solvable problem may be simple and small or may have a larger and longer-lasting impact. For the young woman attacked at the university, she decided to "drop a bombshell," as she described it. After evaluating the pros and cons of her decision, she provided the school newspaper an interview of her experience at the party. Within a week, several other young women came forward and reported similar incidents at the same fraternity's parties. The young women asked for, and received, audience with the director of the intrafraternity council who suggested that the girls file civil charges against the fraternity. While the rape was left unproven, the fraternity quickly lost its charter on the campus and was disbanded.

The young woman told her counselor, "I don't feel healed, but I do feel vindicated. The interview is what turned the tide. Up until that point, I was the victim—the slut. Now, I am the hero. I realize that it could've just as easily gone the other way. I was willing to take the chance, and am just glad that this has turned out in such a favorable way."

Step I.6. Network with Relevant Resources

There is a wide range of established support services for individuals who have been sexually assaulted. Training on appropriate response to rape is mandatory for medical receiving facilities, law enforcement officers, and social service/mental health agencies. Crisis counselors need not reinvent the wheel and feel that they must provide all services. It is more important that the counselor knows about the services offered to the community, and to know how to access and manage those resources. Involvement in the services offered to the rape victim also includes a psychological price that must be factored. The counselor can help the individual to assess the symbolic and energetic cost of relying on the service in favor of resolving and healing the crisis. The counselor serves as educator and can help to teach the role of the service delivery system in recovery, can aid in setting appropriate boundaries, and can assist in the understanding of the limits to the services that are offered.

When dealing with rape, the crisis counselor learns that the timing associated with intervention has a significant impact. For example, often the first response to the attack is from the medical community. The individual attacked will need to be tenderly assisted in each step of the investigation and examination. The counselor serves as advocate and protector and should be aware that this help will potentially be as intrusive as all others. In this role, the counselor can assure privacy and integrity.

Later, the counselor may need to help the individual assess what legal recourse is available in the process. The man raped in the earlier example disclosed that his attack was a gang retaliation for an offense he committed against a rival's sister. While he was strongly encouraged to press charges against his attacker, who was known to him, the man made the decision not to pursue legal action. While frustrating for police, the counselor worked with the individual to heal from the rape in a way that did not include the court.

Phase II: Reorganize

Step II.1. Formulate a Plan for Change

Goals for treatment are contingent on the nature of the assault, the involvement of outside agencies, the degree of the system's disorganization as a result of the assault, and the extent of the support system.

An individual who has been sexually assaulted will need immediate help to restore a sense of personal and environmental safety. Indirect victims, such as spouses and family members, can mobilize their resources to "batten down the hatches."

One woman who was raped in her home asked her family for help. "We secured the windows and doors and changed the locks," reported her husband. Her adult son had an alarm system installed. A young adult daughter said, "Mom had trouble sometimes going from place to place. I would go with her and would be a safety check for her. We even found ways for her to get in and out of the car so that she would feel safer. She needed companions to walk her back and forth from her car to work as well as someone at home when she arrived. This was something that I could coordinate. It made me feel useful."

The woman raped told her counselor, "I couldn't feel good in my own skin. Even as I got some distance from the attack, I could still feel his touch." With the help of the counselor, the woman found a sensitive massage therapist who was able to begin a wellness routine that helped her to feel physically and psychologically stronger. The woman continued to want regular and frequent medical checkups to assess for sexually transmitted diseases. Her health care team was willing and able to accommodate her requests.

The ramifications of pressing legal charges are worthy of careful consideration in the formulation of a plan for change for the victim of a sexual assault. Legal counsel is prudent, as is education to learn the laws related to sexual assault. The clinician can provide instrumental aid to help the individual to assess what the legal system can and cannot offer. The goal for the plan for change should include a "no surprise" rule for sexual assault victims. Violence breaks barriers of trust and security. As the individual learns more about the process of evolving from a rape, each healing step should occur with eyes wide open, which ensures a progressive sense of safety and security.

Counselors should also attend to the restoration of a normative rhythm within the family and intimate system. The individual should be encouraged to speak her peace to those who care about her and explicitly define how they might be helpful.

The woman in the example continued in this vein: "As much as I love my family and friends, after a while they became solicitous and overly protective. They thought they were helping me, but their assistance robbed me of my chance to regain autonomy and independence. I had to get a good deal of help from the counselor to get them to give me enough space to take things on my own. I was surprised that this was one of the hardest tasks. I know they felt helpless and would do anything they could for me. Letting me 'be' was tough for all of them."

Step II.2. Identify Developmental Issues

The sexual maturity of the individual will interface with the experience in interesting and important ways. The younger the individual, the more relevant the developmental level of the family becomes. A rape will interfere with the normative and natural rhythms of the family's functioning and will create disruption for each member as well as the system as a unit.

A mother described the rape of her six-year-old son by an adolescent neighbor: "This teenager tried to tell us that the sex was consensual. What a joke! How can a six-year-old consent to something that he doesn't understand? Of course, he came right to me and his father and told us what had happened. He was physically hurt. We've had to be very careful. My son sees the attack primarily as a physical assault. We see it as much more than that, but are using the counselor to help us gauge our discussions to an appropriate six-year-old level." The counselor, understanding the sexual and maturational levels of six-year-olds, knew that the child could be exploited as much by the family's reactions as by the attack itself.

Consider another example. A teenage girl was raped during an off-campus trip with her high school peers. As ninth graders, students were allowed to go to an overnight trip to a science fair. The girl rebelliously violated the school rules and visited the room of a group of boys from another school. She was assaulted. She told her girlfriends on the trip about the incident but swore them to secrecy. Fortunately, one of the victim's friends was unable to tolerate the anxiety of the secret and confided in a teacher. The entire group needed intervention from the crisis counselor to restore any semblance of balance and order. The girl covered her guilt and shame by projecting anger onto her friend. The friend felt ostracized for her actions, and the rest of the groups chose "sides." Fortunately, the crisis counselor had an understanding of the developmental issues related to young adolescents and was able to intervene on a peerage level which gave some calming to the system and allowed the girls to focus on the attack.

An earlier example recounted the circumstance of an elderly woman who was raped. Eventually, she chose to move into an assisted-living facility and was able to restore a sense of balance and presence to her life. She told her family that while the change was desirable, the precipitant would stay with her. "My independence was shattered. I've always been able to take care of myself, and I can't do it anymore. I feel compromised and I despise the feeling."

While sexual maturity is a component of the assessment process, the crisis counselor is cautioned from overinterpretation. Sexual assault is a violent act. Most recipients of crisis counseling will focus primarily on the violence, assault, and intrusion rather than genitalized sexuality.

Step II.3. Engage Therapeutic Tools

The crisis counselor will find that a reassuring, supportive stance creates a holding environment for an individual who has been sexually assaulted. Gaining trust in the presence of personal attack and betrayal is paramount. The counselor should be reminded that trust is tentative, and in the case of sexual assault, promises made must be promises kept. Reflective listening and allowing the client psychological room to replay the assault in the presence of a safe witness allows for healing.

One client described her experience: "I had to tell the story over and over. It seemed like I remembered every detail, but couldn't get the big picture. That's how the counselor helped me. She listened, patiently and attentively, as I went through the attack in my mind's eye. She was able to ask the right questions to help me to begin to distance from it enough that I began to get a new perspective. That was the best support that I got. That she could listen so well was the help I needed to find a new place in relation to the attack."

Though in most forms of brief therapy, including crisis counseling, there is an obligation to work quickly to enact change, the best adage for providing sound therapeutic interventions to victims of sexual assault is "Don't just do something, stand there." One counselor said, "I have to hold on to my own anxiety so that I won't get in the way of my client's. She is the one who has to live with the pain all the time. I can distance from her distress. If I can sit still, I know that she will be able to resurface much more effectively than if I get overly prescriptive just to tend to my own anxiety."

Step II.4. Assign Homework

That being said, the value of homework is in its connections to others and the outside world. Successful accomplishment of tasks with specific goals allows the individual to participate fully in the counseling process. The nonjudgmental, reflective stance of the counselor is combined with suggestions of steps to encourage the individual's personal and environmental safety. At the very least, the clinician should be attentive to those activities that encourage individuals to see themselves through new eyes that move from victim to survivor to healed. With integration of the rape experience as the overarching goal, the counselor guides the person in the direction of those activities that "make sense."

One counselor described her approach: "Homework for the individual who has been sexually assaulted always focuses around 'What do you need?' and 'How much help do you want from others?' I want her to feel increasingly safe and as though she can provide this sense of security for herself. This may be as simple as making a phone call. It may be as challenging as sitting through legal discussions."

One of the counselor's clients responded: "She very gently said, 'What do you need?' I had absolutely no answer to the question. The best homework assignment that I had was oriented to defining those things that I needed at any given point in time. I learned a very good focusing exercise that helped me to tune in to my most basic needs. Then I was able to ask for, and receive, help."

Step II.5. Support Systemic Rules, Roles, and Rituals

The family of the sexually assaulted victim will be in the presence of a breaking of rules and roles that provide for the environmental safety of the system. The counselor is obligated to look at the system with a nonblaming eye as structures are bolstered to regain the safety that has been lost. Although roles typically do not change drastically for the victim, the guidelines for the functioning of the role change for all involved.

The young woman whose mother was raped spoke with the counselor at one point: "I'm a runner, and have always jogged early in the morning before anyone got up. A good run just started my day in the right way. I never thought twice about my safety until my mother's attack. Now, I wait until midmorning and am running in a more populated area. I am so much more aware of my surroundings. Sometimes I feel like I'm too paranoid and suspicious, but then when I consider that I never thought twice about my safety, I feel like I'm pretty much in the normal range now with my caution."

Consider the young woman who was raped at the fraternity party. While she had defined herself as a "wild child" to the counselor, she began to modify this role to one of advocate. She enrolled in self-defense classes. She talked openly and unashamedly about the rape and her participation in the precipitants to the attack. She gave presentations in psychology and science classes on date rape drugs. Ultimately, she organized a program at her university titled "Take Back the Night." She invited students who had suffered sexual assault to tell their story in a public environment and worked to create a heightened awareness on the campus regarding rape. Fraternities and sororities cosponsored the event, which was ultimately incorporated into the school's rush policy as a required function.

Phase III: Restore

Step III.1. Track Progress Toward Goals

Each time the clinician communicates ways that the individual appears stronger and more capable, the self-identity of that person is shaped toward recovery. The goals in the second phase of treatment should be reasonably concrete so they may be observed easily by others. The counselor will want to keep a focus on the question "How will you know when you are no longer in need of my help?" The question generates a discussion that defines postcrisis functioning.

As one young woman said, "I will never be quite the same. I can say now that my sense of security has been altered, but it won't always be shattered like I thought immediately following the rape. I'll need to be aware of my safety needs in practical ways the rest of my life. I just won't be able to naively assume that I'm safe. Most of the world can do that. But then, most of the world hasn't been raped. If I can "do" safety, then I'll be happy. Like I said, most people just move through the world feeling safe. I'll have to take good steps to make sure I'm okay."

In the presence of the crisis work related to sexual assault, the counselor should remember that no surprises are welcome in the counseling process. Therefore, the counselor must be aware of the indicators toward termination and plan to talk openly about the progress toward goals approximately three sessions before the formal ending occurs.

A counselor described her thoughts this way: "I don't want to track my client so closely that she feels stifled. I do know that there will be many times that I might be able to reframe an experience as progressive and healing if I am attentive. I always want to find those moments that my client can catch herself doing those things that feel more facile, manageable, and natural. I also want to make sure that she knows that I will take my leave at some point in the process of recovery."

Step III.2. Acknowledge Indicators of the Time to Terminate

Astute observation and critical questions to the individual and the members of the family system will help to assess readiness for termination. The counselor should look for markers that indicate a return to precrisis levels of functioning. Role-related responsibilities, natural energy levels, and increased initiative in problem-solving abilities are markers for termination. To the degree that the client is comfortable with "things under control," the counselor can prepare to exit the system.

A client described her experience: "One of the most unhelpful things that anyone asked me was what I had learned as a result of the rape. I felt patronized and humiliated. Fortunately, I had a good therapist. She was able to help me look around myself and to define how I was restoring my life back to where it was before the rape. Certainly, I'm different. I am much more aware of the dangers in the world and I feel much more vulnerable than I would like. I am doing better, though, and feel like I'm well on the road to being okay. Time will need to take its course for me to toughen up again."

The client continued: "I didn't know how reliant I had become on my counselor. My conversations with her began to feel like a refuge, and I felt that she could hold everything that I brought. I thought it was a little odd that she began to talk about termination before I was ready. Now I can see that she really was encouraging me back to health. She was helping me to mark those ways that I could take care of myself. I miss her, but feel like I'm doing what I need to and am glad that she gave me a heads up that she would eventually leave."

Step III.3. Address Future Sources of Stress

A sexual assault tends to put an individual at risk for other psychological problems that may not be readily evident. The context of violence can poison other loving relationships. Such an attack can alter and damage the sense of trust required for deepening intimate relationships, especially if the assault was perpetrated by a known assailant. Rape will change the individual's sense of self in her own and others' eyes. Such an event can cause disruption in normative developmental life transitions. Any developmental change in the individual's life related to the sense of self, for example, puberty, birth of a child, empty nest syndrome, or loss of a job, can place her in a heightened sense of vulnerability and frailty. Knowledge of this phenomenon can help the individual to prepare for life changes. She can shore up her support system as developmental shifts occur, knowing that with any storm of emotions she may need help to navigate.

One woman told this story years after she was raped: "I never knew that I would be so vulnerable to changes after I was assaulted. I thought that, as time passed, I would move on and forget about the damage done. Well, I did move on from the rape, but found that anytime big changes happened in my life, there would be some trigger that took me back to the attack. With continued help from a therapist, I learned that there was a connection imprinted deep in my unconscious that just put me at risk. I now have a therapist that I rely on like I use my primary care physician. This lovely woman knows that I need help from time to time to make it over rough bumps in the road. This is something that I have learned about myself. 'Under any kind of stress?' I say to myself. 'Go and see the therapist. She can help me with perspective and judgment.'"

Step III.4. Refer for Continuing Treatment

As noted, the individual who has experienced a rape may be at continued risk for a recapitulation of stress-related responses to other environmental events. Depending on precrisis levels of functioning or the developmental stage of the individual, longer-term treatment may be indicated. If the individual has a personality disorder or any particular psychological vulnerability, these may become dysfunctional as a result of the assault. The crisis clinician should be attentive to the stress response and make an appropriate referral if necessary after the crisis has been abated.

Step III.5. Exit the System

The crisis counselor described the exit from the system of an individual who suffered a sexual assault: "I met with my client and, over time, helped her to gather a sense of her self. When termination time came, she began to find ways to stay connected with me. While this was understandable, there is a part of me that knew that I must leave or I would create undue dependency that would not help her to fully heal from the attack. We talked at length about the nature of my taking leave from her, and our conversation had a beneficial therapeutic effect. She saw that our termination left her a stronger person, which was a goal of ours from the start."

The termination should communicate a sense of strength and an increased capacity for autonomy and independence. For the clinician, this generosity of spirit should give the client a sense that the farewell is a return to a normative level of functioning. For the client, it is a step into a level of balance.

THE CRISIS OF A LIFE-THREATENING ILLNESS: ACUTE LYMPHOCYTIC LEUKEMIA

About 3,200 new cases of acute lymphocytic leukemia (ALL) are diagnosed each year in the United States. It is the most common type of leukemia for patients under the age of fifteen. While children are at the highest risk for developing the disease, it can occur at any age. It represents a type of crisis that is medical, chronic, and life threatening.

ALL is a disease of the blood. Too many infection-fighting white blood cells, called lymphocytes, are found in the bone marrow and blood stream. Lymphocytes, found in the lymph system, are a colorless, watery fluid present in the lymph vessels. They fight infection in the body by making antibodies to attack germs and harmful bacteria. With ALL, the developing lymphocytes do not mature and become overly abundant. These immature lymphocytes collect in lymph tissue and marrow, crowding out other cells. Anemia develops, since the marrow does not have room to produce red blood cells and platelets. The absence of platelets, which help the blood clot, leaves the body at risk for bleeding or bruising. Without rapid and aggressive treatment, cancerous lymphocytes eventually invade other organs, including the spine and brain.

ALL is difficult to diagnose because of an insidious onset of symptoms, including fatigue and a generalized loss of well-being. Early symptoms are similar to those of the flu. Once diagnosed through bone marrow biopsy, the primary treatment is chemotherapy, but radiation therapy may be used in certain cases. Bone marrow transplantation is currently being studied in clinical trials.

A normal course of treatment for leukemia is a seven-day regimen of continuous intravenous infusion of a chemotherapy agent called cytarabine (Ara-C). Over a two- to three-week treatment period, the patient's white blood count, hemoglobin, and platelets decrease in a process known as bone marrow suppression. A recovery phase follows, where healthy bone marrow regrows. During this period, the individual is at high risk for fever, infections, and bleeding problems.

Even after intensive treatment, some individuals have residual leukemia cells remaining in the bone marrow. This condition, known as "refractory leukemia," gives rise to a relapse of the disease after a period of time of remission. A repeat of the typical course of chemotherapy treatment is required for relapse.

The "cure rate" for ALL has increased over the last twenty-five years. In children, the probability of an extended remission or cure is approximately 75 percent. Of adults with ALL, 60 to 80 percent can be expected to have complete remission following appropriate therapy. Nonetheless, it is a frightening disease that causes intense feelings of fear, anxiety, and helplessness. Counseling provides a source of support for the patient and the family. The systemic model of this text can guide the work of the counselor through the crisis phases of the disease. Suggestions for each step in crisis counseling and examples of interventions follow.

Phase I: Remember

Step I.1. Share the Story

For the individual who discovers a life-threatening illness, the initial crisis is one of recognition and impact. The person will need instrumental aid to learn the nature of the disease, its prognosis, and the most appropriate course of treatment. As always, the crisis counselor's listening skills are critical in the sharing of the story. The crisis clinician should ask questions related to health care access and symptom recognition and should listen closely for thoughts and feelings regarding diagnosis. Involving members of the individual's support system is likely to increase the effectiveness of treatment planning, since the individual will need practical and applied help during the course of treatment.

A twenty-three-year-old fellow told his story: "I had graduated from college and landed this great job as a commercial artist. I have a lovely girlfriend and all was well—or so I thought. I got sick and thought I had the flu. I ran a fever, had some nausea and vomiting, and generally felt lousy for a few weeks. I had convinced myself that I was getting over it when my family noticed that I was losing weight. I went to see an internist. I never had any physical problems before and didn't even know what kind of doctor I should see."

He continued: "The doc thought I had a bad and lingering case of flu and drew blood to check for mononucleosis. He gave me a prescription for antibiotics and told me to go to bed and he'd call if there was anything I needed to know. Well, that night he called me and told me that he was 'concerned' about the results of my blood work. He had already made an appointment for me to see a hematologist/oncologist the first thing the next morning. I called my parents and they were in shock. I didn't even know that an oncologist was a cancer doctor. The next morning, I learned that my blood test results were grossly abnormal and that, in their words, my blood was 'suspicious of leukemia or another blood disorder.' I was scheduled for a bone marrow aspiration the next morning. I freaked the rest of the day and night; I was absolutely terrified. Within three days, I was diagnosed with ALL and was in the hospital to begin chemotherapy treatments. My life was turned upside down."

The fellow needed help to tell his story. Many times, individuals in a health care crisis will not have the language to describe the disease state and will have difficulty recounting the emotional response to learning of the illness.

Step I.2. Validate the Emotional Impact

The client described his life-threatening illness as "a blind side wipe-out." As noted, the fellow was unable to put words other than "freaked" on his emotional experience. The clinician worked and helped this gentleman and his family put words on the distress of the disease.

As a general rule, when working with disease states, the known is always less frightening than the unknown. Validation of emotional impact can be strengthened with knowledge. The crisis counselor is in a position to serve as an educator while the emotionality of the crisis emerges. Evaluating and underscoring the emotionality for realistic understanding, as well as monitoring the cognitive and behavioral functioning, can help the individual feel held and supported while accommodating to a "sick" role.

A nurse who served as an individual's crisis counselor described her function in this way: "I believe the individual needs to ventilate, to air out, and to circulate all of the feelings and thoughts that are likely to emerge. When I sit with someone who has learned of a catastrophic illness, I want to watch for nonverbal cues and the tone of that person's voice as much as I listen for the content of what will be said. There may not be much time for the individual to acclimate to the diagnosis before treatment begins, so it is important for me to help set the stage for ongoing assessment of needs that come from a knowledge base related to the disease." This wise clinician speaks of the need for the counselor to clarify treatment options and misconceptions. Another counselor spoke of her therapeutic stance: "I have to remember that validity is a statistical term and is defined as the accuracy of measuring what is intended to be measured. That's where I see my job in helping to validate the emotional impact. If I can help my client to know 'what's what,' then I can assist and help them ground their feelings in a reality-based experience."

Step I.3. Evaluate the Context of the Crisis

For an individual in the crisis of a life-threatening illness, enough cannot be said about the necessity of social support. As noted, leukemia can strike an individual of any age. For the child or teenager, the diagnosis will have a profound impact on the life of the family. The family support will most likely include members of the extended family system, such as grandparents, who may take an active part in the caregiving responsibilities. For an elderly adult, the context of the crisis will be different. Previous life experience with loss may make adaptation to the diagnosis more graceful. Elders will also be more likely to have established health care relationships, but they may also be isolated from family, widowed, or limited in mobility. All contribute to increased anxiety and fear.

Consider Mary, a seventy-eight-year-old retired schoolteacher who was diagnosed with ALL three years before she requested crisis counseling. During her first round of treatment, she spent one month in the hospital receiving chemotherapy. The leukemia went into remission and she returned to a routine level of daily living. When the disease returned and she relapsed, another round of chemotherapy was prescribed.

Mary had told her adult children after the first course of treatment, "I will never, ever do chemotherapy again." When the relapse was diagnosed, Mary did not want to repeat the chemotherapy, even though family members and health care providers insisted that her prognosis for remission was excellent. She acquiesced to the wishes of her support system but had a difficult and complicated recovery. Her children wanted the treatment but failed to recognize the price their mother paid. Their own family demands limited their support. This example speaks to the nature of the context of the crisis. Mary said, "Learning about the recurrence was not nearly as traumatic as the second course of treatment. I knew how sick I was going to be and I knew that I didn't have the strength to go through the treatment again. Sometimes, ignorance is bliss. Nobody can know how sick chemotherapy can make you. I did the treatments for my family. I know they love me, and I appreciate their love, but I didn't know that I was able to rise to the task of the chemo." Mary asked her counselor to help her tell her family that she would refuse further treatment, should it ever be suggested again. She wanted an inviolable contract with them not to demand treatment that she did not want.

Step I.4. Protect Vulnerable Family Members

When an individual is diagnosed and treated for a life-threatening illness, it is not unusual that other members of the system may be at risk for illness or accident. For the individual fighting the disease, the counselor is advised to make an ongoing assessment for lethality and suicidality. If the disease is terminal, then the risk for suicidality increases and should be assessed and discussed with the individual and members of the support system.

Members of the intimate system may also be at risk. Children may feel unreasonable guilt or anxiety due to parents' illness. Adults may feel particularly helpless when unable to counter the impact of the treatment on a child's illness. The clinician is obligated to speak to the issues of vulnerability and frailty that will surface in the presence of the crisis of a catastrophic illness.

Consider one counselor's discussion with her patient: "When this wonderful young man developed leukemia, I knew he was worried about how his life would continue. He began to talk about what it might be like if he were to die. At one point, I asked him to talk about any feelings of wanting to end his life. He looked at me like I had read his mind. He responded by wondering if I knew that he had thought of suicide. When we talked about suicidal thought as a normative response to dealing with such a disease, the issue was out in the open and we were able to talk about ways that he could feel more support and protection in the presence of the disease."

The young man responded: "I couldn't believe she just came right out and asked me if I thought about ending my own life. I had been thinking about it for days. The thoughts were tormenting and I couldn't find any place for them. Once we started talking about them, I felt more of a sense of peace. I learned that talking about my feelings, even those that I'd just as soon keep to myself, helped to alleviate some of the fear and gave me more of a sense of peace in the face of honesty."

Step I.5. Negotiate a Solvable Problem

There are any number of solvable problems for the individual in the crisis of a catastrophic illness. The clinician should help to prioritize those issues that are most immediate and relevant to personal need. Then, in a stepwise fashion, the counselor helps the client negotiate the terrain that leads to satisfaction of those needs.

The young commercial artist talked about this step: "I didn't realize that mouth sores were going to be complications of the chemotherapy. My mouth felt like I had swallowed ten hot cups of coffee in a row. I kept complaining to my girlfriend and my mother, but all the complaints in the world didn't get me any relief. I tried ice chips, mouthwash, and just about anything that I thought might get me pain control. At the time, the counselor and I talked about ways that I might feel more in charge. I told her that if I could get rid of the mouth sores, I would be happy. She and I made a plan for me to speak to the oncology nurse about the problem. When I did, the nurse said, "I have more drugs than you have pain." She gave me something called magic mouthwash and got a prescription for some medicine that was soothing to my mouth. While I didn't get rid of the mouth sores, I did get relief. I realized that I needed to be the one to speak up when I was in pain. Once I learned that lesson, I felt more in charge of an awful time."

Step I.6. Network with Relevant Resources

There are an abundance of resources that can be called into action for support of an individual and intimate system during a catastrophic illness. Health care, social service, and self-help resources are available in the community, and many may be offered at no cost to the patient.

Fortunately for the young man in the earlier example, the Leukemia Society visited him at his bedside soon after admission to the hospital for treatment. They explained their purpose as an educational and advocacy group and offered him Web site addresses, phone numbers, and brochures to learn about his disease and treatment options. The hospital offered a support group for spouses, which his girlfriend chose to attend. She found that the stress of the disease complicated their intimacy. The group offered a safe environment to explore her feelings and to renew her sense of self in the presence of her boyfriend's disease.

Because of the side effect of the mouth sores, the young man's eating habits became problematic. He was visited by a nutritionist who helped him to make reasonable choices of food that were satisfying. He was also visited by case managers from his insurance company and was assigned an ombudsman from the hospital to serve as his patient advocate. He responded well to the help and assistance offered him. As he said at one point, "I didn't know it was this hard to be sick."

Phase II: Reorganize

Step II.1. Formulate a Plan for Change

A plan for change in the presence of the crisis of a catastrophic illness is dependent on the individual's capacity to accept the diagnosis of the disease and the decision to move forward. Decisions must be made regarding treatment options and directions and quality of life. For the support system, intimates must be clear about the tasks afforded the role of caregiver. Many times, treatment options shift from cure to comfort, especially for those with recurrent disease. Since all decisions have the potential to be life altering based on medical interventions, thoughts for treatment options and care decisions will need to be discussed with the health care team until all decisions can be made in plainspoken language.

The elderly woman with recurrent leukemia had many extraordinary decisions to make. She was given the option of a bone marrow or a stem cell transplant as well as participating in several clinical trials. For such involvement, family members had to be engaged as donors. Each participant was blood typed to check for donor material and informed of the potential to give blood for their relative.

Ultimately, with the help of her counselor, the woman opted for no further treatment. She chose a course of palliative care and informed her health care providers with close family members present. She was given several options of support groups to help with her decisions and family members were invited to participate in group sessions, as well. Hospice services were offered and accepted by the woman. The hospice team was able to support the family as they came to terms with the patient's decision to move into quality, rather than longevity, of life.

Step II.2. Identify Developmental Issues

The diagnosis of leukemia presents multiple disruptions in normative developmental passages. For adult acute lymphocytic leukemia, Erikson's (1959) stages of development provide a relevant frame for discussion. The young adult will struggle with issues of intimacy versus isolation. For the young artist in this example, issues related to sexuality emerged. He worried mightily over the potential of infertility resulting from chemotherapy and suffered a profound disturbance of body image due to the side effects of treatment. As he said, "My body has betrayed me."

His chemotherapy caused many unwanted problems. He lost libidinal energy, his sex drive, and ultimately became sterile. Loss of hair became symbolic of his loss of strength, and for a period of time, he referred to himself as Samson. The disease progressed so quickly that the young man did not have the option of banking sperm, which was a cause of great consternation. During his treatment and convalescence, he and his girlfriend needed to explore alternatives to sexual intercourse as well as coming to terms with the loss of the definition of family defined by children.

For a middle-aged adult, Erikson would point to other developmental issues revolving on the resolution of generativity versus stagnation. For this age group, an individual has concerns regarding the productivity and meaning of life and begins to show genuine concern for others, including spouse, parents, and children. Decisions regarding treatment will in large part be determined on "what's best for my family," as one man said.

For an elderly individual, Erikson describes the stage of development as one of integrity versus despair. The individual in this age group will typically struggle with a sense of self-worth and a review of life accomplishments. Acceptance of death becomes a focus.

The elderly woman in the earlier example described the process to her family: "My dears," she said lovingly, "I've lived a good life and I want to live a good death. If I can accept this, then you will have to as well. While I certainly don't wish to die, I cannot tolerate being so sick that I can't enjoy each and every one of you as fully as I might without another intrusive treatment. Stay close to me and let us live our lives out the best each of us can." Her family was able to hear her and helped to make advance directive decisions. The crisis counselor was well-advised and knew to complete a durable power of attorney, to help the woman to prepare a will, and to make plans for her funeral, all in the presence of the family members she loved and who loved her.

Step II.3. Engage Therapeutic Tools

The individual in the presence of the crisis of a catastrophic illness will respond most appropriately to client-centered interventions oriented to active listening, unconditional positive regard, open-ended questioning, and reflection of deeper insight into the meaning of thoughts and emotions. Creating a holding environment for family members to gather with the sick person is encouraged. The sharing of honest emotionality strengthens the interpersonal bonds of the system and fosters a sense of tensile strength and support among its members. Empathy, acceptance, and sensitivity to each person's emotional needs and capacities is crucial, as is remembering the notion that the individual will live and die in character.

The elderly woman's counselor spoke of this process: "I never felt like I had much to do during this time. While I certainly functioned as an educator in many ways, my primary task was to serve as witness to the process of her decision to care for herself in very personal and private ways. It is an interesting process to work with people who are quite physically ill. While there are so many people who are involved with the person's care, the ultimate decisions rest with the patient, who must live and die with their choices."

Step II.4. Assign Homework

As has been stated in other ways, the task for patients is to become their own best physician. Through teaching and providing educational materials, the patient can be encouraged to make choices that are reasonable and congruent with individual thought, belief, and emotion. Homework allows the individual to proceed at a personal pace and serves as an aid to the establishment of the rhythm of counseling.

As an aside, individuals with a catastrophic illness will often wish to assign homework to members of their support system. The young artist developed a highly reactive sense of smell during one round of chemotherapy. He could not tolerate many odors, including the fragrance of flowers. He asked his caregivers to take flowers from his room, photograph them, and bring the pictures of the arrangements back for display on a bulletin board. Of course, the family members were pleased to be involved with such a creative endeavor. The task gave the man and his caregivers a genuine sense of connection that was transcendent of time and circumstance.

Step II.5. Support Systemic Rules, Roles, and Rituals

The family and support system will have a degree of integrity in the presence of any crisis, including that of integrating a catastrophic illness into the life of the system. The integrity, that is, the bounce, re-silience, and "nature" of the system, is found in its roles, rules, and rituals. The crisis counselor will want to know the dynamics of the system and find wholesome ways to support a return to the functional use of these supports. Even when beliefs differ, the individual and family system will be called on to honor the wishes and enactments of belief in the system.

Family roles must be identified, including changes and shifts caused by the impact of the illness. The traditions of the system should be marked, particularly during transitional times, such as holidays. Those individuals in the system with beliefs that vary from the norm of the system should be heard fully, with their beliefs accepted and incorporated.

For the young man with ALL, blood transfusions were an absolute necessity of care. As the possibility of a bone marrow or stem cell transplant became likely, family members were asked to give blood and be checked as donor candidates. One of the young fellow's maternal aunts was a converted member of the Jehovah's Witnesses faith. In this denomination, blood transfusions are prohibited. She was saddened but adamant that she could not participate in the young man's care regarding transfer of blood. Family members who knew the strength of the aunt's belief system acknowledged and accepted this as a way of loving her and found other ways for her to help.

Phase III: Restore

Step III.1. Track Progress Toward Goals

In this phase, the individual and support system receive feedback on previously set goals. The health status of the individual will strongly influence the trajectory and success of goal accomplishment. The tracking should lead to discussions for care options and choices and should advise the support system of the general status of the individual who lives with the disease.

The elderly woman with ALL was able to track her progress with an accuracy that defied her age. She said, "I am willing to hear any and all possibilities for caring for me. Right now, I am so clear that I do not want any more pain. I stay in discussion with my physicians and nurses and am talking about pain management and quality of life." She was able to sign and execute advance directives and informed her support system of her thoughts and wishes. She reported to her family and friends that she was "at peace" with her decisions and organized a support system to "keep [me] company." Family members were assigned days of the week to be in attendance with the woman, and members of her support system were given meal and personal care duties. When asked by her health care providers about changes in her decisions, she readily replied, "I'll let you know if I change my mind. Right now, I am feeling quite satisfied with my progress." She told her physician, in the presence of her saddened daughter, "This may not be progress toward cure, as you both might wish. It is progress for me, though, to know that I'm more in charge of the illness and of my happiness and comfort."

Step III.2. Acknowledge Indicators of the Time to Terminate

A lasting change in the individual's health and emotional status is a primary indicator for the time of termination. Improvement and remission of the leukemia will give cause for celebration. If the disease does not remit or transplants fail, the status of the disease may move from a catastrophic to a terminal phase. Changes in the physical course of the disease serve as markers for the clinician. As the individual accommodates to the demands of the disease and either relinquishes the patient role or adapts to the new demands of the disease, the counselor will want to prepare to take leave from the system.

The counselors in both ALL case examples had several treatment episodes with each individual and system. In each case, shifts of physical status and prognosis indicated termination. The counselor for the young man had two different courses of crisis counseling in the progression of the disease: one to help to incorporate the devastation related to the diagnosis, and a second when the young fellow relapsed. The second clinician engaged in three courses of crisis counseling with the elderly woman and her family. The third episode was particularly challenging, since the family described themselves as "fighters." Many in the system were disappointed with the woman's decision to opt for palliative rather than aggressive treatment. The counselor's task to help the family reframe the course of treatment as a courageous decision required a sensitivity to the family's view of themselves. The job of seeing alternative forms of bravery and "fight" was particularly tender territory for the family to incorporate.

The elderly woman provided an indication for the time of termination when she brought a meditation to the counselor and asked her to help communicate its message to her family and health care providers. The meditation said, "Cancer has invaded my body, but it need not invade my spirit. There are scars on my body, but there need not be scars on my heart." The woman said, "I believe this, and if my family and friends can hear and accept this with me, things will be better."

Step III.3. Address Future Sources of Stress

The young artist said it best: "You can never go back. Once you've had leukemia, particularly with a relapse, everything from that point forward looks like leukemia. I wear ALL glasses now. A cold? Leukemia. An ache in my ankle? Leukemia. A bad day at work? Leukemia. Everything looks, sounds, and feels like leukemia. My job is to try and stay aware of what is disease related and what is, at least in my new world, normal."

When an individual has suffered from a catastrophic illness, the world is indeed changed. At best, people who have endured such a disease become good physicians to themselves. They learn the language, the treatment options, and the research related to the illness. The crisis counselor plays an effective role in this stage by helping the individual to mark those times and circumstances that might be particularly stressful.

The young man spoke at one point to the crisis counselor about his relationship with his girlfriend. She had been a stalwart supporter through the course of the illness. The young man wanted to deepen the relationship and was worried that his friend was "staying with me just because she felt sorry for me." He and the counselor were able to address the stress of the nondevelopmental life transition that leukemia brought to bear on the relationship and acknowledged the vulnerability of the couple as they moved into more normative phases of their relationship.

Step III.4. Refer for Continuing Treatment

The crisis counselor referred the young couple to a psychotherapist who specialized in work with couples and families. This therapist encouraged the patient to continue his participation in a support group, where he learned to deepen his affective vocabulary and to find more effective ways to allow others to help him.

The elderly woman's counselor referred the family members to bereavement support groups and helped them to accept the resources of the hospice. The family members were reluctant and felt the referrals were made "too soon," and they needed help to come to terms with the disease's trajectory toward their loved one's death.

There will always be good resources for individuals who suffer from catastrophic illness. The community now holds a premium on support activities for most diseases. Following the woman's death, the family incorporated a yearly tradition of participating in a "Shamrocks for Leukemia Day." They would gather, raise money in memory of her, and have a reunion. As the family lived with her loss, several of the family members took leadership roles in survivor organizations and were able to broaden the support for their loved one's memory.

Step III.5. Exit the System

In the leave-taking, the counselor should be aware that while the crisis may be resolved, the chronicity of dealing with the disease may be alive and active. The leave-taking should include a fair amount of acknowledgment of the strengths and positive attributes of the individual and the support system. The clinician may want to self-disclose to the family personal appreciations regarding the individual's and family's resilience in the presence of the crisis. Should the disease result in the individual's death, it is meaningful to find an appropriately congruent way to express condolence and sympathy.

Chapter 10

Integrating the Stress of Crisis

INTRODUCTION

A client said it best: "This crisis just doesn't make sense. It doesn't fit with any way that I understand the world. It's as though my brain has taken leave from my body and I can't make things fit anymore. I feel so stupid and incompetent. My world has been turned upside down." This gentleman speaks to the existential nature of crisis and its ability to take us out of a grounded, predictable life. While all humans understand that change is natural and developmental, most are less flexible to the nature of change than may be believed. At a bone level, Western culture is based on the dualism of science—that things are either "this" or "that," and what is to be believed must be what can be seen and proven. The dominant culture looks to believe those things that are rational, black and white, and easy to categorize. In order to integrate crisis, dualistic investigations in the world eventually have to be put aside, with all prejudice and assumption, in order to meet the world through intuition. The application of the systemic treatment model allows for this process to unfold. Rather than explaining and analyzing the crisis, the individual is encouraged to describe and understand it.

REFLEXIVITY AND AGENCY

Integration of a crisis focuses on working with the individual's awareness by addressing subjective experience and promoting re-

Crisis Counseling and Therapy
© 2007 by The Haworth Press, Inc. All rights reserved.
doi:10.1300/5953_10

flexivity and a sense of agency. Reflexivity connotes elasticity, resilience, and the capacity to bend without breaking. Agency is defined as an action or intervention that produces a particular result. When an individual loses the ability to return to an original shape after having been stretched, a diminished capacity to be in charge of expected results of ordinary actions emerges. Crisis victims begin to doubt subjective experience and lose an internal worldview, including feelings, perceptions, goals, values, and constructs. Essentially, the individual loses potential. Derived from the Latin word *potenia,* meaning "power," potential is a quality or ability that can be developed, leading to future success or usefulness. It is a capacity to functionally expand into something in the future.

In crisis theory, therapists and clients quickly learn that there are few fixed sets of personal traits and environmental attributes. Essentially, things change. As one man said, "My life was shot to hell in a minute. I had no idea that things could change so drastically, so quickly. This will teach me to believe in predictability! I've lost all sense of control." If nothing else, crisis teaches the transience of life. At its most positive, the crisis can be seen as facilitating an emergence, a becoming, a process of being that which is not fixed or characterized by particular traits. In such an effort, the word *being* is taken in its truest verb form, which implies an active and dynamic process. The individual is approached as a work in progress, and the crisis is a detour along the way that holds a great deal of promise. The psychologist and philosopher Rollo May (1958) called this process *dasein,* which acknowledges consciousness and responsibility for one's own choices. The term connotes human potentiality and the process of becoming, rather than life as static. Crisis theory rests on this premise and stresses interaction among intrapsychic, environmental, interpersonal, and biological elements of experience.

Other than the obvious physical changes exacted by a crisis, what makes the critical experience so difficult to bear? Certain assumptions are made that answer the question. First, human beings are "thrown" into the world in the sense that they find themselves in a given situation over which they have not exercised choice. Since they have been jettisoned into this world without an "exit," there is no sense in attempting to understand the individual separate from the context of the crisis. Yet such a fusion of person and environment increases and electrifies anxiety. Individuals become acutely aware of the need to act but have much less certainty about a basis for decision making. In crisis, individuals lose the beforehand knowledge (with any certainty) of how decisions will turn out, leaving them continually under the threat of making a poor choice.

Inherent in the responsibility of critical choice is the notion of responsibility. The state of being *response-able* carries the anxiety of knowing that serious mistakes can be made. Crisis lowers an individual's awareness of whether a particular choice is good or more troublesome in the long run.

Second, not only can crisis be frightening, it can be immobilizing. When the individuals in crisis are confronted with a sense of meaninglessness and a loss of direction for choice, they may be physically, emotionally, and cognitively still to the point of being stuck. If no meaning can be quickly discerned from the crisis, then there is no basis on which to make a decision. This state limits action.

The parents of a child who died of a glioblastoma brain tumor said, "We couldn't get over the fact that there was no medical treatment for our son. As soon as we learned about the horrible news, we took him to a nationally known university hospital. They provided him with state-of-the-art care and did everything humanly possible to save him. He died anyway. We were so stuck in the notion that something could be done, even when we knew everything had been done. We spent hours on the Internet, searching the medical literature looking for treatments, research, and clinical trials that could have been offered to help our child. Everywhere we turned, we ran into huge stumbling blocks and we were right back where we started. The disease was bigger than any of us and it took our son from us much too soon."

The third assumption related to the pain of crisis speaks of the threat of an individual's sense of nonbeing. If it is believed that humans are mortal, then by necessity the person must act and will eventually die. Death is a negation of being and leaves the individual in an open-ended universe with a realm of possibilities. As Prochaska and Norcross elegantly stated, "Nonbeing is the ground against which the figure of being is created" (1999, p. 102). The ultimate truth that all humans will die provides a theoretical and philosophical foundation for choice. In turn, chance, or the randomness of nature, is the ground that determines the limits of human choice. Crisis challenges the individual in being open to the world because it threatens what is known and predictable. Typically, people believe themselves to be the active agents in directing a personal sense of life. In crisis, this sense of direction is lost and the individual becomes an object determined by forces other than free will.

The parents of the child with the brain tumor continued: "We just didn't ever think that our child would die so soon. We believed that we'd get old and die before our children. That's the natural way that things happen in our world. When he got sick and died so suddenly, both of us lost our way. We had plans for him and for his life. We had hopes and wishes and dreams for how he would grow and how we would all continue to live in this world. After his death, we had to search long and hard to find some sense out of all of this. The crisis of his death has taught us lots of lessons, and now we are involved with an organization that supports other parents of children with brain tumors. As we talk about the lessons we've learned with other parents and families, our pain is less intense and softened. We feel less alone."

For the crisis counselor, the phenomenon called *that which appears* requires a presence to maintain openness and to engage as fully as possible with the client. A tragedy as horrific as these parents' story can make any caring clinician flinch with pain. For the parents to be able to live with the change of life enacted by the crisis, they must change the conceptual and emotional setting of the indisputable situation and place it in another framework which will fit the "facts" equally well, which then changes the entire meaning of the experience. Such a therapeutic task has been spoken of in many different ways. Shakespeare said, "There is nothing either good or bad, but thinking makes it so." The philosopher Epictetus expressed this sense when he said, "It is not things themselves which trouble us, but the opinions that we have about these things."

The crisis counselor is obligated to take what the client brings and facilitate the most palatable "opinion" that can be made of the facts. While this sounds like a simplistic notion, the goal is expressed through a shift of cognition and emotion. The parents' counselor described the process in this way: "It wasn't as though my clients were having difficulty seeing the forest for the trees. They were having difficulty seeing the tree because their noses were up against the bark. As I helped them to tell their story, they began to gain a new perspective. They learned that change could take place even if it was beyond the controllable circumstances of the crisis. As they moved through the crisis counseling process, they were able to feel more flexible. Depending on their viewpoint on a particular day, they could see, feel, and think in different ways which gave both parents more of a sense of choice. The perception of choice felt powerful and engaging and helped them to feel less helpless, even though the reality of the crisis left them feeling so fully and completely out of control. Before the counseling, they felt trapped and anguished. After counseling, they felt more of a sense of wisdom and sadness."

The father of the child reflected on this process, as well: "It is really interesting. I had several people offer me platitudes along the line of 'In every cloud there's a silver lining.' These expressions of sympathy left me feeling patronized and sick to my stomach. I've never felt so misunderstood and as thoroughly dismissed. In my therapy, I learned that the facts could not be refuted. They are what they are and have changed my life forever. I learned that I could find some new definition for the problem. I don't like what I found, but I can live with it better than I could with the feeling of being trapped. I can now identify the feeling and use it as a marker for ways that I need to take care of myself and my family in a different way. I believe that it will take years for me to become comfortable with the feeling, but I'm willing to practice and live with it. I've also learned that once I figured out that the trapped feeling is too close of a replication of the original crisis, I can't feel it anymore without having several possibilities of a way out. Now, that's a relief that I can live with." Once this fellow had found a new solution, his view of "reality" was forever changed for the better.

CONFUSION

Most crisis experiences will be reported by therapists and clients as a confusing time. Crisis disrupts routine; bewilderment is a by-product of the situation or state of disorder. One client described her uncertainty: "I felt like the other shoe was going to drop," she said, "and I had a feeling that when it did, it wouldn't be in my favor." She continued, saying, "I guess I had too many choices and none at all. I learned what it meant to have nowhere to turn. I was so confused that I would give myself a headache trying to figure out my next steps."

To integrate crisis, the client will be encouraged to redefine the incident outside of its obvious and conventional "set" of responses. The parents of the child who died of the brain tumor reflected on this statement: "Once we really did give in to the fact that we did everything that we could, we felt a tremendous sense of relief. To get to that point, though, we needed to go over and over and accept all that we could *not* do. Doesn't that sound strange? That's what our therapist helped us to do—to learn those things that we could not control to keep our child alive. Once we were able to have a glimmer of that realization, we could 'save' him in a different way from keeping him alive at all costs. 'Saving' him began to mean helping him to be more comfortable and helping ourselves to spend the quality time that we had with him through his dying rather than chasing rainbows and quacks on the Internet. That was one of the most confusing and painful times of the whole experience with him. Once we got clear about how to 'save' him, things got much clearer and we had better choices than metaphorically knocking our heads against a brick wall."

Confusion sets the stage for a shift in perspective. Using this definition, confusion becomes a welcome process. Disorientation gives individuals an opportunity to engage with the crisis in a new way. Because of crisis, the context of a conventional response gives way to the misunderstandings that arise out of the event. The result is confusion, which cannot be alleviated by any further information that might have reorganized the pieces of the crisis into traditional, tried-and-true means of understanding. Such a state of confusion is uncomfortable, uncertain, and distressing. The need to find an exit from the confusion, by finding a new frame of reference, makes the individual an eager party in experimenting with new information that may provide relief. In the parents' story, the two folks were able to redefine "save" from a medical cure that would keep their son from dying to a spiritual place where they were able to savor the remaining days of their child's life. Saving, that is, storing memories, further allowed them the wisdom to enter other parents' experience with dying children, and seasoned their sadness with compassion and understanding.

Confusion, then, is a marker for change. Once the concrete issues related to safety in the crisis have been addressed, confusion becomes a therapeutic indicator that an impasse can be broken. Confusion gives the crisis counselor an opportunity to lift the problem out of the symptom viewpoint and into another perspective that does not carry the implication of unchangeability. Out of the client's narrative, a congenial and complementary perspective can be fashioned that will help the crisis client to redefine and recategorize the reality of the critical events. Confusion gives the therapist a chance to help the client to change "the rules of the game." The change is a reinterpretation of reality, and a complex task. Resolution of the problem, by presenting a new definition of reality-based circumstances, induces a new view of the given situation. In the new view, the individual is allowed and encouraged to act accordingly.

FEAR AND ANXIETY

The emotions of fear and anxiety are natural in the presence of crisis. Fear mobilizes the individual to the presence or threat of danger. Its trajectory is harm avoidance. Anxiety electrifies the individual. Its psychological direction points toward relief.

Maintaining control and recognizing a need for a sense of safety and purpose are common and natural responses to living in the world. Many people will report a generalized sense of anxiety and fear in postmodern society and feel that it is more dangerous to be living now than it ever has been. Given this heightened sense of stress, it is difficult to reassure an individual when the stress of crisis is added to the psychological "mix." It is a given truth that, in the presence of crisis, a disconnect occurs between facts and fears. When it comes to the perception of risks, facts are only part of how the individual decides what to be afraid of and how afraid to be.

Biologically, the human brain is built to fear first and think second. This is a survival strategy that alerts the individual to threat and danger. Visual information is channeled into two parts of the brain. The first is the prefrontal cortex, located directly behind the forehead. This area provides reasoning and thinking. The other activated area, the amygdala, holds the brain's key emotion center. Because of the way the brain is constructed, visual information gets to the amygdala before it gets to the prefrontal cortex. Before the reasoning and thinking part of the brain has a chance to consider the facts, the fear center is working to avoid harm and find relief.

One client described her response to crisis as "freaking out." She said, "I'm not that kind of person and have never overreacted to situations. Since the crisis, I am easily scared and feel like I stay on a high-alert mode of operation all of the time. It's even hard to sleep, and I've always felt safe and secure in my own bed."

Fear is a component of stress, and understanding this speaks to the fight-or-flight response that has been taught since Psychology 101. When confronted with the perception of danger, the individual begins to pump adrenaline, speeding up the heart, increasing blood pressure, and quickening breathing. Anxiety then begins to feed on itself, reducing the individual's comfort level in his or her own skin. One client indeed used these words. He said, "I was so anxious, I wanted to jump out of my skin." Another said, "I was on pins and needles all of the time."

Appropriate amounts of anxiety nudge the individual out of complacency. Too much, and the individual becomes knotted in irrationality and will do anything possible to relieve pain. Anxiety alters an individual's cognitive appraisal of a given situation. The term is used to describe the process through which people evaluate the meaning of a specific event with respect to its personal significance. Cognitive appraisal requires thought, which anxiety and fear diminish. The greater the amounts of anxiety and fear, the more rapid the initial appraisal of events; deliberation becomes unnecessary and the individual begins to operate on knee-jerk cues for action. Anxiety and fear motivate the individual toward safety and relief from the perception of threat, which may or may not be fact based. Control of self and environment becomes paramount.

Traumatic events commonly violate the individual sense of control, and subsequent attempts to regain that sense can help to decrease the stressful nature of the situation. When individuals are unable to directly control what happens to them, regaining perceptions of being in charge, even indirectly, through any number of attributions, is known to be helpful. This has been called secondary control and is defined as "aligning oneself with existing realities and accepting as unchangeable the nature of the situation" (Rothbaum, Weisz, & Snyder, 1982,

p. 7). Secondary control increases in the face of failed efforts to gain direct control, which is evident in the presence of crisis.

This suggests that attributions made to the crisis event can influence fear and anxiety. The more the sense of control, the lower the fear and anxiety. When an individual feels out of control, the emotional responses of fear and anxiety rise. A sense of imposition and intrusion lowers this personal sense of control.

Trust is an additional emotional factor that influences fear and anxiety. Individuals trust certain sources more than others. Operationally defined as "promises made are promises kept," the sense of trust can be easily broken in the presence of crisis. The perception of competence affects trust. The counselor who is identified as an expert in helping others through trauma has more of a halo of credibility than an individual identified as friend.

Newness and dread also affect fear and anxiety. A new situation is an uncertain situation. As one fellow said about a crisis involving a cancer diagnosis, "It's not that I lost my way. I didn't have a way to start with. I've never been in anything like this in my life. I never had anything more than a physical and had no idea what to do or think about cancer. I didn't even know what type of physician that I needed to contact." Dread also compounds the fear of newness. "I knew it was bad, and dreaded seeing any of my doctors coming around the corner. They always had bad news," the client said. Living with the crisis situation for awhile potentially gives greater understanding. Understanding has the capacity to lower dread.

The more complicated the risk and the less the individual understands its impact, the more natural the emergence of fear seems. The fellow diagnosed with cancer continued, saying, "I was always taught if it walked like a snake and talked like a snake, it was usually a snake. I believed the same thing about cancer. All I knew when the doctor said the word 'cancer,' I said to myself, 'I'm toast.' I was terrified and ready to go ahead and be put out to pasture the minute I heard the diagnosis. Fortunately, I've had good people who have been patient and willing to teach me about reasonable fears associated with my disease. I can simplify all of the medical processes now and can categorize things in my language—not in a complicated medical vernacular. That has been particularly helpful in calming me down. One of the medicines I took caused arrhythmias. Once I could understand it as my heart skipping a beat every now and then, I was able to feel better."

In summary, the best way to reduce the danger to any given risk is to learn basic facts from a reliable, neutral source, so that the rational side of perceptions can hold their own in the contest with natural emotions created by the crisis. The better able the individual is at keeping perception of risk closer in line with what the risks actually are, the happier and more settled the individual will be.

HELPLESSNESS

Survivors of rape, incest, and natural disasters often present an array of symptoms that can be recognized and diagnosed as an anxiety or post-traumatic stress disorder. Such symptoms as sleep disturbance, intrusive memories, flashbacks, and hypervigilance contribute to the diminished capacity of daily living. Loss of personal control, social withdrawal, and loss of meaning have been identified as psychological disruptions resulting from crisis. As has been noted, such symptoms may have lifelong consequences.

In the last two decades, there has been an increasing amount of clinical and scientific interest in the phenomenon of helplessness as a crisis response. Several writers have used the concept of "learned helplessness," coined by Seligman in 1975 as a paradigm for understanding the continuing sense of lost personal control in response to crisis. Such helplessness may be accompanied by a lowered sense of self-esteem, a general disinterest in life, and an increased probability of additional victimization. Seligman reported the condition of helplessness to be a general response of individuals who cease to appreciate the potential efficacy of their actions to influence daily life in adaptive ways.

It is assumed in crisis theory that individual responses to crisis events vary widely, that not all events are equally traumatic for all individuals, and that individual differences in crisis response and recovery are the result of a complex interaction among person, event, and environmental factors. It is also assumed that the core event defined as the crisis will involve inescapable pain.

This sense of pain is amplified when an individual feels helpless because of a lack of options and by finding few, if any, alternative choices to a given situation. For example, the options for a battered wife are limited. She can remain with her children in an intermittently violent home. She can call potentially disinterested authorities and provoke certain violence in the home. She can seek a shelter for battered women but will have to adhere to rules that may exclude living arrangements for children over a certain age. These choices will lead to an increased sense of despondency and despair, not security and the reassurance that life can be better because of her choices. When the environment does not offer alternatives to continued victimization, helplessness emerges.

Some individuals who appear helpless in the presence of crisis may lack the skills needed to resolve the problem. In the context of crisis counseling, the clinician is obligated to assess personal levels of competencies and individual capacity to master complex skills. For example, elderly and handicapped individuals may lack the physical strength to act on their own behalf. Sexually abused young children may be unable to think in a sufficiently abstract way to formulate questions needed to tell others about their predicament.

Some individuals will feel helpless when they do have a sense of true possible alternatives, and the skills necessary to implement solutions, but find themselves blocked by the ineffectiveness of others. This frustrated sense of agency places psychological pressure to abandon efforts at empowerment and efficacy.

For example, a battered woman filed an abuse petition with the court system and obtained a restraining order only to find that the police were not responsive to the implementation of such an order. When her children were abducted by her husband and she was severely beaten, she was blamed by the police for not taking more effective action. She reported feeling helpless.

There are individuals in crisis who appear helpless because they believe that they are not deserving of better. Self-esteem remains low even when the individual has the skills to cope in a more adaptive fashion. This characterological self-blame causes the individual to assume that continued victimization is justifiable punishment for presumed inadequacies.

As an example, a young man who grew up in an alcoholic home was criticized relentlessly. When he found himself in a crisis situation, he responded with a sense of self-blame, saying variations of

"I deserve to have this happen to me." The clear counseling intervention was oriented to providing the individual a sense of efficacy by neutralizing the internal critical voice of his long deceased father.

MOVING TOWARD RECOVERY

Harvey and Falnnery (1991) identify seven attributes which characterize crisis recovery. Recovery is initially defined by the individual's resumption of personal control of the remembering process. Second, memory is linked with affect, with a third step taken when the affect evoked by recalling the crisis is bearable. These affects are tolerable and no longer threaten to overwhelm the individual as they move into more of a sense of personal mastery.

The fourth step of the move to recovery revolves around the individual's understanding of the crisis and of symptomatic responses. Situations and stimuli that stimulate memory of the crisis can be identified and avoided or incorporated. When unavoidable, they can be anticipated and prepared for. The fifth factor in recovery is improved self-esteem. Self-care routines are enhanced, and self-blame is replaced by self-regard. The sixth indicator is the capacity to form and maintain safe attachments. Isolation is resolved and trust and compassion for self and others increase. The individual, through grief, is able to assign some life-affirming meaning to the crisis event, and a sense of purposeful meaning in life again develops.

As stated, recovery from crisis is ultimately dependent on the relevance of various aspects of the individual's efforts to cope with unwanted life events and aversive life conditions. There are a number of aspects to meaning that are critical in people's adjustment to crisis. Such adjustment is conceptualized in a variety of ways.

Meaning can be defined as a perception of significance. It refers to beliefs that organize, justify, and direct a person's striving. Meaning is motivational and is typically framed in terms of its goals. People's goals represent their current identity and their future ideal selves. By definition, goals are hierarchical and give the individual a sense of purpose, even though they may not be acutely aware of some of the more unconscious pursuits of satisfaction.

There are two levels of meaning that are operational during crisis. Global meaning encompasses a person's enduring beliefs and valued goals. It is the awareness of order, coherence, and purpose in one's existence. It implies the pursuit and attainment of worthwhile goals and is accompanied by a sense of fulfillment. On the other hand, situational meaning is formed in the interaction between a person's global meaning and the circumstances of a particular person-environment transaction. Situational meaning encompasses an initial appraisal of the meaning of an event and the search for meaning, either or both of which may affect global meaning. In terms of situational meaning, meaning refers to the significance of a particular occurrence in terms of its relevance.

On further explanation, global meaning refers to the most abstract and generalized level of meaning. It includes an individual's basic goals and fundamental assumptions of self and expectations of the world. It influences an individual's understanding of the past and the present, as well as his or her expectations regarding the future. It is a personal theory of reality and of the assumptive world. Global meaning allows the individual to estimate the benevolence of the world and helps the individual to gauge justice and fairness in response to crisis. The sense of justice has implications for beliefs about the degree to which the world is predictable, understandable, and, perhaps, controllable.

Such beliefs about control are related to a sense of the self and control. Control refers to the extent to which individuals believe they are in charge of destiny and important outcomes. There is a pronounced tendency for humans to search for correlations between actions and outcomes. Generally, individuals have an illusion of control and an exaggerated sense of ability to control chance outcomes. It is the illusion that is shattered in the presence of crisis. People often assume that they can directly control their world, or that they can minimize the likelihood of unfavorable outcomes by engaging in "proper behaviors." These behaviors are tied to a sense of self-worth, which consists of evaluations of one's essential goodness and morality, and evaluations of effectiveness of personal action.

Said again, people derive beliefs about themselves in relation to the world from their understanding of the benevolence, controllability, and fairness of the world and personal beliefs regarding self-worth. Crisis is disruptive to this derivative process. For example, an individual who believes that the world is good and fair may tend to minimize the likelihood that bad things may happen to them. A man who was diagnosed with cancer, for example, complained that "this just isn't fair. I've never done anything to justify my suffering."

Humans have a fundamental need for stability and predictability. A coherence of conceptual systems leads to the tendency for an individual to fit new data into existing beliefs, rather than to modify personal belief systems to fit the stimuli. This is the frustration of crisis. The need for stability requires that the cognitions that maintain a person's beliefs remain flexible in order to accommodate the variety of stimuli encountered in daily life. People will maintain their beliefs by interpreting situations in ways that are congruent with preexisting understandings of the world. Individuals will tend to seek out experiences that confirm their global beliefs, even if these experiences confirm beliefs that are negative. The colloquial "See? I told you so" response supports this tenet.

Situational meaning refers to the interaction of an individual's global beliefs and goals in the circumstances of a particular person-environment transaction. For example, when confronted with the fact of a loved one's death, the initial meaning of that event and the eventual meaning that the individual may derive from it are influenced by the survivor's global meaning. From the perspective of stress and coping theory, situational meaning involves the appraisal of person-environment transactions, which in turn influences how people cope with the demands of those transactions and their outcomes.

In a person-environment transaction, the individual makes an initial cognitive appraisal, where the meaning of the event is evaluated with respect to its personal significance. This appraisal is influenced by the relevance of the event to the individual's belief, commitments, and goals, and by options regarding what can be done about the situation. People make rapid initial appraisals of events; deliberation is unnecessary. Appraisal patterns are based on prior knowledge of and beliefs about certain conditions and their consequences for well-being. The appraisal also has a motivational quality that directs behavior in relation to the importance of the beliefs, goals, or commitments that are threatened in a crisis.

Incongruence, also known as dissonance, between the individual's interpretation of events and its global meaning, leads to a sense of unpredictability and causes the person to question the viability of self-

and worldviews. For example, a man questioned his religious beliefs following the destruction of his community by a tornado. The crisis provided evidence to this fellow that he was, in fact, vulnerable to disaster and not entirely in control of his fate.

Crisis events that impede or render valued goals untenable can challenge an individual's sense of meaning at its most fundamental level. The more central a goal is to an individual, the more likely its obstruction will affect the individual's sense of meaning by diminishing the sense of purpose and direction. The more this occurs, the more distress ensues.

A young man provides a graphic example of this. He played football throughout his middle and high school career and received a college scholarship for athletics. His life's goal was to play for a professional football team. He worked hard and held records for his position as an athlete. Every waking activity was oriented to the acquisition of skills needed to reach his goal. He had dreams of earning income, buying a home for his parents, and mentoring younger boys. In his senior year of college, he suffered a spinal cord injury during a play-off game with a rival team. While he eventually recovered mobility, his football career was ended. This caused an extraordinary degree of distress and pain. His central goal was frustrated and his life trajectory was altered.

MEANING MAKING AND COPING WITH CRISIS

People typically have a number of both emotion-focused and problem-focused strategies available to cope with events they have appraised as stressful. As has been illustrated, crisis circumstances are amenable to active efforts to solve the problem or change the situation. For circumstances that are unchangeable, the impact of the crisis is buffered by responses that control the meaning of the problem. The major task in the management of meaning is to reduce the incongruence between the appraised meaning of the crisis and the person's preexisting global meaning in terms of beliefs and goals.

The resolution of a crisis can be defined when the discrepancy between an individual's current situation and desired goals is reduced to a manageable level. This idea is consistent with cognitive dissonance theory, which holds a primary importance in maintaining working constructions of reality.

The meaning-making process is further defined as successful when an individual achieves reconciliation either by changing the appraised meaning of the situation to assimilate it into preexisting global meaning or by changing beliefs or goals to accommodate the crisis. Such coping processes are continuously mediated by cognitive reappraisals. These appraisals decrease the threatening and harmful aspects of the event and sometimes can even increase its positive aspects.

In the process of coming to terms with crisis, individuals will find meaning as they search for and find some reason why an event occurred and who or what is responsible for its occurrence. Such activity simply helps to make sense out of unfortunate crisis situations. This process, known as reattribution, is positively associated with indicators of favorable adjustment to crisis.

The reattribution process generally begins early in the coping process with the narrative, that is, the telling of the story. Theorists believe that early in crisis, people will begin to make automatic, unconscious appraisals of situations related to cause and effect. By giving voice to thought and emotion, individuals in crisis can shift in the struggle to understand and will find more palatable explanations for the crisis. The shift will continue throughout the counseling process until the individual finds an acceptable, congruent version to situational and global meaning.

The process through which individuals integrate the meaning of a specific situation with belief and personal philosophy tempers and seasons the individual. As one man said, following the crisis revolving the death of his child, "I am a sadder, but wiser man." Positive beliefs about the world come to be seen with maturity, wisdom, and greater tensile strength. Coping effectively with stressful crisis experiences allows people to emerge from crisis with new coping skills, closer relationships with family and friends, broader priorities, and a richer appreciation of life.

The man whose child died continued, saying, "I have learned to think things through in a different way. I am a better problem solver and have learned many lessons about how to ask for and accept help from others. I now know what Tennessee Williams described when he talked about 'the kindness of strangers.' I have a deeper understanding of my emotional life, and know better how to monitor and regulate my feelings so that I can live with some degree of authenticity." These changes are not uncommon.

The extent to which people in crisis are able to integrate the appraised meaning of an event to their daily functioning is related to psychological adjustment. This is consistent with the thought that a general sense of coherence is linked to better adjustment. This integration leads to acceptance and allows people to move on.

References

Aguilera, D. C. & Messick, J. M. (1986). *Crisis intervention: Theory and methodology* (5th ed.). St. Louis, MO: C.V. Mosby Company.

Albom, M. (1997). *Tuesdays with Morrie: An old man, a young man, and life's greatest lesson.* New York: Doubleday.

Allport, G. W. (1937). *Personality: A psychological interpretation.* New York: Holt.

Allport, G. W. (1950). *The individual and his religion: A psychological interpretation.* New York: Macmillan.

Altmaier, E. M. (2002, April). The debriefing controversy: Does psychological debriefing do more harm than good? *Clinician's Research Digest, 20*(4), 5.

Anderson, C. M. & Stewart, S. (1983). *Resistance in family therapy.* New York: Guilford Press.

Anderson, H., Goolishian, H., & Windermand, L. (1986). Problem determined systems: Toward transformation in family therapy. *Journal of Strategic and Systemic Therapies, 5*(4), 1-13.

APA (2000). *Diagnostic and statistical manual of mental disorders* (4th ed., text revisions). Washington, DC: American Psychiatric Association.

Arredondo, P., Toporek, R., Brown, S., Jones, J., Locke, D., Sanchez, J., et al. (1996). Operationalization of the multicultural counseling competencies. *Journal of Multicultural Counseling and Development, 24*, 42-78.

Bandura, A. (1977). *Social learning theory.* Englewood Cliffs, NJ: Prentice Hall.

Bandura, A. (1978). The self system in reciprocal determinism. *American Psychologist, 33*, 344-358.

Bandura, A. (1982). Self efficacy mechanism in human agency. *American Psychologist, 37*, 122-147.

Bandura, A. (1986). *Social foundations of thought and action: A social cognitive theory.* Englewood Cliffs, NJ: Prentice Hall.

Bard, M. & Sangrey, D. (1979). *The crisis victim's book.* New York: Basic Books.

Barrett, R. K. (1995). Contemporary African-American funeral rites and traditions. In L. A. Despelder & A. L. Strickland (Eds.), *The path ahead: Readings in death and dying* (pp. 80-92). Mountain View, CA: Mayfield Publishing.

Barrett, R. K. (1998). Sociocultural consideration for working with blacks experiencing loss and grief. In K. Doka (Ed.), *Living with grief: How we are, how we grieve* (pp. 83-96). Washington, DC: Taylor & Francis.

Bateson, G. (1992). *Sacred unity: Further steps to an ecology of mind.* New York: Harper-Collins.

Crisis Counseling and Therapy
© 2007 by The Haworth Press, Inc. All rights reserved.
doi:10.1300/5953_11

Beck, A. T. (1990). Beck Depression Inventory. Washington, DC: The Psychological Corporation; Harcourt, Brace, Jovanovich.

Beck, A. T., Sokol, L., Clark, D. A., Berchick, R., & Wright, F. (1992). A crossover study of focused cognitive therapy for panic disorder. *American Journal of Psychiatry, 149,* 778-783.

Boss, P. (1999). *Ambiguous loss.* Cambridge, MA: Harvard University Press.

Boss, P. (2001). *Family stress management* (2nd ed.). Newbury Park, CA: Sage.

Brammer, L. M. & Shostrum, E. L. (1982). *Therapeutic psychology: Fundamentals of counselling and psychotherapy* (4th ed.). Englewood Cliffs, NJ: Prentice Hall.

Brewin, C. R. (2001). A cognitive neuroscience account of posttraumatic stress disorder and its treatment. *Behavior Research and Therapy, 39,* 373-393.

Brewin, C. R., Dalgleish, T., & Joseph, S. (1996). A dual representation theory of posttraumatic stress disorder. *Psychological Review, 103,* 670-686.

Bruner, J. (1986). *Actual minds, possible worlds.* Cambridge, MA: Harvard University Press.

Bugental, J. (1987). *The art of the psychotherapist.* New York: Norton.

Burgess, A. W. & Holmstrom, L. L. (1985). Rape trauma syndrome and post traumatic stress response. In A.W. Burgess (Ed.), *Rape and sexual assault: A research handbook.* New York: Garland.

Burnham, B. (1965). Separation anxiety. *Archives of General Psychiatry, 13,* 346-351.

Burns, D. D. (1989). Burns Anxiety Inventory. *The feeling good handbook.* Boston, MA: Brooks/Cole.

Campbell, K. M. & Hills, A. M. (2001). Effect of timing of critical incident stress debriefing (CISD) on posttraumatic symptoms. *Journal of Traumatic Stress, 14,* 327-340.

Caplan, G. (1964). *Principles of preventive psychiatry.* New York: Basic Books.

Carnes, P. & Rening, L. (1994). *27 tasks for changing compulsive, out-of-control, and inappropriate sexual behavior: Therapist's guide.* Minneapolis, MN: Positive Living Press.

Carver, C. S. & Scheier, M. F. (1990). Principles of self-regulation: Action and emotion. In E. T. Higgins & R. M. Sorrentino (Eds.), *Handbook of motivation and cognition: Foundations of social behavior* (Vol. 2, pp. 3-52). New York: Guilford Press.

Corey, M. S. & Corey, G. (1998). *Becoming a helper* (3rd ed.). Pacific Grove, CA: Brooks/Cole.

Cove, E., Eiseman, M., & Popkin, S. J. (2005). *Resilient children: Literature review and evidence from the Hope VI Panel Study.* Washington, DC: The Urban Institute Metropolitan Housing and Communities Policy Center.

Davis, A. D. (1998). *Providing critical incident stress debriefing (CISD) to individuals and communities in situational crisis.* Washington, DC: The American Academy of Experts in Traumatic Stress.

Dowd, E. T. & Olsen, D. H. (1985). Contingency contracting. In A. S. Bellack & M. Hersen (Eds.), *Dictionary of behavior therapy techniques* (pp. 70-73). New York: Permagon.

Eagle, G. T. (1998). An investigative model for brief term intervention in the treatment of psychological trauma. *International Journal of Psychotherapy, 3*(2), 135-139.

Ehlers, A., Macrecker, A., & Boggs, A. (2000). Posttraumatic stress disorder following political imprisonment: The role of mental defeat, alienation, and perceived permanent change. *Journal of Abnormal Psychology, 109,* 45-55.

Ellis, A. (1980). Rational-emotive therapy and cognitive therapy: Similarities and differences. *Cognitive Therapy and Research, 4,* 293-300.

Eliot, T. S. (1936). *Selected writings.* New York: Winggold Press.

Erikson, E. H. (1959). *Identity and the life cycle [Psychological Issues* 1(1)]. New York: International Universities Press.

Erikson, E. H. (1963). The A-B-C method of crisis management. *Mental Hygiene, 52,* 87-89.

Everly, G. S., Jr. (1995). The role of critical incident stress debriefing (CISD) process in disaster counseling. *Journal of Mental Health Counseling, 17,* 278-290.

Everly, G. S., Jr. & Mitchell, J. T. (2000). The debriefing controversy and crisis intervention: A review of lexical and substantive issues. *International Journal of Emergency Mental Health, 2,* 211-225.

Foa, E. (1998). *Treating the trauma of rape (cognitive-behavioral therapy for PTSD).* New York: Guilford Press.

Foucault, M. (1980). *Power/knowledge: Selected interviews and other writings.* New York: Pantheon Books.

Fowler, J. W. (1991). Stages in faith consciousness. In F. K. Oser & W. O. Scarlett (Eds.), *New directions for child development: Special issue on religious development in childhood and adolescence* (Vol. 52, pp. 27-45). San Francisco: Jossey-Bass.

Frank, J. D. & Frank, J. B. (1991). *Persuasion and healing.* Baltimore, MD: Johns Hopkins University Press.

Frears, L. H. & Schneider, J. M. (1981). Exploring loss and grief within a holistic framework. *Personnel and Guidance Journal, 59*(2), 341-345.

Freud, S. & Breuer, J. (1955). Studies on hysteria. In J. Strachey (Ed. & Trans.), *The standard edition of the complete psychological works of Sigmund Freud* (Vol. 2). London: Hogarth Press. (Original work published 1895.)

Friedrich, W. N. (1990). *Psychotherapy of sexually abused children and their families.* New York: Norton Press.

Friedrich, W. N. (1991). *Casebook of sexual abuse treatment.* New York: Norton Press.

Fromm, E. (1966). *You shall be gods.* Greenwich, CT: Fawcett.

Gallup, G. & Linday, R. (1999). *The Gallup poll: Public opinion 1999.* Wilmington, DE: Scholarly Resources.

Garfield, S. L. (1986). Research on client variables in psychotherapy. In S. L. Garfield & A. E. Bergin (Eds.), *Handbook of psychotherapy and behavior change* (3rd ed.). New York: Wiley.

Gartner, R. B. (1999). *Betrayed as boys: Psychodynamic treatment of sexually abused men.* New York: Guilford Press.

Gendlin, E. (1974). Client-centered and experiential psychotherapy. In D. Wexler & L. N. Rice (Eds.), *Innovations in client centered therapy.* New York: Wiley.

Gilfus, M. E. (1999). The price of the ticket: A survivor-centered appraisal of trauma theory. *Violence Against Women, 5*(11), 1238-1258.

Glen, M. (1971). Separation anxiety: When the therapist leaves the patient. *American Journal of Psychotherapy, 25,* 437-446.

Goodyear, R. K. (1981). Termination as a loss experience for the counselor. *Personnel and Guidance Journal, 59,* 347-350.

Greenberg, L. S., Rice, L. N., & Elliott, R. (1993). *Facilitating emotional change: The moment-by-moment process.* New York: Guilford Press.

Hall, T. W. & Edwards, J. K. (2002). The spiritual assessment inventory: A theistic model and measure for assessing spiritual development. *Journal for Scientific Study of Religion, 41*(2), 341-357.

Harvey, M. R. & Falnnery, R. B. (1991). Psychological trauma and learned helplessness: Seligman's paradigm reconsidered. *Psychotherapy, 28*(2), 374-378.

Headington, B. J. (1981). Understanding a core experience: Loss. *Personnel and Guidance Journal, 59,* 338-341.

Hebb, D. (1995). Parenting. In Siegel, D. J. & Hartwell, M. (2003). *Parenting from the inside out* (pp. 34-46). New York: Basic Books.

Hendricks, J. E. & McKean, J. B. (1995). *Crisis intervention: Contemporary issues for onsite interveners.* Springfield, IL: Thomas.

Herman, J. (1992). *Trauma and recovery: The aftermath of violence, from domestic abuse to political terror.* New York: Basic Books.

Hoff, L. (1995). *People in crisis: Understanding and helping* (2nd ed.). Los Angeles, CA: Addison Publishing Co.

Hoffman, L. (1981). *Foundations of family therapy.* New York: Basic Books.

Holmes, J. & Rahe, H. (1967). The social readjustment rating scale. *Journal of Psychosomatic Research, 2,* 213-218.

Hurn, H. T. (1971). Toward a paradigm of the terminal phase. *Journal of the American Psychoanalytic Association, 19,* 332-348.

Imes, S., Clance, P., Gailis, A., & Atkeson, E. (2002). Mind's response to the body's betrayal: Gestalt/existential therapy for clients with chronic or life-threatening illness. *Journal of Clinical Psychology/In Session: Chronic Illness, 58*(11), 1361-1373.

James, R. K. & Gilliland, B. E. (2005). *Crisis intervention strategies* (5th ed.). Pacific Grove, CA: Brooks/Cole.

James, W. (1961). *The varieties of religious experience.* New York: Random House.

Janosik, E. H. (1984). *Crisis counseling: A contemporary approach.* Monterey, CA: Jones and Bartlett.

Johnson, K. (1989). *Trauma in the lives of children.* Almada, CA: Hunter House.

Johnson, M. E. (1988). Influences of gender and sex role orientation on help-seeking attitudes. *Journal of Psychology, 122*(3), 237-241.

Jones, S. L. (1994). A constructive relationship for religion with the science and profession of psychology. *American Psychologist, 49,* 184-199.

Jung, C. G. (1938). *Psychology and religion.* London: Yale University Press.

Kandel, E. (1998). A new intellectual framework for psychiatry. *American Journal of Psychiatry, 155,* 457-469.

Kanel, K. (1999). *A guide to crisis intervention.* Pacific Grove, CA: Brooks/Cole.

Kanfer, F. H. (1980). Self-management methods. In F. H. Kanfer & A. P. Goldstein (Eds.), *Helping people change* (pp. 188-201). New York: Permagon.

Kempler, W. (1973). *Principles of gestalt family therapy.* Salt Lake City, UT: Desert Press.

Kessen, W. (1965). *The child.* New York: Wiley.

Kirkpatrick, L. A., Kellas, S., & Shillito, D. (1993, August). *Loneliness and perceptions of social support from God.* Paper presented at the 101st Annual Convention of the American Psychological Association, Toronto, Ontario, Canada.

Kirschenbaum, D. S. (1987). Self-regulatory failure: A review with clinical implications. *Clinical Psychology Review, 7,* 77-104.

Korner, I. N. (1973). Crisis reduction and the psychological consultant. In G. A. Specter & W. L. Claiborn (Eds.), *Crisis intervention* (pp. 53-65). New York: Behavioral Publications.

Lazarus, A. A. (1981). *Behavior therapy and beyond.* New York: Wiley and Sons.

Lifton, R. J. (1993). From Hiroshima to the Nazi doctors: The evolution of psychoformative approaches to understanding traumatic stress syndrome. In J. P. Wilson & R. Raphael (Eds.), *International handbook of traumatic stress syndromes* (pp. 11-23). New York: Plenum Press.

Lindemann, E. (1956). The meaning of crisis in the individual and family. *Teachers' College Record, 57,* 310.

Lindsey, C.K. (2005). Short term crisis counselling. In James, R.K. & Gilliland, B.F. Eds., *Crisis intervention strategies* (5th ed.). Pacific Grove, CA: Brooks/Cole; pp. 112-114.

Maholick, L. T. & Turner, D. H. (1979). Termination: That difficult farewell. *American Journal of Psychotherapy, 33*(4), 583-591.

Mahoney, M. (1995). *Human change process.* New York: Basic Books.

Mahoney, M. J. (1977). Reflections on the cognitive learning trend in psychotherapy. *American Psychologist, 32,* 5-13.

Marmor, J. (1980). Crisis intervention and short-term dynamic psychotherapy. In Davanko, H. (Ed.), *Short-term psychotherapy* (pp. 237-243). New York: Jason Aronson.

Martin, E. S. & Schurtman, R. (1985). Termination anxiety as it affects the therapist. *Psychotherapy: Theory, Research, and Practice, 22,* 92-96.

Marx, J. A. (1983). An exploratory study of the termination of individual counseling in a university counseling center [Doctoral dissertation, University of Maryland, 1983]. *Dissertation Abstracts International, 44,* 3938B.

Marx, J. A. & Gelso, C. J. (1987). Termination of individual counseling in a university counseling center. *Journal of Counseling Psychology, 34,* 3-9.

Maslow, A. H. (1971). *Religions, values, and peak-experiences.* New York: Viking.

Maton, K. I. (1989). The stress buffering role of spiritual support: Cross sectional and prospective investigations. *Journal for the Scientific Study of Religion, 28,* 310-323.

May, R. (1958). *Existence.* New York: Basic Books.

May, R. (1981). *Freedom and destiny.* New York: Norton.

Mayou, R. A., Ehlers, A., & Hobbs, M. (2000). Psychological debriefing for road traffic accident victims: Three year followup of a randomized controlled trial. *British Journal of Psychiatry, 176,* 589-593.

McGoldrick, M. & Gerson, R. (1985). *Genograms in family assessment.* New York: Norton.

Melnick, J. & Nevis, S. M. (1998). Diagnosing in the here and now: A gestalt therapy approach. In L. Greenberg, G. Lietaer, & J. C. Watson (Eds.), *Handbook of experiential psychotherapy* (pp. 247-260). New York: Guilford Press.

Menahem, S. E. (1996). The care of "anger and hurt": Rogers and the development of spiritual psychotherapy. In B. A. Farber, D. C. Brink, & P. M. Raskin (Eds.), *The psychotherapy of Carl Rogers* (pp. 322-333). New York: Guilford Press.

Michenbaum, D. & Fitzpatrick, D. (1993). *Cognitive behavior modification.* New York: Plenum.

Miller, A. (1994). *Prisoners of childhood.* New York: Basic Books.

Miller, G. (1999). The development of the spiritual focus in counselling and counsellor education. *Journal of Counseling and Development, 77*(4), 498-501.

Miller, G. (2003). *Incorporating spirituality in counseling and psychotherapy: Theory and technique.* Hoboken, NJ: John Wiley and Sons, Inc.

Miller, W. & Thoresen, C. (2003). Spirituality, religion, and health: An emerging research field. *American Psychologist, 58*(1), 24-74.

Minuchin, S. (1974). *Families and family therapy.* Cambridge, MA: Harvard University Press.

Mosak, H. H. & Maniacci, M. P. (1998). *Tactics in counseling and psychotherapy.* Itasca, IL: F.E. Peacock Publishers.

Myer, R. A. (2001). *Assessment for crisis intervention: A triage assessment model.* Belmont, CA: Brooks/Cole.

Myers, D. G. (2000). The funds, family, and faith of happy people. *American Psychologist, 55,* 56-67.

Norcross, J. C. (1990). An eclectic definition of psychotherapy. In J. K. Zeig & W. M. Munion (Eds.), *What is psychotherapy?* San Francisco: Jossey-Bass.

Pargament, K. I., Smith, B. W., Koenig, H. G., & Perez, L. (1998). Patterns of positive and negative religious coping with major life stressors. *Journal for the Scientific Study of Religion, 37,* 710-724.

Peake, T., Bouduin, C., & Archer, R. (1988). *Brief psychotherapies: Changing frames of mind.* Newbury Park, CA: Sage.

Pedersen, P. B. & Locke, D. C. (1996). *Cultural and diversity issues in counseling.* Greensboro, NC: ERIC Counseling & Student Services Clearinghouse.

Perry, J. (1993). Mourning and funeral customs of African-Americans. In Irish, D. P., Lundquist,K. F., & Nelson, V. F. (Eds.), *Ethnic Variations in Dying, Death, and Grief* (pp. 51-65). Washington, DC: Taylor & Francis.

Piaget, J. (1983). Piaget's theory. In P. Mussen (Ed.), *Handbook of child psychology* (Vol. 1). New York: Wiley.

Polster, E. (1995). *A population of selves.* San Francisco: Jossey-Bass.

Prochaska, J. O. (1979). *Systems of psychotherapy: A transtheoretical analysis.* Chicago: Dorsey.

Prochaska, J. O. & Norcross, J. C. (1994). *Systems of psychotherapy*. Pacific Grove, CA: Brooks/Cole.

Prochaska, J. O. & Norcross, J. C. (1999). *Systems of psychotherapy: A trans-theoretical analysis* (4th ed.). Pacific Grove, CA: Brooks/Cole.

Quintana, S. M. & Holahan, W. (1992). Termination in short-term counseling: Comparison of successful and unsuccessful cases. *Journal of Counseling Psychology, 39,* 299-305.

Rainer, J. P. (1998). A family systems approach to grief. In L. VandeCreek (Ed.), *Innovations in clinical practice: A source book* (Vol. 16, pp. 179-190). Sarasota, FL: Professional Resource Press.

Rainer, J. P. (2002). Bent but not broken: An introduction to the issue on chronic illness. *Journal of Clinical Psychology/In Session: Chronic Illness, 58*(11), 1347-1350.

Rainer, J. P. & McMurry, P. E. (2002). Caregiving at the end of life. In J. P. Rainer *Journal of Clinical Psychology/In Session: Chronic Illness, 58*(11), 1421-1431.

Richards, P. S. & Bergin, A. E. (1997). *A spiritual strategy for counseling and psychotherapy*. Washington, DC: American Psychological Association.

Rogers, C. R. (1980). *A way of being*. Boston: Houghton Mifflin.

Rose, S., Bisson, J., & Wessely, S. (2001). Psychological debriefing for preventing post traumatic stress disorder (PTSD) [Cochrane Review Abstract]. *Cochrane Library, 4.*

Rothbaum, F., Weisz, J. R., & Snyder, S. S. (1982). Changing the world and changing the self: A two-process model of perceived control. *Journal of Personality and Social Psychology, 42,* 5-37.

Rutter, M. (1985). Resilience in the face of adversity: Protective factors and resistance to psychiatric disorder. *British Journal of Psychiatry, 147,* 598-611.

Sartre, J. P. (1946). *Existentialism and humanism*. London: Metheun.

Schneider, J. (1984). *Stress, loss, and grief*. Baltimore, MD: University Park Press.

Schneider, K. J. (1998). Toward a science of the heart: Romanticism and the revival of psychology. *American Psychologist, 53,* 277-289.

Schneidman, E. (1973). Crisis intervention: Some thoughts and perspectives. In G. A. Specter & W. L. Claiborn (Eds.), *Crisis Intervention* (pp. 9-15). New York: Behavioral Publications.

Seligman, M. E. (1975). *On depression, development, and death*. San Francisco: Freeman.

Selye, H. (1975). *Stress without distress*. Scarborough: Signet.

Shafranske, E. P. & Gorsuch, R. L. (1984). California psychologists' religiosity and psychotherapy. *Journal of Transpersonal Psychology, 16,* 231-241.

Shafranske, E. P. & Malony, H. N. (1996). Religion and the clinical practice of psychology: A case for inclusion. In E. P. Shafranske (Ed.), *Religion and the clinical practice of psychology* (pp. 561-586). Washington, DC: American Psychological Association.

Shapiro, E. (2002). Chronic illness as a family process: A social-developmental approach to promoting resilience. *Journal of Clinical Psychology/In Session: Chronic Illness, 58*(11), 1375-1385.

Shapiro, F. (1996). Eye movement desensitization and reprocessing (EMDR): Evaluation of controlled PTSD research. *Journal of Behavior Therapy and Experimental Psychiatry, 27,* 209-218.

Siegel, D. (1995). Memory, trauma, and psychotherapy: A cognitive science view. *Journal of psychotherapy practice and research, 42*(2), 93-112.

Slaikeu, K. A. (1990). *Crisis intervention: A handbook for practice and research* (2nd ed.). Boston: Allyn & Bacon.

Smokowski, P. R. (1998). Prevention and intervention strategies for promoting resilience in disadvantaged children. *Social Service Review, 72*(3), 337-364.

Solomon, R. M., Gerrity, E. T., & Muff, A. M. (1992). Efficacy of treatments for post traumatic stress disorder. *JAMA, 268,* 633-638.

Spezzano, C. (1993). *Affect in psychoanalysis: A clinical synthesis.* Hillsdale, NJ: Analytic Press.

Tinsley, H. E., Bowman, S. L., & Ray, S. B. (1988). Manipulation of expectancies about counseling and psychotherapy: Review and analysis of expectancy manipulation strategies and results. *Journal of Counseling Psychology, 35,* 99-108.

Van der Kolk, B. A., McFarlane, A. C., & Van der Hart, O. (1996). A general approach to treatment of post-traumatic stress disorder. In B. A. Van der Kolk (Ed.), *Traumatic stress: The effects of overwhelming experience on mind, body, and society* (pp. 231-237). New York: Guilford Press.

Vaughan, F., Wittene, B., & Walsh, R. (1996). Transpersonal psychology and the religious person. In E. P. Shafranske (Ed.), *Religion and the clinical practice of psychology* (pp. 483-509). Washington, DC: American Psychological Association.

Wachtel, P. L. (1977). *Psychoanalysis and behavior therapy.* New York: Basic Books.

Walters, D. S. (1997). A study of the reliability and validity of the Triage Assessment Scale. Unpublished doctoral dissertation, University of Memphis, Memphis, Tennessee.

Watson, J. C. & Greenberg, L. S. (1996). Emotion and cognition in experiential therapy: A dialectical-constructivist perspective. In H. Rosen & K. Kuelwein (Eds.), *Constructing realities: Meaning making perspectives for psychotherapists* (pp. 300-313). San Francisco: Jossey-Bass.

Werner, E. (1993). *Overcoming the odds: High risk children from birth to adulthood.* Ithaca, NY: Cornell University Press.

Werner, E. & Smith, R. (1989). Resilient youth: Perspectives on coping and sources of security. In E. Werner (Ed.), *Vulnerable but invincible: A longitudinal study of resilient children and youth* (pp. 191-198). New York: Adams, Banister, Cox.

Wexler, D. B. (1991). *The Adolescent self: Strategies for self-management, self-soothing, and self-esteem in adolescents.* New York: Norton.

White, M. (1993). Deconstruction and therapy. In S. Gilligan & R. Price (Eds.), *Therapeutic conversations* (pp. 38-43). New York: Norton.

White, M. & Epston, D. (1990). *Narrative means to therapeutic ends.* New York: Norton.

Worthington, E. L., Jr. (1986). Client compliance with homework directives during counseling. *Journal of Counseling Psychology, 33,* 124-130.

Yalom, I. (1970). *The theory and practice of group psychotherapy.* New York: Basic Books.

Young, J. E. (1994). *Cognitive therapy for personality disorders: A schema-focused approach.* Sarasota, FL: Professional Resource Press.

Zinker, J. (1977). *Creative process in gestalt therapy.* New York: Brunner/Mazel.

Index